WORLD WAR II
at
CAMP HALE

WORLD WAR II
at
CAMP HALE

Blazing a New Trail in the Rockies

DAVID R. WITTE
Foreword by Flint Whitlock

THE
History
PRESS

Published by The History Press
Charleston, SC
www.historypress.net

First published 2015

Manufactured in the United States

ISBN 978.1.46711.854.5

Library of Congress Control Number: 2015947678

CONTENTS

FOREWORD

During those first few, frightening months of America's involvement in World War II, there were hundreds of military camps, bases and posts that sprang up all across the nation practically overnight. Young men (and women, too) had to be quickly converted from civilians to soldiers, sailors, airmen and marines.

Most of these newly created camps were utilitarian in the extreme, with cookie-cutter wooden barracks, headquarters buildings, hospitals, training facilities and recreational centers emerging from fields, swamps, deserts and forests—wherever the government could purchase a few hundred thousand acres of otherwise little-used land.

One of the most unusual of these camps suddenly—from April to November 1942—appeared 9,250 feet up in the Colorado Rocky Mountains. It was named Camp Hale and, from mid-1942 until the summer of 1944, would be the home of America's only army division specially trained for mountain and winter warfare: the 10th Mountain Division.

Located on U.S. Highway 24 between the Colorado towns of Minturn and Leadville and one hundred mountainous miles west of Denver, Camp Hale offered the kind of terrain perfect for training men to live and fight in an inhospitable environment. (The war had already involved heavy fighting in some of the coldest and most mountainous areas of Europe.)

An army of ten thousand workmen spent those eight months in a massive wartime construction project—draining the high-meadow swamp; removing the thick undergrowth of foliage; straightening the twisting Eagle

River; rerouting Highway 24; putting in roads, streets, water and sewage facilities and power plants; adding railroad spurs to the warehouse area; and building a rifle range, a combat village, an artillery range, two ski-training areas and much, much more. All told, there were more than eight hundred structures of every description that were erected in this, the highest of all U.S. Army posts. In addition, there were barns and stables and veterinary facilities to house and take care of some four to five thousand pack mules and horses that the division would need to haul artillery and supplies into the trackless mountains.

Once the camp began to take shape, into this wilderness location—where the air is thin and the snow on the surrounding peaks never melts—pulled hundreds of troop trains carrying thousands of young men who had either volunteered or had been drafted into the ski troops. The training was impossibly hard. During the winter, there was skiing (cross-country and downhill) from morning until night. In the summer, there were long marches and rock-climbing drills that tested the soldiers' stamina and courage. All year long, there was unending physical conditioning in the thin air and exercises designed to teach survivalist skills and turn flabby city boys into rock-hard mountain soldiers capable of defeating a ruthless enemy in some of the most difficult environments on earth.

Until now, the story of Camp Hale has been told piecemeal in various publications and documentary films. David Witte has performed a great service for all history buffs by creating this fascinating, richly detailed and thoroughly researched portrait of a unique place. Drawing on a considerable amount of original source material and locating scores of photographs that have rarely, if ever, been published, he has woven together a narrative of an army camp that served America for only a brief time but that has gone down in legend.

He has also done what few writers have done: turn a geographic location into a living, breathing entity.

So bundle up, put on your mukluks and fur-lined parka, wax your boards, grab a canteen full of hot joe and immerse yourself in a read that will take you on a journey to a chilly, windswept place that today exists only in memory but that is imbued with glory brought to it by the greatest generation.

FLINT WHITLOCK
10th Mountain Division descendant and coauthor of
Soldiers on Skis: A Pictorial Memoir of the 10th Mountain Division

PREFACE

S itting in the barren, flat and compressed land of the Eagle Valley, just
north of the Continental Divide in the Sawatch Range of the Colorado
Rocky Mountains, are the remnants of a once bustling and booming army
cantonment. The roar of steam engines and train whistles are all but silenced,
and the firing of M1 rifles is a distant thought of the past. No more calling
of cadence and singing of songs remains as the land glimmers in the cool
mountain air and gleaming summer sun. However, small signs on the side of
Highway 24, which one can miss in the blink of an eye, share a brief glimpse
into the past of this majestic land and the wartime activities that once rumbled
the valley. The remaining concrete foundations and support beams presently
on the land reveal little about the story of the tens of thousands of men and
women who served and trained at Camp Hale during the years of World
War II. While various other information plaques around the valley help the
casual visitor envision a city of white barracks and other buildings, much of
the history of the area has been untold. What remains is a true American
story of ingenuity, determination, racial conflict and overcoming adversity
to obtain something never done before. The history of the cantonment is a
worthy story to be told due to the significant social and economic impact the
camp had on its workers, the nearby Arkansas River Valley of Colorado, the
army's future cantonment development and the mountain and ski troopers
who were stationed there. This is the untold story of Camp Hale, Colorado.

The land of the Eagle Valley has intrigued me ever since I was a eight-
year-old boy riding through the Rocky Mountains on Highway 24 on one of

my annual summer family vacations to Colorado. Every summer we packed up the minivan and drove the 1,040-mile, fifteen-hour trip from Lombard, Illinois, to Monument, Colorado, to visit family and to enjoy the mountains. For our family, vacations were never about getting away but rather about getting to the mountains. The Colorado Rockies have always interested me, with their majestic peaks at elevations above fourteen thousand feet, higher than most Americans will ever see and feel unless driving up to the top of Pikes Peak or Mount Evans. I began climbing the "fourteeners" at the age of nine and have not stopped since. The combination of the adventure and the history that lies within these rugged mountains is something that keeps drawing me back. Though I had completed all fifty-four fourteeners by the summer of 2015, Colorado remains a yearly destination for my family.

One summer in college, as I continued to climb Colorado's fourteeners, I worked at a small Lutheran outdoor adventure camp in eastern Oklahoma where I learned rock climbing and repelling in the Ozark Mountains of Arkansas. I have taken these skills and continue to apply them to my mountaineering in Colorado and to the rock climbing I continue to do around the country. During this same time in college, my interest in skiing also grew as I took to the slopes in Breckinridge, Vail, Keystone, Copper Mountain, Arapaho Basin, Monarch and Ski Cooper. No doubt, my frequent trips to Colorado in both the summer and winter months shaped my interest in the state's history and with the people who live in this unique part of the country.

In my graduate school years, while I was working on a degree in public history in Little Rock, Arkansas, my fascination with material history and local history began to flourish. While being pressured by colleagues and friends to write on something local in Arkansas, I decided to branch out of the state and tackle Camp Hale with vigor. Between my academic interest in history, my fascination with Colorado, my love of rock climbing and skiing and my current position as a chaplain in the U.S. Army, Camp Hale seemed like an ever more enticing part of history as its remnants continued to call out from the valley. My intentions on writing a book to chronicle the history of Camp Hale were sealed one spring day in March as I skied down the slopes of Ski Cooper. The small gift shop tucked into the side of one of Ski Cooper's main buildings reminds visitors that the resort once served as the main ski training slope for soldiers at Camp Hale. However, I could not help but notice a void in the knowledge of the resort's past—namely, the army cantonment that brought it into existence. As I ate my lunch in the small resort restaurant, I observed the mountain rucksacks, skis, poles and boots from America's finest in World War II lining the surrounding walls of the building. This history had to be told and needed to be made official in the selected works of World War II history.

When I was nine years old, the Eagle Valley of Camp Hale was nothing more to me than just another mountain valley. However, questions began to rise in my mind about that beautiful rubble-filled landscape. I could not help but ask myself the question as to why anyone would want to build a small city and push people through army Basic Combat Training in such a desolate and harsh place? Who were these people who built and occupied the camp? Why did they choose a small valley just north of Leadville for such an operation? After completing army Basic Combat Training myself during the warm summer months at Fort Leonard Wood, Missouri, I knew there was something special about the land in Eagle Valley and the people who built, lived and trained there. By all means, it was no Fort Leonard Wood. There was nothing ordinary about constructing a city at 9,250 feet in less than nine months to conduct army Basic Combat Training in addition to winter warfare and ski training.

These combined influences led me to begin my research. My study of Camp Hale began in the beginning of 2010, just under a year after Congress began debating a bill to turn what remains of Camp Hale over to the National Park Service. I started my studies at the Denver Public Library, Western History and Genealogy Department, which has the archives for the 10th Mountain Division in World War II and a majority of the newspapers, construction documents and memoirs of soldiers and personal papers of people involved in the building of Camp Hale. Subsequent research took place at the Lake County Public Library in Leadville, which is the archive for the *Camp Hale Ski-Zette*, Camp Hale's newspaper, and the *Camp Hale Construction Completion Report*. Many conversations with Camp Hale veterans, local Leadville residents and members of the National Association of the 10th Mountain Division have brought forward valuable information. However, the core of this book is in the three years of research done in the primary source documents of Camp Hale and the surrounding areas. Hundreds of hours were spent reading through more than two thousand pages of newspapers, around five hundred pages of government documents and hundreds of pages of memoirs and in viewing or conducting several interviews.

This book is well suited for any enthusiast of military history, World War II, race relations, women in the military or the 10th Mountain Division. It is also very pertinent to aficionados of Colorado history, including those interested in local economic impacts, the Arkansas River Valley, Eagle

Valley, the railroad, skiing, mountaineering and how the state supported the war effort in World War II. May the sacrifices made by all in the history of Camp Hale live on through this work so that what the men and women did in support of victory in World War II will never be forgotten.

Acknowledgements

S pecial thanks go to Mr. Dennis Hagen and Ms. Coi E. Drummond-Gehrig of the Denver Public Library for their assistance in my research. Dennis provided much-needed knowledge in accordance with the documents available to help with this topic. Coi provided many of the rich images included in this book. Also, special thanks go to Ms. Janice Fox at the Lake County Public Library. Janice went out of her way to help me in viewing hundreds of pages of newspapers on microfilm. This book could not have been completed without her willingness to support me given my limited research time in Colorado. Lastly, thanks go to Dr. Carl Moneyhon and Dr. Raymond Screws of the University of Arkansas at Little Rock for their advice and guidance on writing this work. Additionally, thank you to Dr. Bobby Roberts, director of the Central Arkansas Library System, for his constructive criticism of my work.

This book is written in honor of both of my grandfathers, Erwin Witte and Kenneth Wachtel, and my grandfather-in-law Robert Jones. My beloved grandfathers and grandfather-in-law inspired me to write about the sacrifices of the greatest generation. Erwin Witte served during and after World War II in 1945 with Detachment E, 283rd Company, 3rd Military Government Regiment, European Theater of Operations. Kenneth Wachtel served during World War II in "E" Company, 4th Infantry Regiment, Illinois Reserve Militia. Robert Jones served during World War II in Oran, North Africa, in 1943 as a combat medic and ended the war with the 262nd Station Hospital at Mussolini's headquarters in Aversa, Italy, European Theater of Operations.

INTRODUCTION

The events that led to the building and the occupation of Camp Hale, will no doubt be written in the pages of history in the years to come.[1]
—Rene L. Coquoz, author and resident of Leadville, Colorado

World War II at Camp Hale: Blazing a New Trail in the Rockies is the story of the United States Army's choice to start training mountain troops for combat in World War II and the subsequent development of Camp Hale, Colorado, in order to accomplish this task. It begins with a look into how increasing interest in skiing in America, along with the work of a few influential civilians and deteriorating conditions in Europe, helped convince the army to train mountain troops. For the first time in American history, the army began construction of a cantonment devoted entirely to the elite training of a small, division-size element of mountain troops.

The construction of the post proved to be an unprecedented event not only for the army but also for the volunteer civilians who made the sacrificial decision to leave their homes and work in an inhospitable environment. These individuals answered the government's call for wartime support of the military and helped change the army, Colorado and the preparedness of soldiers for combat in Alaska and Italy during World War II. As a result of this work, engineers changed the army's standards for the construction of cantonments and opened up a new camp capable of cold-weather and mountain warfare training. The exceptional nature of Camp Hale will be analyzed given the time limitation put on the project, the choice of land, initial earth moving work, the high elevation and its impact on workers and soldiers, racial conflicts, community support from local towns and the desire for the final product to be as self-sustainable as possible.

The terms "ski troops" and "mountain troops" are used interchangeably throughout because they refer to the same group of soldiers. However, defining the soldiers as mountain troops is a better description considering that these soldiers were versatile and trained in much more than just skiing. Veterans of the 10th Mountain Division use both terms in their memoirs but often prefer "ski trooper" because this sets them apart from other soldiers in the army and is what made them famous around the country during their training at Camp Hale and also in the Rocky Mountains after the war. However, first commander of the 87th Mountain Infantry Regiment, Lieutenant Colonel Onslow Rolfe, made it clear to his soldiers from the beginning that they were "Mountain Troops" and that skiing would play only a minimal part in their training. Mountain troop training made Camp Hale special to the army and influential in helping win the war in Europe.

Therefore, the following pages are the story of one of the most challenging and unique engineering feats of World War II. The construction of Camp Hale and its occupation is a story of sacrifice, devotion, struggle and endurance. The personal stories and memories of those who built the camp are integral and essential for this work. May these stories live on in history for the sake of the greatest generation.

1

SKI TROOPERS

I feel that Colorado is in a favored position this year.[2]
—*Paul Nesbit, lecturer for the Colorado state advertising and publicity committee*

In the spring of 1942, the U.S. Army began construction of a new home for its Mountain Training Center (MTC) and 87th Mountain Infantry Regiment at Pando, Colorado. Camp Hale, as the army later named it, "was a camp unlike any other" that became the first military cantonment constructed for the basic training and specialized training of ski troops and mountain troops in America.[3] The cantonment owed its existence to the decision of the U.S. Army, heavily influenced by a civilian population ready to assist, to form infantry units capable of fighting in severe cold and mountainous conditions. Beginning during World War II, these troops went to Camp Hale and trained for mountain warfare, eventually forming the elite mountain unit, the 10th Mountain Division, that continues to operate today.

The idea of training ski troopers in America began long before the United States entered World War II. Having and maintaining troops capable of fighting on skis at high elevation and in arctic conditions first developed within the army in America in 1938. The army began experimenting with mountain troops using the 3rd Battalion, 2nd Infantry, at Fort Brady, Michigan.[4] The army issued four hundred pairs of skis to the unit's members for their use, but in all reality, they saw little action. The soldiers saw the skis more as a leisure time activity than as combat essential. As a result, they did not take the training as seriously as originally planned. However, the battalion commander, Colonel Krohner, appropriated the skis while forming the first winter warfare unit and pressed onward with a determination to make them a part of his unit whether the soldiers saw their tactical usefulness or not.

The 3rd Battalion transformed its appearance in the fall of 1938 into that of a distinct ski trooper unit. The uniforms consisted of old-type breeches, wrap leggings, campaign hats and standard-issue GI shoes.[5] Soldiers even made their own sleeping bags out of two sewn-together shelter halves and two standard-issue army blankets. They carried the old World War I–issue khaki rucksack and wore white cooks' clothing as snow camouflage.[6] However, the unit quickly proved to be insufficiently trained and ill equipped and reverted back to regular infantry shortly thereafter. Unfortunately, the army's first experiment in winter warfare had closed, and the army showed little interest in returning to it. The command realized that if soldiers were to be trained in mountain and winter warfare, they would need expert advice, equipment and knowledge to be able to survive. This short-lived and underappreciated experiment in mountain warfare started a bitter and long-lived trial that seemed to face opposition from many in the army for years to come.

The reality of having modern alpine ski troopers first developed in World War I when several companies of skiers were used as reconnaissance ski patrols and attacking units in the Vosges Mountains by the French and Germans.[7] This reality continued to develop in America in 1939, with a growing awareness of Finland's utilization of skis in its fight against the Soviet army in an inhospitable environment that had snow covering the ground during the majority of the year.

Seasoned veterans of skiing and some within the U.S. Army saw the outnumbered Finnish troops, who utilized their quick shock troops on skis in an attempt to stop the Soviet war machine, as an effective resistance. However, this did not immediately convince the U.S. Army of a need for specially trained ski troopers. As a matter of fact, the army needed much more convincing by civilians and civilian organizations before it ever decided to start training ski troopers in large numbers. This convincing took years to happen while America entered into World War II after the Japanese attack on Pearl Harbor in December 1941.

America's interest in the mountains and skiing stemmed not only from Finland's defense against the Soviet invasion in 1939 but also from a few events preceding America's entrance into the war. Civilian curiosity in skiing certainly had an impact on the army's choice to train ski troopers. No civilian proved to be as influential in getting the army to recognize the need for ski troopers as a Massachusetts skier named Charles Minot Dole.

Minnie Dole, as friends often called him, grew up an outdoor enthusiast and became a member of the New York Amateur Ski Club. In 1938, he and Roger Langley formed the National Ski Patrol Committee (NSPC) as a part of the National Ski Association of America (NSAA) to provide emergency aid to skiers who fell and were injured on the slopes. Dole and Langley, before anyone else in America, first saw the need for the army to train ski troopers who could defend a historically vulnerable border in the northern part of the contiguous United States and actively tried to convince the army on this matter by sending thousands of letters to General Marshall and President Roosevelt.[8]

In order to garner more support and to ensure the NSPC stood behind his ideas, Dole mailed out a memorandum to national ski patrolmen, stating that the government might wish to train troops in ski patrol work.[9] He sought their cooperation by giving them a questionnaire that detailed the responsibilities the ski patrol could potentially have should the military decide to ask for their help. To the satisfaction of both Dole and Langley, the questionnaire came back with over 90 percent of the members voting in favor of offering the patrol's services.[10] Dole and Langley now had the backing and the momentum to be successful.

Another significant influence came from European skiers who came to America in the prewar and early war years. Individuals such as Otto Schniebs, Hannes Schneider, Walter Prager, Peter Gabriel, Ludwig "Luggi" Foeger, Friedl Pfeifer, Ernst Engel and Torger Tokle either joined the mountain troops, helped with training them or influenced the army in some way to develop a mountain force. Additionally, the two sons of the Baron George von Trapp family, Werner and Rupert, left Salzburg, Austria, in 1939 and became naturalized citizens of the United States. Both trained at Camp Hale and eventually fought with the mountain troops in Europe.[11]

Nevertheless, not all of the influential skiers of the time period came from Europe to America. One of the most famous American skiers and mountaineers, Paul K. Petzoldt, joined the ski troops as a private, after becoming famous in America for his expeditions in the Himalayas and for his yearly ascents of the Grand Teton in Wyoming.[12] His fame brought even more attention to the mountain troops from across America. He taught safety techniques and methods for evacuating casualties at high elevations while he served in the Medical Detachment as a medic.[13] Upon arriving at Camp Hale, a Mountain Training Center in-processing sergeant asked him which unit he wanted to join. He responded that he wanted to join the 10th Reconnaissance Troop after hearing about its notoriety. The sergeant responded, "I'm sorry they only take good climbers and skiers in that outfit."[14] Who could blame the sergeant for his mistake in not knowing that only Camp Hale, among all army cantonments, seemed to be inundated with celebrity recruits who brought civilian skills the army had never utilized before.

During that same month of February 1940, the army held its first ski fighting maneuvers in its history at Camp Pine, New York, with the 28th Infantry Division.[15] Soldiers moved supplies on skis and fought a mock battle using tactics learned from the Finns in order to experiment more than the army ever had in mountain and winter warfare. Colonel C.M. Dowell of Fort Niagara, commander of one of the units of the 28th Infantry, commented that these maneuvers had demonstrated "one of the greatest national defense advances in American History."[16] The *Lewiston Evening Journal* further quoted him as saying, "It is in the best interest of the army to be able to carry out its mission any time, anywhere."[17] Unfortunately for Dole, these sentiments of Colonel Dowell were not the same for the War Department—at least, not yet.

Finally, at the end of the summer of 1940, Dole and John E.P. Morgan (treasurer of the NSP) traveled to Washington, D.C., and met with army chief of staff General George C. Marshall. Marshall gave the two men his assurance that the U.S. Army was keeping some units in the Snowbelt region through the coming winter to experiment with training and equipment for cold-weather fighting.[18] This assurance turned into an order from General

U.S. ski troops wind up maneuvers with night firing at Camp Pine, New York, on February 28, 1940. *Author's personal collection.*

The 28th Infantry Division, Uncle Sam's own "ghost" army, at Camp Pine, New York, on February 28, 1940. *Author's personal collection.*

Marshall, establishing six army "ski patrols" that trained at different locations around the country.[19]

The purpose of the patrols was to "select men…to be taught the use of skis, snowshoes, and the fundamentals of camping and travelling in the snow and high mountains."[20] These patrols commenced both in the East with the 44th Infantry Division ski patrol around Old Forge, New York, and in the West with the 3rd and 41st Infantry Division ski patrols at Fort Lewis, Washington, which later moved to Mount Rainier National Park's Longmire Headquarters from December 7, 1940, to February 22, 1941.[21] Private Harald Sorensen, coach of the 44th Infantry Division Ski Patrol, reminisced about his arrival at Old Forge, writing, "There was life at Old Forge when our train rolled in—(brass band and all the "trimmins.") We enjoyed that most naturally. But we were soon awakened to the fact we were there on business. It was the business of proving the feasibility of the adoption of a ski patrol unit as a permanent branch of the U.S. Army."[22]

However, by the spring of 1941, the army had declared the ski patrol experiments a success and disbanded the units due to a lack of snow in the

Northeast and a permanent change of station.[23] Dole continued to press for the establishment of two training camps—one in the East and one in the Northwest—while his letters commenced on to Washington.[24] Thankfully, Dole's letters were not in vain, as General Marshall, in April 1941, ordered his subordinates to find a suitable training site for a much larger mountain infantry division adept at skiing and climbing.[25]

This decision did not technically prove effective until November 15, 1941, when Secretary of War Henry L. Stimson and General Marshall stated that the 1st Battalion (Reinforced) 87th Mountain Infantry Regiment would be activated at Fort Lewis, Washington.[26] However, the army never intended for Fort Lewis to serve as the permanent home for ski troopers. As early as June 23, 1941, the Headquarters Company of the 8th Corps at Fort Sam Houston, Texas, recommended in its report of investigation that "a cantonment for mountain and winter warfare training for a triangular division, be located in the Pando, Colorado, area."[27] Exactly one year from the date of the orders for the formation of the 87th Mountain Infantry Regiment, the army finished constructing Camp Hale.

2

THE CHOICE OF PANDO

The Pando area received a heavier annual snowfall than
any other large area in Colorado.[28]
—*Board of officers from the 8ᵗʰ Corps Area, Fort Sam Houston, Texas*

Finding a suitable location for a winter training camp for ski troopers challenged the army because of the unique requirements. Never before in its history had the army desired to find a location large enough for an entire division to conduct daily training, including the basic training for a special group of infantry soldiers called ski or mountain troopers.[29] What the army needed in order to satisfy the desires of its chief of staff included a large area for training and living, an easily acquired territory and an accessible area by train and highway.

Though the army already had ski patrol units in the 1st, 3rd, 5th, 6th, 41st and 44th Infantry Divisions and conducted winter warfare training at Fort Snelling, Minnesota, by April 1941, General Marshall admitted that winter warfare maneuvers on a large scale had not yet been accomplished due to a lack of funding but that the army did desire them.[30] In order for the army to accomplish these maneuvers, it had to obtain a training site large enough to give a division freedom to move. As a result, in April 1941, General Marshall ordered his subordinates to find a suitable training site for a much larger mountain infantry division adept at skiing and climbing, which began the army's search that eventually ended with Pando. This new command of Marshall's abandoned all previous pursuits for a location, including the once viable and sought-after Great Sand Dunes National Monument on the western face of the Sangre de Cristo Mountains near the Colorado–New Mexico border and started a new search for the ideal location.[31]

Following Marshall's orders to find a suitable location, Colonels Nelson Walker, Charles Hurdis and U.S. Forest Service worker Robert S. Monahan investigated sites in the West during the summer of 1941 that were suitable for a one-division camp housing fifteen thousand men for year-round training in winter and mountain maneuvers.[32] Colonel Orlando Ward, secretary to army chief of staff General Marshall, countered the cantonment proposal with the idea that divisions currently stationed in the vicinity of high mountainous terrain should utilize field camps for temporary training instead of moving great distances to other posts.[33] This idea did not go far, as Colonel Harry L. Twaddle, acting assistant chief of staff, G-3 (General Staff Section, War Department Operations and Training) shot it down, writing,

> *The training of units in mountain warfare by having such units move to suitable high mountain terrain and camp for short periods is a make-shift method and entirely inadequate…*
>
> *Troops operating in mountains will normally encounter high altitudes, snow and low temperatures. They must be accustomed to life under such conditions. The camping problems alone are tremendous. Troops must actually live and train the year round under high altitude conditions if we are to obtain any worthwhile results. There is no case where realism in training is more appropriate…*
>
> *Fort Lewis is about sixty miles from terrain which is barely satisfactory for this purpose. Camp Ord and San Luis Obispo are about one hundred miles from suitable terrain.*[34]

Colonel Twaddle's response showed how serious the army was becoming at this point in finding a suitable location in order to train mountain troops correctly with the most realistic conditions.

However, Colonel Ward was not about to give up on his quest to identify the new training location(s). After being rejected once by Colonel Twaddle, he immediately countered with a proposal on April 25, 1941, for the new cantonment to be in the vicinity of Bend, Oregon.[35] Once again, newly promoted Brigadier General Twaddle rejected this due to the fact that the area had a short snow season, bad rock, an inadequate water supply and dangerous dust conditions. This did not sit well with Colonel Ward, who then passed along the chief of staff's decision to temporarily not allocate any new funding for a mountain camp. Though this was a roadblock to the approval of such a site, the idea of a high mountain training site was still being given full consideration.[36] Thus, General Twaddle, Colonel Nelson Walker, Colonel Charles Hurdis and U.S. Forest Service worker Robert S. Monahan continued on in their search and in their proposals for more experimentation and training in mountain warfare.

As the higher-ups continued to drag their feet on the mountain training site, the summer of 1941 quickly began to fade away, and the prospects of having the project completed by the winter diminished significantly. General Twaddle and Minot Dole knew this but continued to press Washington to act. In addition to pushing for a mountain training site, the G-3 continued to insist on the formation of an entire mountain division. Within a ten-day timespan, from July 15 to July 25, 1941, General Twaddle, along with two other lieutenant colonels from G-3, sent memorandums to the chief of staff, Army General Headquarters, Major General Lesley J. McNair, and argued once again that the army needed a unique mountain division.[37] McNair was still not convinced. His response back on August 5 to Lieutenant Colonel Mark W. Clark, G-3, expressed that the need for a mountain division in the United States was questionable.[38] He further explained that an existing infantry division should be utilized. Within this division, one infantry battalion and one artillery battalion should be designated for conducting special operations in difficult mountainous terrain.[39] This response almost replicated that of Colonel Ward to General Twaddle. Apparently, there was a disconnect between the War Department G-3, the Army General Headquarters and the Chief of Staff's Office. Only one out of the three firmly believed in the necessity of a mountain division and a unique mountain training site.

However, as events began to unfold in Europe, specifically in Italy in the fall of 1941, the opinions of the army changed and were reaffirmed by the War Department about the need for a mountain division and a mountain training location. The U.S. military attaché to Italy reported back to the War Department that the Italians had twenty-five thousand killed, ten thousand of whom froze to death while retreating into the mountains after a failed attempt at taking Greece through the mountains of Albania, and an irreparable loss of morale.[40] These Italian troops ventured into the mountains unprepared, untrained and unable to deal with the cold climate conditions. The report further noted that it would be very difficult for the United States to improvise well-trained and well-equipped troops from line divisions for mountain warfare.[41] Another report came into the War Department in July from the American minister in Switzerland, given to him by a German informant, that revealed the Germans were working on training special mountain troops for combat in Alaska and the American and Canadian Rockies.[42] As a result of these reports and other various factors, the army began to change its mind, and the War Department became more serious about an American response. Eventually, Minnie Dole received a letter from Secretary of War Stimson and General Marshall on October 22, 1941, stating that on November 15, the army would activate the 1st Battalion (Reinforced) 87th Mountain Infantry at Fort Lewis, Washington.[43] This battalion became the first in the history of the army to begin mountain warfare training on a larger scale than a single patrol.[44] Other, smaller training exercises continued, such as the training of ski paratroops at Alta, Utah, but did not materialize into anything larger.[45] Dole received a green light to recruit mountain troops, and this he did well.

Charles McLane, the first soldier recruited for the 87th Mountain Infantry, showed up at Fort Lewis with a suitcase, a pair of skis and War Department orders to join the "Mountain Troops" after the activation of the 87th.[46] The major at corps headquarters greeted him and said, "Lad you are the Mountain Infantry. You're a one man regiment."[47] Once other soldiers

"Original Ski Troops and Patrols," (Gum, Inc., 1941). Recruiting advertisement slipped into packets of gum were intended to gather interest in the ski troops. *Author's personal collection.*

52. UNCLE SAM—SOLDIER

Ski Troops and Patrols

Because Uncle Sam's Army may be called upon at some time to go into action in the frozen north, Infantry troops who are stationed in camps where a lot of snow falls are given training with skis and snow shoes. The training tests the ability of one or more battalions of each division to get around in deep snow. It also gives more advanced training to small groups of specially selected individuals organized into patrol units who operate for long periods of time under all weather conditions and on all types of ground. Some are made up in groups for advanced training in battle tactics with rifles and hand grenades. They are employed in war time like cavalry to surprise the enemy and are valuable as scouts. The instruction is given by qualified officers of the Regular Army and by expert skiers of the National Guard and Reserves.

Save to get all these picture cards showing Uncle Sam's soldiers, sailors, marines, airmen and civilians in training for NATIONAL DEFENSE.

Copyright 1941, GUM, INC., Phila., Pa.   Printed in U. S. A.

Back side of original "Ski Troops and Patrols" (Gum, Inc., 1941). This recruiting advertisement promoted pre–Camp Hale ski training. *Author's personal collection.*

began to arrive, McLane further commented, "We guessed at the odds of the Regiment's surviving that first week."[48] Initial uncertainty reigned at Fort Lewis for months, but as time went on, the mountain troops started to distinguish themselves from the other units. The 87th was considered so unique that it began to be called America's "Foreign Legion."[49]

The army had learned many important lessons from the ski patrol experiments and now applied those lessons to the development of the 87th, taking into account the unique nature of mountain warfare.[50] No one factor changed the mind of the army and finally influenced the War Department to begin training ski and mountain troopers, even though the reports from Italy and Switzerland turned out to be the turning points. If Dole and the National Ski Association had not prepared, instructed and guided the army in the development of mountain warfare, it never would have been prepared to take on this unique training. Nevertheless, once the army committed to mountain warfare training, it invested itself completely, which eventually resulted in the construction of Camp Hale.

Original postcard showing ski troops on Mount Rainier, circa 1942. *Author's personal collection.*

In addition to the announcement of the activation of the 87th in November, the army established the Mountain Winter Warfare Board to design and test equipment suitable for mountain troops.[51] The army ordered all training and testing to be accomplished at Fort Lewis, Washington. It also chose Fort Lewis as its initial training location for the 87th primarily because of its proximity to mountains and because of the already established ski patrols that operated out of the post. No other army post in the country, except Fort Ethan Allen, Vermont, offered mountainous terrain within a reasonable driving distance.[52] Fort Lewis, however, provided little geographical assistance to the newly formed 87th and the Mountain Winter Warfare Board in testing equipment due to its lower elevation. As a result, many of the ski troopers of the 87th spent time sixty-two miles to the east at Paradise and Tatoosh Lodges in Mount Rainier National Park.

Lieutenant Colonel Onslow S. Rolfe, commander of the 87th, looked at several locations beyond Mount Rainier, including Mount Baker, Mount Shuksan and Mount Hood, for temporary training purposes.[53] However, Mount Rainier offered the best lodging in two two-story hotels at 5,400-foot elevation, along with excellent skiing conditions.[54] The 87th Mountain Infantry soldiers made the official move from Fort Lewis to Paradise Lodge on February 14, 1942, and commenced with ski training shortly thereafter.[55] The lodge gave ski troopers of the 87th a step up in comfort compared to a typical army barracks because initial constructors built it to serve as a vacation resort.[56] With an average snow depth of 20 feet, it provided soldiers with ample opportunities to ski right from the front door, as the snow at times piled up past the second floor, leaving only the third floor with a view out the window. Meals were brought in on trucks from Fort Lewis and prepared in the lodge's kitchen. For the most part, the soldiers loved Paradise Lodge because the skiing conditions were great, the accommodations were

Mountain troops from the 87th Mountain Infantry Regiment set up camp at Mirror Lake below Mount Rainier in July 1942. *Author's personal collection.*

Original Eighth Annual Silver Skis Open Championship program on April 11–12, 1942, on Mount Rainier. *Author's personal collection.*

comfortable and the conditioning made them stronger and tougher than most other soldiers in the army.[57] During the eight-week training period for ski instruction, soldiers skied for six hours a day, six days a week, through rain, shine, sleet and snow.[58] The 1st Battalion, 87th Mountain Infantry, at Mount Rainier even participated in local ski races put on by the Washington Ski Club. On April 11–12, 1942, the club invited the mountain troops to participate in the Eighth Annual Silver Skis Open Championship, which it hosted right on Mount Rainier. For the civilians, the race gave them an opportunity to support America's finest in the army. For the ski troopers, it

WELCOME TO THE YANKS!

SAY, how's the skiing on Mt. Fujiyama, Mr. Moto? The Yanks will be over for the suki-yaki championship in, oh about 1943.

As a sort of a preview for more serious conquests to come, U. S. army ski troopers are guests in the Silver Skis this Saturday afternoon, up here on the big dish of ice cream called Mt. Rainier.

Welcome to the Yanks!

This spectacular event was planned by The Post-Intelligencer for the double purpose of (a) calling the skiing world's attention to the superlative ski terrain in the Northwest and (b) stimulating interest in the great outdoor sport.

Since its inception in 1934 the race has done both.

This war year when some athletic programs are in full retreat, the Silver Skis are riding high, wide and handsome. The presence of a score of U. S. army ski troops makes it the greatest race of them all. For among these lean, weather-beaten, leather-tough fighting men are the best racers from Maine to California.

Not that it is a cinch that the military will win it. Not with such talented civilian competitors as Martin Fopp, Bill Taylor, Hugh Bauer, Hans Grage, Matt Broze and a lot more. But the presence of the army gives the event a patriotic flavor.

Never a race for sissy-pants, the Silver Skis is more than ever a thrilling test of skill, stamina and daring.

To the competing runners, in the Big Parade, we extend our best wishes, and the same goes for the women and the juniors. But The Post-Intelligencer and the Washington Ski Club give a special welcome to the gallant men in the United States army.

ROYAL BROUGHAM.

Back side of original Eighth Annual Silver Skis Open Championship program on April 11–12, 1942, on Mount Rainier, promoting the ski troopers' presence at the event. *Author's personal collection.*

gave them a chance to show off their skills and to interact with some of the best skiers in the world. The times were cordial, and both sides desired for the races to be fun.

While some in the 87th excelled at skiing and produced a show for the spectators on the mountain, others found a different way to entertain at Paradise Lodge. Lieutenant Richard Look organized a "Government Issue Choir" that sang every Saturday night at Paradise Lodge for weekend civilian skiers who came to Rainier.[59] The choir later became the Regimental Glee

Club and became quite famous around Washington after Lieutenant John Jay began promoting them. The soldiers gained a reputation for being "the singing skiers of the 87th."[60] They chronicled their history through a song they wrote called "The Ballad of Oola," in which they added a new verse for each new part of their history.[61] Eventually, these skiers wrote a competing song to their ballad that expressed their disdain for donning snowshoes on Mount Rainier. The skiers balked at not skiing and subsequently wrote a song titled "Sven," in reference to the cousin of Oola. In this song, they cleverly told Sven to "take your snowshoes and burn them, sister" because "snowshoes have no use."[62] The men of the 87th took great pride in their singing and encouraged civilian skiers to learn their songs because they were bound to hear them on the slopes after the war. It became a small means for the mountain troops to begin promoting their existence across the country.

For the mountain troops early on, they struggled with getting the message out about their mere existence in order to recruit. The soldiers knew quite well that one battalion of ski troopers at Paradise and Tatoosh Lodges could not make a big difference in an army set on conventional destruction of the enemy. The army obtained Paradise Lodge, along with Tatoosh Lodge, on contract from the National Park Service (NPS) from February to June 1942. The NPS worked hand in hand with the War Department and Lieutenant Colonel Rolfe to create the best training environment available in and around Paradise Lodge. However, Paradise and Tatoosh Lodges could only handle about four hundred men, and Fort Lewis served only as a base of operations. In addition, the NPS forbade the use of any type of live ammunition within its borders. This inhibited the soldiers from practicing live fire exercises, including the use of blank ammunition. The NPS even went as far as having to grant special permission for the soldiers to carry empty rifles in the park.[63]

Eventually, this proved to be makeshift and inadequate, as General Twaddle warned in his letter to Colonel Ward about any camping location chosen as a temporary training area right off a major army post.[64] Also, the Western Defense Command continually pressured Lieutenant Colonel Rolfe for troops to help in defending the West Coast.[65] This bothered Rolfe because it often took his troops away from training and distracted them from the mission of gaining knowledge and experience in mountain warfare. Finally, on May 1, 1942, the army activated the 2nd Battalion, 87th Mountain Infantry. Exactly one month later, on June 1, 1942, it activated the 3rd Battalion, 87th Mountain Infantry. Thus, by the end of the contract on June 1, the army had two battalions at Fort Lewis and one in Mount

Mountain troops, in snowshoes, haul supplies on Mount Rainier on March 23, 1942. *Author's personal collection.*

Mountain troops on Mount Rainier on March 23, 1942. *Author's personal collection.*

Rainier National Park.[66] Paradise and Tatoosh Lodges simply could not accommodate two more battalions for training. Thus, the search that began in April 1941 by General Marshall's directive concluded four months earlier than the end of the Paradise Lodge contract, making Pando, Colorado, the replacement location for training mountain troops of a division size in winter warfare.

After authorizing the search for the perfect location for training mountain troops in April 1941, it took the army and the War Department slightly under a year to affirmatively settle on Pando, Colorado. The initial reports the army received identified West Yellowstone, Montana, as the best choice. This location, on the edge of Yellowstone National Park, fulfilled all the requirements for the cantonment, including access, via a good railroad line; level ground for barracks and artillery practice; and a friendly community nearby.[67] However, the War Department quickly found that this location contained habitat for the nearly extinct trumpeter swan. Preservationists warned the army about the impact artillery and human beings would have on the endangered species.[68] Specifically, Frederic Delano, uncle of President Franklin Delano Roosevelt, led the Wildlife Conservation Committee's fight against the army.[69] Frederic's opposition proved to be no match for the army, and eventually, the War Department abandoned the site.

Pando must have always been under consideration because there is a War Department letter, dated May 12, 1941, that had in its subject line "Plans for Increased Housing for the army—West Yellowstone, Montana area, and Pando, Colorado, area."[70] Since Pando remained on the list of possible locations as early as May 1941, the army began to further investigate its feasibility. Consulting engineer R.J. Tipton of the Constructing Quartermaster, 8th Construction Zone, Fort Sam Houston, Texas, conducted an engineering survey of Pando and filed a report of his observations on June 7, 1941. Shortly thereafter, the War Department sent a board of officers from the 8th Corps Area, Fort Sam Houston, Texas, to conduct a more thorough examination of the area than what Tipton completed. In addition to making use of Tipton's survey, the board of officers "gathered information from local inhabitants in the Eagle County area, from an officer of the U.S. Forestry Service and from an actual reconnaissance of the Pando area."[71]

The board's trip to Colorado did not end with just an examination of Pando. While in the area, the board of officers gathered information on other "locations in the mountainous regions of the Corps Area that might afford suitable locations to meet the requirements of the cantonment site in question."[72] As part of its further investigation, the board interviewed chamber of commerce officials in various towns and officials of several railroads operating in the New Mexico, Arizona and Colorado areas. After further examination, the board concluded in its report that "the Pando, Colorado, area [was] suitable for the particular type of cantonment site required by the War Department directive."[73] Not only did they conclude that it was suitable, but they also determined that it met the War Department's requirements more fully than any other location in the 8th Corps Area. In their analysis of other areas where snow conditions were sufficient to meet the War Department's requirements, they determined that these locations were so inaccessible that they were unsuitable for a cantonment site for a large division of troops.[74]

Pando had unique advantages over other locations, including the fact that it resided at around 9,250 feet in elevation, nearly 3,000 feet higher than West Yellowstone, Montana.[75] Originally, this may have been viewed as a positive by the army until it realized that 9,250 was much taller than any of the mountains of Italy where the 10th Mountain Division saw combat in World War II. Even the 87th Mountain Infantry Regiment's combat in the Aleutian Islands never reached the altitude that Pando provided for the ski troopers. However, even from the initial development of the ski patrols at Fort Lewis and in the East, the original purpose for organizing the U.S. mountain troops was to repel a hostile attack on North America, which may have included attacks at elevations such as Pando's.[76] Thus, the choice of Pando made more sense with this initial assessment for the purpose of the mountain troops.

Three other Colorado locations contended with Pando when the board of officers made its final recommendations to the Adjutant General's Office of the 8th Corps Area. Aspen, Colorado, located in the Roaring Fork Valley of the Elk Range, initially showed promise until the army realized that the location was too small, the railroad that traveled through it too old and deteriorating and most of the land privately owned by ranchers.[77] The Colorado Midland Railway once operated through Aspen but ceased major operations in 1918 as shipping business dropped off and moved to other railroads in the area. Not only did the railroad cease operations, but also on October 22, 1920, officials received orders to "start junking the Aspen branch."[78] Eventually, the old Midland grade to Aspen was converted into an automobile route and remained this way until 1943. The second location, Ashcroft, Colorado, had excellent ski terrain but lacked space and had only a forest service truck trail going through the area.[79] The third location, Wheeler, Colorado, lacked a railroad and was too remote to accommodate the number of soldiers and supplies necessary for standard operation. The closest railroad, located eighteen miles away in Leadville, only made Camp Hale more appealing as a choice compared to Wheeler.

Thus, the board of officers, led by Colonel James O'Conner of the 4th Army Engineers, submitted its report after visiting Pando on June 13, 1941, making three recommendations.[80] First, it recommended Pando as the location for a mountain and winter warfare training center not to exceed a population of twenty thousand. Second, if the army desired to have the cantonment completed by the spring of 1942, the board recommended beginning construction by July 1, 1941.[81] Third, the board recommended that a housing project for the families of noncommissioned officers be included in the construction plans, with a location near the camp or adjacent to Leadville.[82] The army began working on all of these recommendations after the Adjutant General's Office received them on June 27, 1941. The establishment of Pando as the training site for ski troopers also resulted from extensive experiments by several army units, including the 1st Battalion of the 87th Mountain Infantry Regiment, Company B of the 503rd Parachute Infantry Regiment and outfits at Fort Devens, Massachusetts; at Camp McCoy, Wisconsin; at Fort Meade, South Dakota; and in Alaska.[83] These units refined and determined what was absolutely necessary for a mountain training post. Pando soon became the army's most modern large engineering project turned military cantonment.

Pando, located west of the Continental Divide along the Denver & Rio Grande Western Railroad near Tennessee Pass, eighteen miles northwest of Leadville, Colorado, had a population of about three hundred people when the army started looking into it as its primary location. National Forest Service land surrounded the proposed cantonment, providing ample space for maneuvers.[84] Captain Adrien R. Aeschliman of the 126th Engineer Mountain Battalion commented that the land was "so barren that even a crow wouldn't fly over it without carrying its lunch."[85] The secretary of agriculture gave the War Department permission on July 15, 1941, to use 179,000 acres of Holy Cross, Arapaho and Cochetopa National Forest land without restrictions for military training and "furtherance of the war effort."[86] Snow conditions met and even exceeded the army's expectations, as forestry supervisor John B. Leighou, of Glenwood Springs, reported that the Pando area received a heavier annual snowfall than any other prospective area in Colorado. Snow began to fall around October 1 and did not stop until early June, creating an ideal location for ski troopers to train. One writer for the *Camp Hale Ski-Zette* wrote that "snowfall at Pando is not like the snowfall in most parts of the United States. Pando, it would seem, has a one-track mind as far as weather is concerned. When it starts snowing, it keeps snowing."[87]

The level valley contained enough space at a high elevation for an entire division to train. Mountains surrounded it and rose up to elevations in excess of fourteen thousand feet, with some containing snow year-round.[88] The board of officers saw the natural bowl of Eagle Valley as a positive in June 1941. They labeled the bowl "quite important" given the strong winds that moved through the mountains.[89] The natural bowl blocked many of these winds during the winter months, making living conditions a bit more hospitable. Ironically, this positive turned out to be the biggest negative of the location because once the trains started to run multiple times a day through the valley on the Denver & Rio Grande Western Railway, the engines spewed black soot from the coal-powered boilers into the air, and it remained trapped in the valley.[90] Lieutenant Charles C. Brown of the 87th Mountain Infantry Regiment reiterated this point in a song his regiment wrote while serving at Camp Hale that noted, "This Pando she sure is nice country. It's the best doggone place I've been put. The weather is fine, and I'm having a time, but I yust [sic] can't get used to the soot."[91]

The most significant negative initially identified by the board came from a perceived lack of social outlets for the troops. The board wrote in

Train with three engines pulling rail cars up to Tennessee Pass above the Pando Valley on February 7, 1944. *Courtesy of the Denver Public Library, Western History Collection, Phil O'Rourke, TMD-705.*

its report that Leadville "affords little recreation conducive to the morale of a command. The morals of Leadville are said to be on a rather low plane. This presents an additional difficulty."[92] As a solution to this problem, the board proposed strict military control in conjunction with cooperation from local and state police. In addition, it proposed the idea of getting the Denver & Rio Grande Western Railway to provide furlough trains to Denver and Colorado Springs for soldiers to take advantage of on leave. The type of soldier that the board of officers expected to inhabit Pando was one that most likely did not require as much recreational outlets because the wilderness surrounding Pando provided ample opportunities for hunting, fishing, climbing and skiing.[93]

Another positive of the site resulted from the work in prior years of lumbermen who logged and cleared the mountainous area around the cantonment site, making it suitable for ski courses. The Eagle River, only a few feet wide at the time, meandered through the middle of the proposed cantonment area providing a source of fresh water for the camp. In addition to the Eagle River, the board found several other freshwater sources to sustain a camp of up to twenty thousand people. The site originally contained springs and streams flowing from the mountainsides, which gave the board assurance of abundant water. However, the most significant source of water that the board identified at the time came from Homestake Creek, located within two miles of the northwestern end of the cantonment site.[94] Thus, the board gave an affirmative recommendation for Pando to the adjutant general, with the positives outweighing the negatives.

The history of Pando, between the towns of Leadville and Red Cliff, is one that is unique and telling about the land. P.G. Worcester, acting dean of the graduate school and head of the Department of Geology at the University of Colorado at Boulder, wrote a letter dated November 10, 1944, to Erl H. Ellis, Denver lawyer and temporary resident of Pando during the construction of Camp Hale, in which he detailed some of the early geological developments of the region. He wrote,

> *Before the Pleistocene glaciation occurred, Eagle River joined Homestake Creek just about where the main road joins the Homestake Creek road at present. Then during the glacial epoch, a very large glacier occupied the Homestake Creek Valley, and a large terminal moraine was deposited just about at the junction referred to above. This moraine makes the very irregular topography between Pando and the road junction on Homestake Creek. Eagle River was dammed up and a lake basin was formed, where*

Eagle Park is now. Finally the lake over-flowed and Eagle River was forced to cut a new channel, which is now the deep narrow canyon occupied by the river and the railroad, beginning about two miles northwest of Pando and extending down nearly to Red Cliff. In time the lake was drained, but the broad, flat floored valley between Pando and the foot of Tennessee Pass represents the floor of the old glacial lake.[95]

The earliest inhabitants of the valley were Ute Indians, who resided in the region until the second governor of the Colorado Territory, Governor John Evans, negotiated a treaty with them on October 7, 1863, in which the Utes surrendered the territory.[96] This agreement opened the territory to exploration, settlement and eventually mining.

Miners first moved into the area surrounding Pando around 1881, when they discovered gold west of Pando around present-day Gold Park and Holy Cross City. These individuals established the town of Gold Park, now a site of ruins along Homestake Road (Colorado 703), which branches off from U.S. Highway 24 and heads west.[97] About two and a half miles northwest of Gold Park, miners established the small mountain town of Holy Cross City. Holy Cross City had a population of about three hundred at its peak and contained a mill, boardinghouse, assay office, justice of the peace, school, general store, post office and several cabins.[98] An iron flume carried ore down to Gold Park until the ore played out by 1883, and the city dwindled down to a single family by the end of the year.[99] Human beings other than Ute Indians may have inhabited Eagle Valley and the surrounding areas before these miners arrived at Gold Park. During the leveling process of Eagle Valley, engineers ran into an unexpected challenge in July 1942, when they discovered and further excavated the relics of earlier inhabitants. Excavators, while digging for a water main, found relics consisting of three cast-iron spittoons, each weighing approximately six pounds, one corroded rifle barrel and a Chelsea cream pitcher.[100] These may have been the remnants of a small mining group in the valley or a traveling group of explorers. Regardless, nothing in historical records indicates that any large settlements sprang up in Eagle Valley in the preceding centuries.

During the 1880s and early 1890s, Leadville and the surrounding mines flourished with activity and investment from businessmen in the East. However, with the repeal of the Sherman Silver Purchase Act in 1893, the bottom dropped out of the price of silver, cutting its value in half. Silver mines shut down by the dozen and resulted in about 90 percent unemployment among the workforce of Leadville by the summer of 1893.[101] Some miners turned to gold, but silver prevailed in the Leadville area and the surrounding regions. The end of the nineteenth century was plagued by miners' strikes and disillusionment in Leadville and the surrounding area. Author Christian J. Buys wrote that "the Cloud City had metamorphosed into a more typical mountain mining town, struggling to make ends meet."[102] However, the early 1900s brought a brief glimpse of hope to the Leadville area as gold mines in 1901 yielded their highest production of gold in the history of the Leadville Mining District.[103] The 1910s and 1920s economy of Leadville fluctuated, but the town's population continued to decline and eventually reached its lowest number in 1932, with only about 3,400 people residing in the town. In that same year, the city recorded the most suicides it had seen in its history as workers could not find jobs. In addition to this problem, the city treasury ran out of money to pay the bills in 1932, putting stress on the town as a whole to figure out a way to survive.[104] The largest industry in the town besides mining from 1920 until 1933 was bootlegging. Times were tough for Leadvilleites as more people left the town seeking jobs. Though Leadville's three railroads dropped down to one, the Denver & Rio Grande Western Railroad, only one major business folded during the Great Depression. The remaining businesses kept industry alive in the town and served the small but manageable population.[105]

By the end of 1933, business began to pick up slightly in Leadville as CWA, WPA and CCC work camps and projects sprang up around the area, providing jobs for young men.[106] However, Leadville never resoundingly saw true prosperity return until the arrival of thousands of workers to Pando from April to November 1942, along with the ski troopers shortly thereafter. America in general did not lift itself out of the Depression until war production began around the country, turning out hundreds of thousands of tanks, planes and other war-related goods.

As a resident of Pando, Erl H. Ellis had a vested interest and spent several months researching its origin and history. He sent letters to various businesses and individuals with connections to the area. He started sending letters around August 1942 and continued his research into 1945. In his letter writing, he contacted officials from the Denver & Rio Grande Western Railroad Company, Black & Veatch Platt Rogers Inc., the University of New Mexico and the Eagle County, Colorado clerk and recorder. The following information came from the period correspondence of Ellis about Pando.

In a letter dated January 22, 1945, Ellis received a response from Arthur Ridgway, chief engineer of the Denver & Rio Grande Western Railroad. Ridgway recounted a short history of the railroad's involvement at Pando, starting with the railroad's use of Pando as a narrow-gauge station along its western line. The first recorded occupation of Pando came in 1902. In July and August of that year, the Denver & Rio Grande Western Railroad Company purchased land for an ice pond.[107] By October, it had finished constructing initial ice harvesting facilities and began minimal operations. By the end of 1902, the railroad had constructed an icehouse with additional support buildings nearby. As a result, the company harvested its first significant crop of ice in the winter of 1902–3, using its own "B&B" labor force. The company force harvested ice for a few years with an occasional year's crop harvested by contract.[108] It shipped most of the harvested ice out to other areas along the train line for storage because its equipment served only in the harvesting process, including tracks and loading machinery at Pando, instead of cold storage preservation. The work never proved to be easy for these early railroad workers given their lack of mechanical power equipment necessary for heavy lifting and moving. Workers completed all of their initial work through the use of draft animals and pulley systems. Despite these difficulties, the primitive system did not inhibit their first harvests, which turned out to be small but worthwhile.

As time moved on, Pando slowly obtained mechanical power equipment to cut and remove ice from the pond and load it onto train cars. Business quickly picked up with both eastern-bound fruit trains and local refrigerated traffic as the Pando icehouse increased production.[109] In 1922, Denver & Rio Grande workers cut 48,297 tons of ice from the Pando ice pond, peaking in 1935 with 48,893 tons, the largest annual crop the icehouse ever produced. In addition to ice production, the Pando area also supported sawmills, which operated extensively between Leadville and Pando, providing lumber to the area. Though ice production soon ended, the lumber mills continued to supply wood throughout the building of Camp Hale. As expected, the announcement by the army of the construction of a military cantonment at Pando was not the first time workers began to settle in Eagle Valley. The three-mile-long flat on the Eagle River soon changed dramatically from a simple railroad depot with two houses into one of the most sophisticated army cantonments in the country during World War II.[110]

Erl Ellis also corresponded with individuals to figure out the origin of the name "Pando" for the area of the Eagle Valley where the Denver & Rio Grande Western Railroad built its railroad depot and icehouse. In his earliest correspondence with the Denver & Rio Grande Western Railroad Company, on August 25, 1942, he learned that a Mr. George Pando from either Michigan or Wisconsin lived as a farmer and prospector in the area prior to 1883. At around this time, Denver & Rio Grande records reveal the first mention of the station of Pando.[111] Other records indicate that George Pando and his wife conducted a small station there for freighters operating in the district. In a letter to Erl Ellis dated two days later, the Eagle County clerk and recorder verified the information about George Pando.[112]

However, other sources revealed a different origin. In a response to Ellis's letter to R.M. Duncan of the University of New Mexico–Albuquerque Department of Modern Languages on November 22, 1944, Duncan wrote that the word *pando* derived from the Latin *pandus*, which means "curving" or "bulging." The Spanish people in the area often said, "Estoy pando," meaning "I am full," after a big meal.[113] As a result, the claim is that the locals changed the name of the area from Eagle City to Pando. Duncan also claimed that locals sometimes applied the word to a river that meandered or even that ran slowly over level territory.[114] The Eagle River fit this definition well given its meandering through the flat, three-mile-long Eagle Valley. The exact origin of the name may never be known, but Ellis provided a few legitimate explanations.

Pando's history contains few significant events or contributions to the area beyond the impact of the icehouse, but it did prove to be ideal for the army's choice for a training area for ski troopers. The once soggy swamp, riddled with boulders, wildlife and quiet sounds of running water, soon had a new beginning as a unique and unprecedented army cantonment.

3

THE ARMY'S DEVELOPMENT
OF PANDO

*Never in the United States was there another construction job like Pando, and I
hope there never is another one.*[115]
—*Pando construction worker*

The U.S. Army was already three months into its Pearl Harbor–related
mobilization of troops when it began to finalize its intentions to build
an army cantonment at Pando, Colorado, near the end of February 1942.
The army desired a better location than its contracted ski area at Paradise
Lodge in Mount Rainier National Park, to train a division of ski troopers for
wintertime maneuvers at high elevation.[116] To the army's delight and the ski
troopers' advantage, Pando became the top choice. By 1942, the valley served
primarily as a railroad depot for the Denver & Rio Grande Western Railroad,
making the army's acquisition of it fairly easy on March 31, 1942.[117] The
Herald Democrat received two telegrams from Congressman Robert F. Rockwell
and U.S. senator Eugene D. Millikin, both stating that the War Department
approved the cantonment at Pando.[118] As a result of the final approval and
the orders to begin building, the army gave out the first two contracts totaling
around $5 million, well over initial estimates and a paltry sum compared to the
overall cost of the project.[119] With the time limitation put on the project, the
lack of initial housing, the preliminary earth-moving work to make the valley
suitable for buildings, the high elevation and the desired final self-sustainable
product, engineers faced an inimitable task.[120]

Many geographical considerations influenced the decision by the
Headquarters Company of the 8th Corps at Fort Sam Houston, Texas, to

recommend that Pando and Eagle Valley be the location for a "cantonment for mountain and winter warfare training for a Triangular Division,"[121] but time constraints in acquiring the land proved to be an important factor also. Before army engineers began construction, the land on which Pando sat and the surrounding Eagle Valley had to be obtained from various private owners and other government and nongovernment entities. Fortunately for the army, most of the private property was owned by one individual: Frank J. Byers.[122] Byers owned 1,027 acres of the total 1,532 acres acquired for the cantonment proper.[123] Of the other 505 acres of land, the army acquired 317 from three private owners, 101 acres from the Denver & Rio Grande Western Railroad and the remaining 87 acres from the State of Colorado.[124] Condemnation proceedings, started by U.S. district attorney Thomas J. Morrissey, began on April 13, 1942, in the U.S. District Court in Denver to acquire 1,060 acres of the land.[125] The proceedings moved quickly and gave the army immediate control. Quick land acquisition became an influential part in the choice of Pando and ultimately worked out well for the army, whose plan was now to begin construction by the spring of 1942. The only exclusion granted in the Camp Hale Military Reservation to a private landowner included allowing fifteen thousand sheep to continue grazing on the condemned land.[126]

Time constraints for the project also demanded that Leadville, the closest city to the cantonment with a sizeable population, provide assistance for the construction project in two ways. First, the June 1941 investigative group from Fort Sam Houston obtained agreements from the mayor of Leadville, John Cortellini, and the City Council to provide a full-time district health unit and health board consisting of army physicians and nurses.[127] The county commissioners of Lake and Eagle Counties and the Colorado State Board of Health agreed to assist with this addition. Army engineers had little doubt that the project would require thousands of civilian workers, resulting in the need for exemplary healthcare to make sure that workers stayed healthy and continued to work on the cantonment to meet the deadline. Second, the army estimated that the construction project itself would double the population of Leadville, demanding leisure activities, restaurants, public facilities and places to stay.[128] Not only were the businesses of Leadville supportive of the project, which would bring much-needed consumers to their establishments, but the entire city also started thinking about the impact Pando would have on it in the future. An April 2 article in the *Herald Democrat* expressed the possibility that many of the ski troopers would want to return to Leadville after the war with their families as businessmen to take up a vocation in the area where they had once skied and trained.[129] This wishful thinking in April 1942 came true after the war, as soldiers returned and contributed to a boom in the local ski industry.[130] Nevertheless, the problems of the day still loomed large, and housing became one of the biggest issues for army engineers. Leadville, located almost twenty-one miles away, lacked adequate housing and could barely spare rooms for workers.[131] The other small towns in the area, including Red Cliff and Minturn, provided even less housing opportunities than Leadville.

J. Hunter Carroll, safety and sanitation inspector for Pando during construction, identified the real underlying problem with housing, writing, "The difficulties attendant to building Uncle Sam's training camps for our soldiers becomes all the greater when these camps are located away from our thickly populated centers where housing and feeding conditions for the men enter into the picture. Such was the condition confronting the Pando Constructors in the erection of Camp Hale."[132] Major Rulon J. Ballard, chief engineer in charge of construction at Pando, reported this concern four months into construction when he commented in the camp's construction newspaper, the *Pando Echo*, that "because of the numbers of workers on the job and the fact that Pando is in a more or less isolated spot, some inconveniences naturally arise. These must be taken in stride and every effort put forth to do your job to the best of your ability and in the spirit of working for your country and not for yourself on just another job with good wages."[133] Ballard made this patriotic appeal to workers to make sacrifices in their life by living and working in the harsh conditions of Pando. As proven through many of the war bond drives made throughout World War II, appeals to patriotism worked in garnering support. In this case, getting people to agree to live in a train car or tent for a few months proved to be the challenge for the army. The vacancy rate in Leadville, Red Cliff and Minturn hovered around zero, and the few available houses within a radius of forty miles of Pando did not conform to habitable standards.[134] Neither Leadville nor Red Cliff had a population large enough to provide adequate needs for workers, resulting in significant challenges for the army.

Owners in Leadville had boarded up homes and abandoned them in the previous decades due to a decline in mining and business; most were uninhabitable.[135] However, this unfortunate event did not stop workers from coming to Camp Hale seeking jobs. Construction brought in large numbers of workers and some families of skilled workers who could afford to house them in the area. "Workers migrated into Pando hundreds at a time from every state in the union and from all walks of life."[136] Whatever housing opportunities Leadville offered, Pando workers took. "Every house, hotel, camp ground and available lodging was taken and hundreds slept in tents and trailers, some even in their cars."[137] One individual by the name of Roy D. Price from Ocate, New Mexico, entered town with his pickup truck, a bedroll and a hitchhiker named Lawrence M. Stevens. Both individuals came in search of the "good money" that they had heard about. However, neither individual knew of a place to stay and subsequently could not find any available housing. As a result, Price parked his truck outside town, and both individuals slept in it until they could find work the next morning.[138] At the Vendome Hotel in Leadville, owner F.W. Henson partitioned two banquet rooms off the lobby into one-cot stalls for one dollar a night. He also allowed patrons who arrived late when the cots were full to crash on the lobby chairs for no charge at all.[139] Similarly, Sheriff Angelo Travison turned the Lake County Jail into housing as a last resort for those who came into town without anywhere to stay. Those seeking a bed were given a jail bunk for the asking price, except on Saturday nights, when the jail typically filled up with individuals who decided to drink more than they could handle at the local saloons.[140] Even army officers found quarters in their offices early on since constructors had not built officer housing yet.[141] With a population of only about six thousand in Eagle County, the location of the cantonment, and seven thousand in Lake County, the location of Leadville, workers had to be imported from around Colorado and the surrounding states, adding to the housing problem.[142] Regardless of the issues that arose from the time constraints put on the construction project, none of them effectively derailed the progress as engineers moved on with their plans.

Army engineers originally planned in April 1942 for a camp housing 20,353 officers and enlisted men and 11,288 animals. The army designated it Pando Job No. T 1-1.[143] By May 11, 1942, the numbers had dropped to 16,392 officers and enlisted men and 3,925 animals under Pando Job No. T 1-5.[144] Engineers studied the area and learned quickly that the half-mile-wide by two-mile-long crescent-shaped glacial valley did not contain enough room for buildings to house comfortably all the people and animals proposed. Also, the severe winters with heavy snows posed another threat to packing buildings and training areas into the limited cantonment space. With such a meager amount of space in Eagle Valley, engineers worked diligently in developing a plan that could be accomplished in the time allotted and would fit into the designated area. As a result, Pando soon obtained the nickname "Stando" as buildings quickly consumed space, and workers joked about having standing room only when the camp was completed.[145]

Army officials designated November 15, 1942, as their goal to have the cantonment completed.[146] With actual construction of the camp not beginning until April 10, this gave the engineers and workers only seven months before the treacherous Rocky Mountain snows significantly covered the valley. To the detriment of the workers and the advantage of the incoming ski troopers, winter came early to Pando yearly and left late.[147] Army surveyors, who estimated that there would be only about eighty-six days free from freezing at the cantonment's elevation, emphasized starting construction early so that underground utility construction and concrete foundations could be finished by October 1942.[148] Local inhabitants of Leadville and Red Cliff, knowledgeable about the climate, also advised this so that frequent delays did not result. They advised that much of the inside work, utilities and furnishings could be done into the winter months.[149] Engineers labeled the foundations and subsequent construction of the barracks and mess halls priorities, with the understanding that even after the ski troopers arrived, the inside furnishings of other buildings could be completed. Also, the workers needed the barracks and mess halls as soon as the constructors completed them to improve housing conditions for the thousands in the workforce.[150]

As the area had only a few days above freezing in this season, speed was of the essence in building Camp Hale. As a result, construction costs increased significantly as many workers labored overtime to complete as much as possible in the time allotted. Also, the awarding of contracts to certain companies resulted in them being much higher on the average than at other cantonments. First, many firms with broad experience were reluctant to bid on jobs because of the rapid speed desired in construction. Second, many firms steered away from working in the unusual cold conditions at 9,250 feet of elevation. Third, government payments and reimbursements to contractors and vendors early on faced a delay because the majority of workers who processed the payments were unskilled in government procedures. The unwillingness of other contractors to work certain jobs often stuck the designers of the camp—Black & Veatch of Pueblo, Colorado, and Platt Rogers of Kansas City—with the responsibility to complete them.[151] These two companies had organized and formed Pando Constructors by the beginning of work on April 10.[152] As a result of Pando Constructors' complete devotion to the job, the army in its completion report wrote that they had "performed much more than the context of their contract…and have overcome many difficulties beyond their control, and have prosecuted all work necessary to bring the completion of Camp Hale to a successful conclusion."[153]

The War Department Office of Chief of Engineers initiated the process to establish contractors for the project on April 3, 1942. On April 7, the chief of engineers awarded Pando Constructors the first two construction contracts.[154] During World War II, the Army Corps of Engineers usually acted as the contracting and supervising agent of the federal government.[155] Thus, the Corps of Engineers gave these contractors authority to recruit personnel, engineer, survey, procure, design, provide professional supervision and oversee the construction of all facilities to serve the troops, animals and all others assigned to the camp.[156] These jobs, starting with personnel recruitment, were started early in April 1942 in Denver at the old Mining Exchange building by a few key individuals from Black & Veatch and Platt Rogers.[157] One of these individuals, J.R. Smith, chief electrical engineer (1942–43), said their initial philosophy was to "hire everybody—then weed out incompetents" since they knew that a shortage of labor existed in the area.[158] A construction project of this magnitude demanded thousands of workers, and Pando Constructors refused to allow this potential impediment to stop them from beginning construction. The U.S. Employment Office initially paid entry-level workers a generous sum of $1.10 an hour, higher than most businesses in the country during World War II, and guaranteed a job to these individuals until at least November 1942.[159] Higher wages, along with government job security, recruited workers to the isolated area of Pando.

Though housing remained limited, work began quickly at two different locations. In Denver, at the Mining Exchange building, engineers started planning and hiring while Captain R.J. Ballard, the army's area engineer, took charge at Pando. On April 10, when work first began on the camp, Pando continued as a railroad station, with two houses in the proper area of the cantonment and an icehouse. The town overlooked a subarctic flat, knee deep in slush that froze hard on cold nights.[160] The primitive setting for construction did not dampen the spirits of the engineers as thirty to forty railroad cars, with engines releasing thick black smoke, made their way up from Denver that day with supplies for the camp.[161] As hired workers began to trickle into Pando, the army advertised for more workers and the *Herald Democrat* also called for interested individuals to stop by the bank building in Leadville and talk with the U.S. Employment Office. Trucks ran back and forth between Leadville and Pando carrying workers from the Employment Office to the camp to begin unloading lumber and other supplies. Apparently, individuals took notice of the army's call for workers and began showing up directly at the camp, only to be sent to Leadville to fill out applications at the

Pando Constructors' War Department identification. Black and Veatch of Pueblo, Colorado, and Platt Rogers of Kansas City, joined in April 1942 to be Pando Constructors. *Author's personal collection.*

Employment Office.[162] Confusion abounded at first in the hiring process, but a system soon developed to get workers signed on in Leadville and then sent to Pando.

As more workers arrived, the question of housing still worried army engineers and civilian contractors. The board of officers from the 8th Corps, which made an initial assessment and report on Pando on June 23, 1941, recommended that work trains rented from railroad companies be utilized to house workmen until sufficient housing could be built on the camp. The report identified a number of sidings available in the cantonment that could be extended with temporary spurs to house a large number of railroad cars. One unknown authorized document recorded that the first workers did indeed take up residence in the railcars and turned the railroad siding into a "swarming town."[163]

Given the lack of housing opportunities in both Eagle and Lake Counties, it was necessary to make provisions for housing workmen at the site. Construction commenced on a total of eighty-seven temporary prefabricated barracks and twelve mess halls to house and provide messing facilities for 2,465 workers.[164] Captain Ballard commented that the structures "would be of a temporary construction and not of brick or other 'permanent type' materials."[165] The temporary camp started on April 15 and was completed by July 15, 1942.[166] None of the original temporary structures initially had heat, electric lights or water.[167] The workers lived as did earlier miners who frequented the area and endured harsh winters in a similar fashion.[168] Only three days after construction started on the temporary camp, Pando Constructors completed the first mess hall on April 18, under the managerial control of John F. Person and his assistant, E.E. Perry.[169] J. Hunter Carroll praised both of these individuals for their untiring and relentless devotion to keeping the mess halls functioning throughout the seven months of construction, even during the coldest of mornings and afternoon thunderstorms. As permanent construction began on the large troop barracks, workers utilized them with the understanding that once the ski troops arrived, they would take the space. Though these facilities were made available to employees at Pando, workers were allowed to settle wherever they chose either in the camp or somewhere in Leadville and the surrounding area.

Chief electrical engineer J.R. Smith settled off the Pando cantonment because his family resided with him. Because Smith came late to Pando, due to his earlier work in Denver on planning for the cantonment, all of the available houses, apartments and rooms for rent were taken for miles around the Pando Valley.[170] Smith and his family, and three other engineers with families, found "four 1-room cabins without running water, non-heated, non-insulated 2 holers out back—with wood burning cook stoves that served

Inside a mess hall at Camp Hale, Colorado. *Courtesy of the Denver Public Library, Western History Collection, Curt Krieser, TMD-807.*

to heat also—a table, a bed—shelves on the wall and a curtained off corner for clothes."[171] Smith further described the cabin as having ice-cold linoleum floors that never warmed up, two bare lamp drop lights, unpainted walls and ceilings and two metal-framed beds with simple four-inch mattresses.[172] To make matters even worse, "black monsters snorting and belching smoke" rolled by like an avalanche in the night.[173] Smith, along with the three other families he resided with, stayed sixteen and a half miles from the cantonment in the confluence of Gore Creek and the Eagle River near Minturn.[174] Many workers like Smith traveled treacherous roads through snowy, sub-zero temperatures to make the trek to Pando daily whereas workers without families found locations closer to the cantonment.

In addition to the temporary housing constructed at Pando, the army also organized a trailer park a mile north of the cantonment site that housed 1,050 workmen and families in 603 trailers at the peak of its population on September 5, 1942. Around this same time, the army also built a school for the approximately 300 children in the trailer park with funding from the National Bureau of Education. The school, located within the boundaries of the camp in section twenty-one, was in one of the permanent warehouses near the trailer park.[175] Also, a little-mentioned camp located about a half mile northeast of Pando consisted of forty tents and two barracks.

Mexican American workers, hired mostly from New Mexico, lived on their own, segregated from the rest of the other Pando workers.[176] At the peak of construction, about 345 Mexican American workers lived in this camp and supported the efforts at Pando.[177] Overall, approximately 5,100 hired workers and 3,525 Black & Veatch and Platt Rogers employees found housing in permanent cantonment buildings during the peak period, and approximately 2,800 resided in nearby towns, tourist camps, temporary shacks and trailer sites off the cantonment.[178] No significant delays resulted from the housing crisis, as workers endured the often squalid conditions in order to obtain one of the coveted government jobs during the war.

By the end of April, the heavy work of molding the land into a flat, solid foundation began. Pando Constructors and the Army Corps of Engineers first addressed geographical matters in preparing Pando Valley for construction before any permanent structures went up. The Pando cantonment, located in a glacial valley about one half mile wide and five miles long, was a "subarctic swamp for much of the year."[179] The Eagle River meandered sluggishly through dwarf willows and swamp grass on its way through the valley making S curves across the land.[180] It obtained its water from rainfall and the spring runoff from the immediate surrounding peaks, which rose in excess of ten to eleven thousand feet.[181] The valley, filled with wildlife and tumbled boulders and once a haven for big game hunters, provided challenges for the engineers to tackle before any major buildings went up. The first task the Pando Constructors took on included rerouting the Eagle River so that it no longer created the swamp terrain in which muskeg prevailed.[182] Engineers estimated the muskeg to be on average about four feet deep in the middle of the valley, creating serious problems for its removal, as heavy machinery sank into the ground before it could cut away any trees. "Into this freezing morass, where even the bulldozers bogged down, plunged crews of men who chopped out seventeen miles of willow trees by hand to shift the course of the river and drain the swamp."[183] Many acres of trees, including pine, spruce, willows and sagebrush, were later chopped or uprooted so that the camp could be built in as compact a space as possible."[184] Not only did workers get cold and wet during the day, enduring occasional snowstorms and sloshing through the ice and slush cutting down

Opposite, top: New Eagle River channel, Camp Hale, Colorado. *Courtesy of the Denver Public Library, Western History Collection, Pando Constructors, Black & Veach and Platt Rogers Inc., TMD-591.*

Eagle Creek, Camp Hale, Colorado, 1944. Notice the straight and contained flow of the river through camp as a result of early construction. *Courtesy of the Denver Public Library, Western History Collection, Phil O'Rourke, TMD-792.*

trees, but they also had to endure the cold nights in unheated temporary living structures surrounded by bare walls.[185] One worker reminisced about his first impression upon arrival at Pando. He wrote that the train conductor "unceremoniously dumped [him] on the other side of the tracks and told [him] to walk up to the barracks—through the mud, over the rocks to a barren barrack room that looked like a cell."[186] As work commenced on the valley floor removing vegetation, constructors removed the ice plant, taking away the last traces of Pando, prior to the army's adoption of the area. Engineers from Platt Rogers of Denver, chief contractor of Pando Constructors, had built the railroad's icehouse twenty years before and now returned to tear it down and move it to Wilmore, near Wolcott, Colorado, to make room for more train tracks at Pando.[187] This officially opened the valley floor for what came next: a complete overhaul of Pando.

Earthmovers followed the straightening of the Eagle River and the draining of the swamp. Heavy machinery gouged and dragged two million cubic yards of earth from nearby mountainsides and leveled it over the ice and slush of the valley floor.[188] This spectacular engineering process added significant costs to the project and formed the Pando Valley into the landscape that travelers see today from Highway 24. Evidence of the scraping and gouging of the mountainsides to fill in the valley can still be seen along the valley floor leading up to the mountain slopes today. "Never in the United States was there another construction job like Pando," many an experienced workman and veteran engineer declared.[189] Despite the difficulties, work continued, and the engineers stayed on track to finish on time.

After the river had been rerouted and molded into a canal that ran straight north and south through the cantonment, workers began to fill the oxbows the river once created in order to flatten out the land and make it suitable for buildings. As part of this process, the construction crew announced toward the end of work time that it was about to close a loop. Individuals, carrying pails of water and wet gunnysacks, swarmed around the banks while a few individuals waded into the water with seed forks and stabbed the trout, throwing them onto the shoreline. That evening, the workers living on the cantonment held a fish fry.[190] In addition to this removal of the fish, workers from the Colorado Fish and Game Commission trapped two hundred beavers from the marsh, dismantled their dams and moved them to a new home in Colorado where their environment would not be disrupted.[191] The once pristine wilderness environment, surrounded mostly by the Arapaho National Forest, now roared with the sounds of freight trains, bulldozers, earthmovers and hungry workers filling mess halls and barracks.[192]

In sequence with the clearing, filling and leveling of the Pando Valley, the War Department, in cooperation with Colorado State Highway engineer Charles D. Vail, decided to move a portion of Highway 24.[193] Both entities decided that the famed trans-American highway should run straight from Tennessee Pass, located on the Continental Divide, down to Pando under Job No. Pando T 1-4, May 6, 1942.[194] Engineers thought the move was necessary because the road made a sweeping curve through the proposed cantonment ground, which interrupted planned locations for barracks and buildings. Other factors—such as the requirements of having controlled entrances to the cantonment area monitored by military police, slow traffic regulations and the elimination of traffic congestion and traffic hazards in the cantonment—made the move necessary.[195] The new route, at a cost of around $400,000 and an engineering marvel of its own, cut off three miles from the original route through the valley and followed the Denver & Rio Grande Western Railroad along the outside of the western side of the camp.[196] The Colorado State Highway Department rerouted all through traffic during construction from Leadville to Minturn, over Fremont Pass and Vail Pass on State Highway 91 and U.S. Highway 6, increasing the distance by about fourteen miles for a short period of time.[197] Once constructors straightened the Eagle River and rerouted U.S. Highway 24, Captain Ballard took charge of a crew of surveyors and began running lines totaling four miles along the valley floor.[198] These lines later helped arrange the barracks and other buildings into the limited space. Four major roads (A through D) led through the span of the camp, with one (D Street) continuing into the ordnance ranges on the far southeastern part of the valley. In order to conserve space within the three roads, engineers combined buildings for special uses into fewer buildings. This also resulted in shorter distances within and between battalion areas, which helped soldiers when temperatures dropped below zero.[199] Though late-April snowstorms brought minor delays in filling the marsh, rerouting U.S. Highway 24 and various other tasks, construction efforts moved on, and by May 1, buildings were beginning to be completed across the camp.

By the middle of May 1942, the cantonment only had about 150 workers laboring forty hours, five days a week.[200] However, this number soon jumped significantly as the U.S. Employment Office sought and hired more workers from around the country. A *Herald Democrat* reporter visited the cantonment on May 11 and reported that the construction work was mainly confined to preparations for the larger force of workers that would build the cantonment. Temporary buildings were going up rapidly. Buildings already standing in the vicinity from the Pando Depot were utilized, and railroad spurs were laid to handle material for the camp when it arrived.[201] Lieutenant William D. Mitchell, the army's executive officer in charge of the field headquarters, commanded by Captain Ballard, still resided in his makeshift office in a railroad car on the siding. Even though no major permanent structures had gone up by the middle of May 1942, Pando had quickly turned into a city in the middle of an alpine valley.

The increase in workers meant an increase in the amount of supplies coming into camp. Trains utilized the Denver & Rio Grande Western Railway for bringing supplies to Pando and also as one of the main transportation routes to haul war materials through the Rocky Mountains.[202] Given the steep grade of the tracks at close to 4 percent in many locations, three locomotives often pulled a train over Tennessee Pass toward the Continental Divide.[203] Powered by coal, each one of these locomotives released thick black smoke into the Pando Valley. In addition to the locomotives polluting the valley, steam from stoker-fired coal furnaces heated every one of the newly constructed buildings in the cantonment, adding more black smoke to an already tainted valley.[204] To make matters worse, the beautiful rolling green mountain sides and tree line–breaking ridges surrounding Pando Valley helped trap and hold cold air and smoke, thus creating a vacuum of dirty, stagnant air.[205] Unfortunately for the Pando workers and even more so for the ski troopers when they arrived, individuals contracted what became known not so affectionately as the "Pando hack" by some and "Pando-monia" by others. Robert B. Ellis, a soldier of F Company in the 85th Mountain Infantry, wrote in his memoirs about the "Pando hack" and the unique geographical nature of Camp Hale:

> Upon arrival by train at Camp Hale, I quickly discovered what distinguished the camp and the ski troops from all other military facilities and units in the U.S. at the time. These factors included the camp's isolation from all normal human habitation, its extreme altitude, a climate unequaled in severity for snow and cold, the smoke and dust-laden air filling the basin where the camp was located and its impact on our health, its extraordinary physical demands despite the absence of accustomed levels of oxygen, and the high intelligence and education characteristic of its newly arrived volunteers.[206]

Some workers ended up in the infirmary due to the Pando hack while others simply quit their job because they could not handle the respiratory challenges in the valley. Other workers demanded "double wages" or they were done with their work.[207] Though the soot affected some workers, it did not create a large enough problem for the Colorado Safety and Sanitation Inspectors to step in and make changes.[208] The trains continued to run daily, bringing in thousands of pounds of supplies to Pando.

Camp Hale infirmary around the winter of 1942–43. *Author's personal collection.*

Finally, one other major factor contributed to construction difficulties. The cantonment sat at a higher elevation than any other army camp in the country, resulting in unprecedented weather difficulties and health problems. According to Mr. John B. Leighou (forestry supervisor, Glenwood Springs, Colorado), in 1941, the Pando area received a heavier annual snowfall than any other large area in Colorado. Snow began to fall in Pando around the first day of October and lasted until about the first of June.[209] In an average winter, 12 feet of snow stayed on the valley, and temperatures dropped to as low as negative thirty degrees Fahrenheit on the surrounding mountain peaks.[210] The high altitude and its effects on the body also challenged workers, especially those from the Midwest, the South and other places of lower elevations. Just as it later affected the ski troopers, it caused dizziness, lack of sleep and fatigue for some workers when they first arrived in Pando.[211] One soldier commented that at high elevation, "you are so short of breath you can hardly go on but you go on somehow and catch your breath later. The same way when you are working, if you pick up a shovel about 1 minute you have to stop for breath. After all, we are up between 10 & 12,000 feet."[212] Many were not used to the lower air pressure, the 20 percent relative humidity and the 30 percent less oxygen at 9,250 feet.[213] On top of the natural effects of snow and altitude, the Pando Valley occasionally experienced earthquakes that rattled buildings and knocked pictures off the walls.[214] Steep and treacherous mountain roads challenged soldiers inside and outside Camp Hale, resulting in at least one death due to a jeep that fell 1,000 feet off a mountain trail in between Leadville and Aspen.[215] Pando did not offer a hospitable environment for workers, but construction continued on regardless of the high altitude and its effects on weather, workers and transportation.[216]

The War Department desired all along for Pando to be a self-sustainable unit in the middle of the Colorado Rockies. The cantonment eventually grew into a city nearly as large as Colorado Springs in 1942 but contained much less area. Army engineers and site planners agreed that the cantonment, when completed, had the capability of housing sixteen thousand soldiers in a ten-thousand-man camp area.[217] This created unprecedented challenges for engineers to figure out all the logistics, including matters like keeping one of the cantonment's minor sources of fresh water, the Eagle River, from freezing in the winter.[218] Thus, the cantonment relied on five deep wells at the south end of the valley for most of its water, storing it in tanks just north of the hospital.[219] Every other army base or camp constructed shortly before or during World War II relied on basic utilities and recreational opportunities from nearby cities or towns and also on a standard army layout for cantonments. Leadville offered some of these amenities but not enough to sustain the camp.

Throughout 1942, Leadville was far from being a desirable recreational town. Workers and soldiers had to travel about eighteen miles to get there. The War Department showed much less concern for Pando workers mingling in the affairs of Leadville and, at times, encouraged them to take a break and enjoy Leadville's hospitality. However, Leadville stayed off limits to soldiers stationed at Camp Hale until February 24, 1943, due to its lingering red-light district and other perceived immoral temptations. Pando did, however, offer local recreational opportunities, such as hiking, climbing, fishing, wrestling matches and shows in the warehouses and other buildings, easing the strains of long workdays.[220] However, the camp, with its harsh conditions, often struggled to bring traveling shows in for entertainment. The fact that other people refused to even travel to the place they lived provided the soldiers at least small amusement. The social outlet issue eventually became such a concern to the Mountain Training Center that it requested that the cantonment receive a special service officer.[221] However, Army Ground Forces (AGF) rejected this request.

Another unique aspect of the cantonment came from its modifications to the standard army training program as established by the Army Ground Forces. Major Jefferson J. Irvin, G-3 for the Mountain Training Center, worked to modify enclosures one, two and three of the standard training directive to better meet the requirements for mountain troops.[222] General Rolfe faced a difficult situation in meeting the training needs of soldiers that included both basic training and mountain training. The army equipped the Mountain Training Center with a staff equivalent to that of an infantry division for training purposes, which neglected the fact that the center also needed staff for specialized mountain training.[223] One officer covered both training positions, which later proved to be a deficiency at the MTC when observers witnessed the impact of this duel coverage at the fiasco of the Homestake Peak Maneuvers. However, not all blame can be placed on the Army Ground Forces, as the Mountain Training Center's Headquarters table of organization actually called for four captains to help as liaisons to the main training officer in the specialized areas of skiing, rock climbing, dog management and packing.[224] To the detriment of the MTC, these positions were never filled, as these individuals never arrived at Camp Hale.

In conjunction with the lack of local facilities and recreation in Leadville and the modifications to training, the army dealt with another significant change in the deviations at Camp Hale from the standard army cantonment layout. According to an engineer's news article in the *Pando Echo* from September 15, 1942, Pando Constructors built the parade grounds, recreational area and warehouse area in completely different locations from the traditional site plan standards for army camps due to the topography and limited area at the cantonment site.[225] Not only did the army modify the cantonment layout, but it also modified about thirty-three different structural designs from its standard to accommodate skiers and ski equipment. All modifications to the layout and structures took time to disseminate and come to fruition, adding yet another level of complexity to an already complex project.

Specifically, engineers added more space into heater rooms and added ski rooms into barracks, allowing soldiers to dry clothing and equipment and store, wax and repair skis when needed.[226] Each two-story barracks was well insulated and had blower fans to ensure even heat distribution throughout.[227] Also on the buildings, engineers modified the roof framing and wall framing to support fifty pounds per square foot, assuming an accumulation of about six feet of snow or eight to ten inches of ice on the roofs. In order to prevent dangerous ice from forming on the eaves of the roof projecting from the heated portion of the building, engineers cut back all of them to one foot.[228] Constructors eliminated all canopies over windows to save on lumber and labor and to prevent ice buildup. In addition, workers installed no gutters or downspouts to conserve metal and labor, as well as prevent ice buildup. Roof pitches increased on all buildings from the standard pitch of five to twelve feet to eight to twelve feet, preventing excessive snow and ice buildup on the top and reducing the potential for roof collapse. All buildings housing men contained half-inch insulation board in the floors and walls. Even this modification did not completely prove sufficient, as Philip A. Lunday and Chuck Hampton, veterans of the 126th Engineer Mountain Battalion, commented that the barracks walls were "constructed almost exclusively of wood siding, [and] offered little more protection than a cardboard box."[229] They further explained that "cold winter nights in the barracks [were] only slightly better than being outside on the ground." On the exterior walls, asbestos-cement shingle siding, which was abundant in the area, of oyster white lined the walls. Veteran Dick Over recalled that every night during the winter and summer to combat the extreme dry air of the mountains, the soldier assigned to barracks duty threw a bucket of water down the middle of the barracks onto the floor to increase the relative humidity.[230] Nearly every modification to the camp resulted from a need for conserving supplies, an abundance of a certain item in the area or the fact that extreme cold conditions existed for much of the year at Pando.

The existence of snow, ice, consistent cold weather and dry summers led to many other unique challenges at Camp Hale. During the winter months, when temperatures dropped below freezing, engineers recommended that soldiers keep a faucet open slightly to act as a bleeder for the water service. They also recommended that fire hydrants and sewer lines be inspected periodically to make sure they did not freeze. Sewage treatment slowed during the winter months due to the cold temperatures preventing the growth of bacterial life in the treatment process.[231] Additionally, by the end of 1943, almost all army vehicles at Camp Hale, including jeeps and trucks, were fitted with a "Winterization Kit," which consisted of a gasoline heater to keep the motor and battery warm during the night while not in use.[232] The Camp Hale Completion Report even went as far as identifying over twenty companies and their role in maintaining all of the electrical, heating and refrigeration facilities. Should any one of them fail, the cantonment would come to a standstill in

Drilling F Company, 86th Mountain Infantry Regiment, in between barracks. *Courtesy of the Denver Public Library, Western History Collection, Ralph W. Hulbert, TMD-706.*

some of the coldest months of the year.[233] Each company pledged at least a one-year warranty on its equipment to ensure the engineers of the quality of work upon installation.[234] Finally, the winter months often times disrupted the laundry service since Camp Hale did not have its own laundry company and facility until January 1944.[235] The cantonment utilized the overcrowded Denver Quartermaster Laundry service, which proved inefficient due to transportation and distance factors.[236]

The summer months also provided challenges to a cantonment completely surrounded by forest. Nearly every summer issue of the *Ski-Zette* warned soldiers of the risk of forest fires and their benefit to the enemy if one were to burn part or all of the forest surrounding Camp Hale. Not only did Camp Hale train its own soldiers to fight forest fires, but the Forest Service and the Corp of Engineers also conducted training programs at Camp Hale to ensure a proper response should one occur.[237] The high elevation of the cantonment also forced the Camp Hale bakery to modify its "formula" for making bread because the thin air affected the yeast.[238] Pando never ceased to provide challenges for the Army Corp of Engineers and Pando Constructors, who continued on with construction.

By the middle of 1942, when construction began at Pando, the Army Corps of Engineers had already taken diligent steps to ensure that

Mountain troops in jeeps at Camp Hale on December 29, 1942, testing the capability of the jeep in deep snow. *Author's personal collection.*

cantonment construction around the country went efficiently and quickly in an organized manner. However, Camp Hale might have been the exception. As early as December 23, 1940, the inspector general of the U.S. Army, Major General Virgil L. Peterson, wrote to General Marshall advocating that the army begin forecasting requirements for cantonment construction in the future so that housing and material shortages would not plague the Quartermaster Corps (QMC) and the Army Corps of Engineers as it had in previous years.[239] These forecasts were successively turned into terms of projects. The preparations, as proposed by Major General Peterson, resulted in the Army Corps of Engineers choosing sites acceptable to both users and builders, improving standard layouts and structural plans, establishing better labor relations and providing better over all forward-looking organization.[240] Unfortunately, Fine and Remington did not evaluate the outcome of these goals of the army in 1940 with their actual implementation at Pando. Truthfully, the Quartermaster Corps and the Army Corps of Engineers were not in a position to be able to evaluate the needs of Camp Hale and to predict the necessary materials to complete this project. As stated already, this made Camp Hale an exception to this general policy and, for all intents and purposes, gave the constructors the authority to continue building with whatever materials they could acquire.

As a result of the varied supplies, unique nature of the constructing and natural conditions at Pando, the improved standard layouts for cantonments were dropped almost immediately for a more advanced and specialized layout. However, the army's forward-looking organization still resulted in labor and material shortages at Pando throughout most of its construction. Though all of these factors brought challenges to Pando, the Army Corps of Engineers did succeed in meeting its construction schedule. At least a portion of this success may be attributed to what Leadville offered Pando.

Pando relied on its own ingenuity for much of its sustenance, but Leadville did provide some support. As already mentioned, Leadville eventually gave Pando a recreational outlet and a few housing opportunities. In addition to these, newly promoted Major Ballard and Lieutenant Mitchell identified another act of support by Leadville while attending a joint meeting of the Leadville Chamber of Commerce, Junior Chamber of Commerce, Lions Club and representative businessmen at the Manhattan Café in Leadville.[241] Lieutenant Mitchell thanked Leadville businessman J.V. Bradley and his crew for installing a phone line between Leadville and Pando while enduring snowdrifts and painful snow burn.[242] Pando's electric power supply did not originate in Leadville, but the lines built to the camp carrying the power came from there. Pando's electric power supply originated from two power plants: the Shoshone Hydro Plant near Glenwood Springs and the Valmont Steam Plant near Denver. The Public Service Company of Colorado ran the one-hundred-kilovolt transmission line from the Robinson substation, located between Glenwood Springs and Denver, to Leadville since Leadville had sectionalizing facilities that protected high-tension lines with over-current trip oil circuit breakers going into Camp Hale.[243] The army paid the utility company $17,000 to relocate three and a half miles of line along with the construction of additional lines and facilities for Pando.[244] Also, the two directors of the camp asked the people present to provide high-quality food not only for the workers but also for the ski troopers when they arrived. The Leadville representatives present at the meeting gladly promised to comply with the suggestion. Leadville's impact on Camp Hale and Camp Hale's impact on Leadville were eventually mutually supportive and contributed to both economic and social growth in the town and the camp.

By June 1, 1942, Pando Constructors and U.S. Employment Offices had hired approximately 400 workers, who labored in the Denver Office, but

U. S. Mountain Troops on Skiis

CAMP HALE DEVELOPMENT

A little more than a year ago only a railroad station, a couple of buildings and an ice house overlooked the valley of swamps and lakes where Camp Hale, home of the Mountain troops now stands. The camp was begun April 10, 1942 with construction beginning May 1. Several thousand workers and carloads of machinery came in. The valley was drained and filled. Rapid construction of barracks and buildings began on an enormous scale---continued through the summer.

In June the camp was dedicated and named after General Irving Hale, Colorado veteran of the Spanish-American War. In September the first Army units arrived while construction work was being wound up. And by late fall Army trucks and soldiers had replaced civilian workers. Basic training and maneuvers were under way, Camp Hale assumed its role as a full-fledged training camp for Mountain troops.

Original Leadville Lions Club 1943 tourism brochure, including an advertisement for Camp Hale and for Pando Constructors. *Author's personal collection.*

most of them needed a place at Pando to begin working. Since field workers at Pando finished constructing an engineering office and barracks near the Pando Depot to house the technical personnel of 350 men and 80 women, a massive move "by car caravan" was made to the Pando Valley location on June 1.[245] According to J.R. Smith, chief electrical engineer, "detailed instructions were typed, duplicated and issued to each of the workers to insure [sic] a safe and orderly move. The instructions gave such specifics as starting time, location, what kind of clothes to wear—watch out for snakes, deer, bear, and rushing streams, where to meet for lunch (near Dillion [sic]), and arrival time in Pando."[246]

Workers were not the only ones moving from Denver to Pando. The U.S. Post Office finally took an interest in the cantonment also. Beginning June 1, a substation of the Denver Post Office moved into Pando. The station operated like a suburban post office, even though it resided 120 miles away from Denver.[247] Denver already had experience in handling army mail because it served as a center for distribution of large amounts of it across the Rocky Mountains. Business picked up at the main Denver distribution center as the Pando cantonment's influence extended beyond the Arkansas Valley.

For the U.S. Employment Office, at the request of Pando Constructors and the Army Corps of Engineers, the hiring of workers for Pando never ended during the months of construction. In the middle of May, Major Ballard and Lieutenant Mitchell asked Leadville businessmen if they could spare stenographers for the camp so they could start going through the thousands of pages of documents that had already accumulated and take care of the expected train carloads of documents to come.[248] On June 9, an "urgent request" went out from the Pando Constructors for fifteen material clerks, ten warehouse clerks, ten first cooks, ten second cooks, ten third cooks, twenty dishwashers and twenty waiters.[249] As the number of actual constructors increased, so did the number of support jobs for these individuals. Pando Constructors acted like a small army of soldiers in which the construction workers, or "infantry," did the building and the support staff served them so they could continue with the mission.[250] Nearly all support for the workers came in-house at Pando, reflecting the army's emphasis on creating a self-sustaining post.

In many ways, the Pando Constructors functioned as part of the army, especially in using army equipment. Many contracted civilian engineers quickly understood that not everything worked in the army as intended. Chief electrical engineer J.R. Smith ran into this firsthand when the army first notified him that it had acquired two surplus diesel generators of two

Sign at Camp Hale that stood during construction of the cantonment, encouraging workers to be diligent and on time with completion of the camp. *Author's personal collection.*

different makes and speeds. Smith made it known to the army that the generators only worked together when synchronized to carry the load for the barracks and the engineering office. Possibly out of fear of not having a heated office or electricity to work late, Smith knew that he had to make them work. He commented on this instance, writing, "This was typical of all work involved in the building of Camp Hale—specify what you want—but take what you can get—and make it work—you cannot wait for anything—as the signs out in the field with the picture of Hitler say 'We've got a date with this son-of-a-bitch—lets [sic] not be late!'"[251]

After a little under three months of construction, Pando changed from a remote, marshy railroad depot and icehouse to a bustling city of engineers, workers, army planners and families. The *Saturday Evening Post* once described the area as "one of those whistle stops that would cause the passengers from behind the car windows to remark, 'Can you imagine anyone living there?'"[252] Toward the end of June 1942, thousands of people did indeed live there and called it home. By the end of June, Pando was no longer called Pando. Buildings began to go up across the valley, providing housing for workers. A vision of the past became reality in less than three months, changing the landscape of the Eagle Valley forever.

4

From Pando to Camp Hale

A civilian army-in-overalls has performed a miracle![253]
—Denver Post *writer*

Construction progressed quickly in the summer months at Pando, bringing in a new era to the camp. The time finally arrived for Pando to obtain a formal name and establish itself as a military cantonment of the U.S. Army and not just a construction site. On June 23, 1942, the headquarters of the 7th Corps Area at Omaha, Nebraska, announced that the cantonment at Pando would be henceforth named after Brigadier General Irving Hale.[254]

Hale, born on August 28, 1861, in Bloomfield, New York, moved with his family to Denver, Colorado, at the age of five. He graduated from West Point in 1884 at the top of his class with one of the highest ranks ever attained by obtaining a score of 2,070.4 points out of a possible 2,075. Upon graduation, the army commissioned him in the Corps of Engineers, where he served for six years. In 1890, he left the army and came back to Colorado to serve as manager for the General Electric Company of Denver. On May 1, 1898, Hale reentered the army as a lieutenant colonel in the Colorado National Guard. Shortly thereafter, the army promoted Hale to full colonel, and he became the commander for the 1st Colorado Volunteer Infantry Regiment. The army ordered the volunteers in April 1898 to go to the Philippines to support the war against Spain. Hale proved his military abilities at the Battle of Manila in August by leading the regiment in the capture of the capital city. As a result, the army promoted him to brigadier general. Seven months later, in March 1899, Hale was shot in the knee while scouting enemy positions at

Camp Hale postcard sold at the Camp Hale Post Exchange (PX) (1942–45). *Author's personal collection.*

the Battle of Meycauyan. Nevertheless, Hale returned to combat at Luzon a month later and earned the Silver Star for his gallantry. Finally, on October 1, 1899, Hale left the army for good and returned to Denver.[255] In his postwar years, he helped form veterans' organizations that eventually developed into the Veterans of Foreign Wars in 1914 and became known as the founder of Denver's first electric tramway system. Hale suffered a paralytic stroke in 1911 from which he never fully recovered. He died on July 26, 1930, in Denver. He left a legacy in Colorado unmatched by any military general in the history of the state.[256] As a result, the army adopted his name and called the high-altitude cantonment Camp Hale.

This was not the first time the army made use of General Irving Hale's name for a military site. A section of Camp Merritt near San Francisco became Camp Hale while soldiers of the 1st Colorado Volunteer Infantry Regiment resided there from May 21 to July 1, 1898.[257] However, the Pando cantonment was the first time a military post in Colorado was named for one of Colorado's longtime heroes.

The 7th Corps' announcement on June 23 was the beginning of Camp Hale, the army's first ski trooper training camp in American history and the site of one of the largest construction projects the state of Colorado had seen at the time. As construction moved into the end of June and the beginning of July, buildings continued to go up at a rapid pace. The summer months provided engineers with the best possible weather and conditions for construction. With the increase in productivity came a demand for more workers to accomplish the tasks. A shortage of unskilled labor in and around Leadville resulted in the U.S. Employment Office once again seeking new laborers from outside the state.

One group of Mexican American migrant workers, primarily from Taos, New Mexico, came to Camp Hale for work.[258] Out of these workers, 285 came from Taos and 60 came from around the state of Colorado. Of the approximate 345 Mexican Americans who worked at the camp, about 95 percent worked as laborers and the other 5 percent as carpenters or foremen.[259] For many, deep engrained patriotism for the United States dominated their decision while others came for the high-paying government contractor jobs that Camp Hale offered. One worker commented in the *Pando Echo* that he felt a special duty to help the war effort after learning that 160 "Taos County Boys" were in the Bataan campaign and still missing in action.[260]

A Taos native named Juan F. Romero led the group from New Mexico to Camp Hale and became the "padre," or father, of their small community, half a mile northeast of the camp. Romero proved to be well suited for the job. He owned a 340-acre ranch, a filling station and several tourist cabins near Taos, blessing him with leadership experience and respect from his fellow Taos men.[261] His leadership role soon became more important than the small group of Mexican Americans ever imagined at Camp Hale.

On June 22, 1942, Major Rulon J. Ballard, the army engineer in charge of construction at Camp Hale, dismissed 282 of the New Mexican and 60 Coloradoan Mexican American workers. One day later, on the twenty-third, Senator Dennis Chavez of New Mexico fired back at Ballard in Washington, D.C., by appealing to his superior, Major General Eugene Reybold, chief of army engineers, about the dismissal, which he claimed was "because they were Mexicans."[262] Major Ballard responded to the report insisting that the media "greatly exaggerated" the incident, saying:

What happened was precisely this: I went out to look over the job and saw too many who assumed this was a WPA project. I demanded of the contractor that he correct the situation. We're paying good wages and for overtime work we're paying $1.20 an hour and we're entitled to our money's worth. A certain group of people did not deliver; they were loafing. Their training was not suited to this work. A large percentage of these who had never had such training were terminated as building workers but were *offered work on the railroad at exactly the same pay. They refused to accept, apparently because they felt the work was too heavy. We are not interested in employing any persons who will not deliver.*[263]

Senator Chavez refused to be bullied, even by a field-grade officer such as Major Ballard. He threatened to take the story to the floor of the U.S. Senate unless he stood corrected for "this un-American outrage."[264] Chavez went on to assert that all the individuals involved were "full fledged Americans" and that many had friends and relatives who fell at Bataan.[265] He ended his remarks on the twenty-third by saying, "Now to be denied the right to work because they are supposed to be Mexicans is certainly not in keeping with what we are supposed to be fighting for."[266] That same day, Chavez received assurances of support and protest if needed from Senator Edwin C. Johnson of Colorado until the army resolved the matter.

The night before the final decision, the evening of the twenty-fourth, Chavez continued to question Ballard's actions. He said that the loafers "certainly should have been fired, but did the major investigate the 345, or make the innocent one pay for the specific ones that he speaks of?"[267] Also, he found it odd that "out of 345 loyal American citizens the major couldn't find any one who were [*sic*] qualified and efficient."[268] Chavez knew Ballard had made a mistake, and he refused to back down in getting the situation corrected.

Three days after the incident and before any of the Taos Mexican workers left for New Mexico, military authorities thought they had resolved the issue. On the twenty-fifth, Major Ballard reported that "competent workers have been returned to their jobs at Pando."[269] These workers totaled 288 out of the 345. He covered for his folly by making a case to the media that the army needs as many competent workers as it can get and that they are wanted badly only if they are willing to give their country a full day's work. He added that "the job has got to be done and persons willing to work and fitted for the task are being employed regardless of race, religion or color."[270] Ballard's tone clearly changed from his remarks on the twenty-third, when he insisted that he had made the right decision. Nevertheless, resentment still lingered over the decision as he advocated only for people willing to give a full day's work to return to Camp Hale.

Ballard sent a complete report of the incident to Major General G. M. Robins, assistant chief of the army engineers in Washington, D.C. General Robins then informed Senator Chavez that the army called the workers back to work on a railroad spur in the camp and that the situation had been resolved. Chavez, satisfied with the decision, remarked that the army "apparently wants to do the right thing about this serious matter."[271] Shortly thereafter, he remarked that the dismissal of the 345 workers was a "wholesale blitzkrieg" and expressed hope that the army would never again permit such a disgraceful thing to occur.[272] He repeatedly asked rhetorical questions similar to those he asked on the twenty-fourth as to why the innocent paid for the poor work ethic of a few and why Major Ballard found nobody qualified and efficient enough to stay working at Camp Hale. Of course, Chavez knew the answer to these questions, but he wanted to make it clear to the public once again that Major Ballard had made a bad decision and that the army needed to make sure that it never happened again.

Once the army decided to reinstate the workers, it quickly focused on damage control. Colonel Carl H. Jabelonsky, the army's district engineer in Denver, traveled to Camp Hale on the twenty-fourth. He reported the next day that, with the workers back at their jobs and a full report on the labor difficulties at Pando submitted to Washington, "the matter is at an end so far as we are concerned."[273] Nevertheless, the matter proved to be far from over mostly due to the colonel's mishandling of the situation after declaring it over and because of the statements he made about the Mexican American workers. Colonel Jabelonsky continued to defend Major Ballard, which hurt the army's chances of minimizing the damage to its reputation at Camp Hale. He attempted to take part of the blame off Major Ballard, saying, "The difficulty arose largely because of the men themselves. They were not suitable for construction work and were transferred to railroad construction. They seemed not to like it, and left of their own accord. Naturally when men are being paid 80 cents an hour we expect them to produce. They are coming back to work now in groups of ten and fifteen."[274] The army could not get its story straight: Major General Reybold and Major General Robins thought that it had been settled, but Major Ballard and Colonel Jabelonsky continued to fuel the flames of controversy.

Major General Robins and other military officials in Washington, D.C., soon learned that the situation had not been completely settled. As a response, the army sent out from Washington, D.C., Barron B. Beshoar, regional minority group representative for the War Production Board, and Colonel John Kirkpatrick, representative of the office of the chief of engineers. On Friday, June 26, Beshoar announced that his investigation "had shown discrimination against Spanish-American and Negro workers on the project."[275] Beshoar then proceeded to write an agreement that the army had to abide by and dragged Colonel Jabelonsky along with him in making a joint statement titled "To Reinstate Workers."[276] This statement showed the public that the army now meant business in getting individuals back to their jobs. The first point of the statement guaranteed the dismissed workers that all individuals qualified would be reinstated upon their application without regard to racial origin. The second part assured the workers that if the army, War Production Board or any other governing authority found any foreman or superintendent responsible for discrimination based on race, creed or color, that individual would be dismissed. The third point demanded that the army establish bunkhouse facilities and mess halls for all employees, regardless of race, creed or color. At the time, the Mexican American workers resided at a small camp half a mile northeast of Camp Hale that had forty tents and two barracks. This third point stipulated that the army had to provide adequate facilities for workers on the working grounds. Finally, the fourth point established standards for hiring that said that any future hiring would be conducted on the basis of the merit of the individual without regard to race or religion.[277] Beshoar promised that compliance with the agreement met the demands of the Minority Groups Branch of the War Production Board and thus ended any further investigations.

Colonel Kirkpatrick reported that the Mexican American workers also expressed satisfaction with the statement and the guarantees it provided. Therefore, the conference of representatives of the army, the contractor and the discharged employees on the twenty-sixth ended the conflict. As a result, Colonel Kirkpatrick sent telegrams detailing the arrangement to U.S. senator Eugene D. Millikin of Colorado and Governor Ralph L. Carr of Colorado. Similar telegrams went to U.S. senator Edwin C. Johnson of Colorado, Governor John E. Miles of New Mexico and Senator Dennis Chavez of New Mexico.[278] Finally, in the last part of Beshoar and Jabelonsky's statement, they made it clear to the public that the order against discrimination applied to any other war projects in the region, which backed up previous statements made by President Roosevelt and the War Department prohibiting racial discrimination.[279]

With the racial discrimination case now under control, the army put its focus back on construction. It continued to seek new workers as the heart of the summer of 1942 moved along, providing the best weather for efficient and speedy construction of the camp. The housing issue continued to plague the army and its contractors as more and more people flooded into Camp Hale, which filled the barracks and other temporary housing to near capacity. Carpenters continued to work on more barracks, with the expectation of them being finished within one to two weeks. One day in August, five work crews consisting of sixty-one carpenters and four shinglers each decided to see how fast they could build five barracks.[280] Each started early in the morning trying to outdo the other teams. One team finished construction in seven hours and forty-five minutes, cutting off more than three hours from the national record for barracks construction. The building "was a regulation two-story, 63-man barrack made of prefabricated material for the greatest possible warmth, and complete with the exception of plumbing, doors, screens and other finishing touches."[281] At 4:00 p.m. on that day, the army called all contestants to a barbecue in which the losers purchased beer for the winners as part of a camp-wide celebration. With the camp still struggling to provide housing, Leadville authorities stepped up their promise to support the camp in whatever means possible. On July 23, 1942, city authorities opened up the Leadville High School Gym, located on East Sixth Street, to a portion of the nearly two thousand workers expected to arrive in the city in the near future.[282] Lake County officials provided other quarters for workers, including the school lunch sites at the county building and at East Fifth and Poplar Streets in Leadville.[283] In addition to the housing, city officials planned meals for around two hundred of the incoming workers. Overall, Leadville contributed significantly to the success of construction at Camp Hale, benefitting the cantonment and the city itself in the summer of 1942.

Help with housing also came from areas other than Leadville. On September 5, 1942, the *Pueblo Chieftain* newspaper reported that an old Civilian Conservation Corps (CCC) camp established along the banks of the Arkansas River about twelve miles west of Cañon City in a little-known town called Parkdale was packed up and shipped to Camp Hale.[284] The CCC had established the camp in Parkdale almost a year prior to the move and subsequently closed it in July 1942 to get it ready to move. At its peak of operation, the camp housed a maximum of two hundred men. The "deluxe camp" of thirty buildings was "moved lock, stock and barrel" to Camp Hale in the beginning of September and took laborers from Fremont County ten days to reconstruct the buildings for use by government employees at Camp Hale.[285] Housing for about two hundred more workers became available quickly, increasing the demand for qualified individuals to contribute to the development of Camp Hale. The army once again sought all available people, regardless of race or ethnicity, to endure the harsh weather at the cantonment and help finish construction.

By the end of September, a war manpower commission representative called for Spanish American and Negro construction workers for Camp Hale and assured them they no longer needed to fear discrimination on the job.[286]

Beshoar, the man who twice before accused Camp Hale of discriminatory practices, now declared that race prejudice at the site had disappeared.[287] He also assured Mexican American and African American workers from around the country that Colonel Jabelonsky had corrected the conditions that gave rise to the complaints and that adequate housing accommodations, including heat and mess hall facilities, would heretofore be provided for the minority groups.[288] One of the most reassuring acts to the minority workers made by the army came with the reassignment of Major R.J. Ballard from his position as project engineer. As a replacement, the army chose Harold E. Berglund of Denver to be the construction superintendent for the project contractors.[289] This change eliminated the source of the original problem and began a new era of leadership at the cantonment.

Beshoar finished his assessment of the newly reformed Camp Hale, saying, "I am convinced that Spanish-Americans and Negroes need have no further fear of going to Pando. They will be given the same treatment as any other workers."[290] He even took the making of amends one step further by asking the Mexican American and African American workers to help the U.S. Employment Service find a few hundred workers. The employment office promised to pay all of the project workers, regardless of race or ethnicity, eighty cents an hour for a forty-hour week, with average earnings, based on an actual workweek of seventy hours, about sixty-eight dollars a week, including overtime.[291] The incident that once rocked the military cantonment now faded away into history as new opportunities opened for workers of all races and ethnicities.

Throughout the months of September and October, Camp Hale began to show new signs of life, booming with patriotism while tackling unique problems. One sign of patriotic success included the cantonment's sale of war bonds. War bonds allowed the government to purchase thousands of tanks, planes and other weapons for the fight against the Axis powers. During the month of October, Camp Hale workers averaged around $50,000 in sales a week.[292] Prior to this time, workers had to travel to either Leadville or Red Cliff in order to make bond purchases or send money orders to Denver. In the beginning of October, the Treasury Department and Platt Rogers organized a simple means of allowing workers to cash their paychecks free of charge at an armored motor service of Denver booth located in the camp.[293] Next to this door, volunteers manned a bond order booth where they helped individuals fill out the paperwork for bond sales and then sent workers across the street to the post office, which issued the bonds. Fourteen clerks worked daily to process bond sales at the post office while around thirty women, mostly stenographers and wives of workmen, solicited bonds to the workers on the weekends.

Women often took the lead at Camp Hale during its construction in the sale of war bonds as many of their husbands labored throughout the camp.[294] One stenographer and volunteer on the weekends, Elizabeth (Betty) Bennett, set an all-time two-hour sales record for war bonds by selling $680 in bonds on a single Friday night.[295] A big board positioned in the most prominent place of the camp encouraged a spirit of bond buying and competition, as it listed the names of subcontractors and how much of their paychecks they gave up to purchase bonds. For example, the employees of Walter and Eric Oberg, brick subcontractors, put 40 percent of their paychecks into bonds. Another individual by the name of D.A. Matheson, a guard earning $44.55 a week, lived off one paycheck for every four months and then put the other three into bonds. Camp Hale workers truly exemplified a spirit of patriotism toward the war effort not only in working overtime to complete the cantonment but also in the purchasing of war bonds.

A few unusual problems hit Camp Hale during the fall of 1942 that tested the camp's resilience in keeping people motivated and driven toward completion. First, a rumor spread quickly around the camp at the beginning of September that working conditions had deteriorated to poverty levels at Camp Hale. This discouraged some workers from staying and others from moving to the cantonment and taking a job. The Commissary Board of Directors addressed the rumors swiftly by saying that a "majority of these rumors [are] unfounded."[296] The board did recognize that occasional discomforts had caused personal dissatisfaction and inconvenience but that they continually put forth an honest attempt to correct justified grievances. In more specific words, the board issued a statement posted in the *Pando Echo*, which said, "The person who promiscuously complain, or exaggerate their dissatisfaction to the extent that it would cause workmen to leave this project or prevent others from coming here, are performing an activity that is un-American. Pando is no Bataan Peninsula."[297]

Another rumor circulated a few days later in September that alleged the government had frozen workers in their jobs, preventing them from leaving. However, the *Pando Echo* exposed this rumor, writing, "The rumor that maliciously spread around the camp that all personnel would be frozen to their jobs is entirely unfounded and without base. Our United States is a free country and as long as our colors fly she will remain so. The personnel of Camp Hale and of any other camp is free to do as they please."[298] Neither the army nor the Pando Constructors ever froze jobs at Pando. Management used positive and legal methods for the recruitment of new workers.

Other problems, not fueled necessarily by rumors, hit Pando also. The close living conditions, especially within the trailer park, resulted in at least three fires in the camp in the month of September. The first fire broke out on a ridge above the sewage disposal plant and burned part of the forest, coming within one hundred yards of the trailer camp. This fire, as army firemen later determined, started from a spark from a nearby coal-powered locomotive.[299] Two other fires broke out in the trailer park due to exploding gasoline stoves and faulty heating equipment. As the days grew colder, fire became more important and also more of a hazard in the camp.

Crowded living conditions provided another problem for the Safety and Sanitation Department of the cantonment. In addition to its primary job of overseeing the mess halls and the safety of workers in the construction sites, the Safety and Sanitation Department had to manage "100 barracks for workmen and women, five tent and auto-trailer camps, ranging in size from capacity of fifty men to the largest one containing eight hundred trailers with population of 2000, [and] check up and sample regularly the water supply for the whole camp."[300] To make matters even more difficult, almost every section of the camp was supplied from a different water source. Since the government's rationing made gasoline and tires a scarce commodity and safety inspectors had to make frequent trips to all different parts of the camp, a corral of forty riding horses complete with saddles was provided for Captain Batot and the other inspectors and field personnel.[301] These inspectors soon obtained the nickname "sore inspectors" for a couple different reasons. From the inspectors' points of view, their frequent riding made their bottoms sore while workman associated them with a different kind of sore—the type that never found anything right on the work site and was always correct in their assessment.[302] These squabbles never amounted to anything more than a brief bickering, driving workers and inspectors to compromise with the conditions of the camp. Engineers slowly learned more about the unique problems of their high-altitude cantonment once the camp neared completion.

Also, at the end of the month of September, a story broke in the local papers about two boys being caught for theft at Camp Hale. Unfortunately for the residents, the story turned out to be true, and the two eighteen-year-olds, William Leatherman of Pueblo and Vernon Young of Colorado Springs, were turned over to the authorities at Camp Hale, charged with stealing army blankets.[303] Even with the remote location and high altitude, the camp suffered from some of the same problems that the rest of the country faced. Nevertheless, these events did not impede progress, as the War Manpower Commission announced a need for another three thousand workers for Camp Hale at the beginning of October.[304]

Once October came, army officials knew they had to move quickly before the deep snowstorms blanketed the Pando Valley floor and eliminated all chances of finishing construction. In an announcement on October 6 by Walter F. Scherer, special representative of Harold Berglund, the new project manager at the camp, publicized that the construction project demanded three thousand more workers before the end of the week or progress may not meet the scheduled demands.[305] Prior to Berglund's takeover, apparently inefficiencies in the contracted system between worker and management, as seen with the Mexican American discrimination incident, led to construction gaps, slow downs and other nonracial discriminatory practices. The *Herald Democrat* reported on the sixth that Berglund had fixed these issues, which included supervisors and workmen eating in different locations and staying in different barracks and other buildings not meeting suitable living condition standards as approved by federal authorities.[306] Most likely, army officials sacrificed federal standards for the cantonment and its workers in order to speed up construction and move in as many workers as possible. As long as complaints did not reach outside the camp, construction continued as planned.

Berglund's changes not only made life better for the workers already at Pando but also added an extra incentive to prospective workers. In addition to these improvements, the U.S. Employment Office continued to offer carpenters, laborers, steamfitters and all other types of mechanics, seventy hours of work a week, with laborers drawing $0.80 an hour and $1.20 for every hour in excess of forty, or $68.00 a week. Carpenters received $1.50 an hour and time and a half for overtime while working a seventy-hour week.[307] Employment officials, desperately seeking workers within the state, promised to even pay round-trip transportation costs for workers coming from Denver if they agreed to work for at least thirty days. Camp Hale officials continued to entice these workers by describing how a small city existed at the cantonment for the benefit of the workers, including a school, a jail, a police force and mess halls.[308]

By the end of October, the focus in Pando had switched briefly from the recruitment of workers and construction to the arrival of ski troopers. Lieutenant George Shimmon, public relations officer at Camp Hale, announced during the last week of October that the army sought ski troopers first and foremost from the local population of Colorado.[309] More importantly, he emphasized that the army now allowed potential draftees and interested soldiers to choose which service they desired to enter.[310] This change in army policy potentially prevented local Colorado boys from getting stuck in an undesired army unit with an undesired job. While Lieutenant Shimmon continued recruiting enlistees, he also encouraged college graduates—including doctors and dentists—who were potential officer candidates, to give the ski troopers a try for at least three months and then attend an officer training school.[311] He requested on the twenty-ninth that all men interested leave their name and address with the local *Herald Democrat* office.

The next day, another announcement went out in the *Herald Democrat* to the citizens of the Arkansas River Valley seeking eighteen- and nineteen-year-olds for ski trooper training. Specifically, the army sought mountain climbers, skiers, outdoor recreational sportsmen and individuals who had worked with pack animals.[312] Soldiers who enlisted with a background in one of these fields quickly advanced through the ranks and were offered the opportunity to become instructors of other soldiers who lacked such experience.[313] One example of this was Private First Class Clarence E. Gilbert. Being a native of Vermont, he came to Camp Hale and quickly moved up through the ranks as his skills earned him an instructor position. Not only did his rank go up, but his assignments and details also diminished as ski instructing became his first priority. In a letter back home to some folks in Vermont, he wrote, "I was made (P.F.C.) when I got back, after my furlough. I am now a ski instructor at Camp—all day. So I have know [*sic*] details such as guard or K.P.—at present. But I peel a mean spud!"[314] Ski instructors at Camp Hale became a close-knit group of soldiers, and many of them already knew one another from before the war. One instructor, Private First Class Henry J. Perkins, made this point when he wrote, "The camp seems to be just one big gang—besides the new friends I work and ski with, most of my old friends, too."[315]

With the completion of construction at Camp Hale and the relocation of the Mountain Training Center (MTC) imminent, the army began recruitment and training programs that it had never before undertaken. Originally recruited by civilians, ski troopers made up a unique part of the army with a defined set of skills that the army needed at Camp Hale before training began. Unlike every other type of military job, for which the army sent soldiers off to schools to learn the trade, the army had no school for ski troopers. It envisioned for Camp Hale to be its newest school, a mountain and ski trooper school.

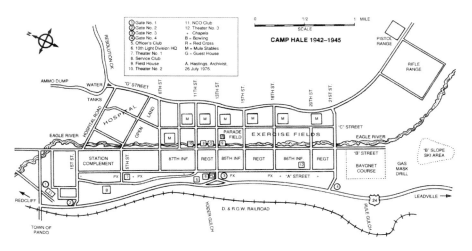

Map of Camp Hale looking from the west to the east. *Courtesy of Andy Hastings, used by permission of Flint Whitlock and Bob Bishop,* Soldiers on Skis: A Pictorial Memoir of the 10th Mountain Division.

Standard army chapel at Camp Hale, Colorado. *Courtesy of the Denver Public Library, Western History Collection, David B. Allen, TMD-753.*

November 1942 finally came at Camp Hale and marked the beginning of the most pivotal month in the camp's history as engineers finished up the last projects and ski troopers started to arrive. Though the army officially stood by its original completion date of November 15, 1942, construction continued beyond this date even after the ski troopers arrived. Nevertheless, the camp neared full functionality in November and showed more signs of life than it ever had before. At the end of the first week of November, the camp had its first wedding of Mr. Leoland Edwards and Miss Jeanne Thompson, two construction workers whose courtship came to fruition around the same time the camp's construction ended. The two married on November 7 at the army's newly completed chapel, under the camp's newly arrived chaplain.[316]

While the social life at Camp Hale expanded, engineers scraped together some of the last projects to complete the camp and got as many of the civilian workers out of the barracks as possible so the ski troopers could move in. One of these projects cost the army dearly. By the end of October, most buildings were up, and the army was focused almost entirely on getting in equipment for heating, plumbing and electrical systems. However, with the expansion of buildings across the Eagle Valley landscape, the camp electrical distribution system did not keep up. Some of the distribution line pole holes were not dug and installed by December when the ground froze to about seven feet.[317] Chief electrical engineer J.R. Smith reminisced about this expensive mistake in his memoirs when he wrote:

> *If anything approaches the impossible—it is to dig an eight foot hole in frozen ground. Tons of wood was burned at hole locations for 30 to 48 hours—then dynamite removed two or three feet of half thawed dirt and rock—then logs again—reblasting until the depth was obtained. By then it looked more like a crater than a pole hole. The costs ran to as much as $600.00/hole, even in those days!*[318]

Army engineers and Camp Hale construction workers once again took on these unprecedented struggles with the patriotic satisfaction of knowing that Camp Hale would eventually help make a difference in ending the war.

By the middle of November 1942, around the official completion date for the camp, thousands of workers still resided at Camp Hale. They daily devoured three tons of potatoes, two tons of coffee, 1,920 cans of milk, three thousand loaves of bread, seven hundred pounds of butter and 20,160 eggs at thirty different mess halls![319] Not only did the mess halls have to feed these workers, but they also had to serve the ski troopers. With no surprise, Camp Hale already bustled with activity when the ski troopers arrived, creating a welcoming atmosphere for them.

The army now started moving men into barracks as fast as they became available.[320] Upon final completion of the camp in the middle of December, Camp Hale consisted of hundreds of buildings with thousands of civilian workers still residing there. The completed camp contained housing for 16,662 soldiers, 124 civilians, 4,002 stable animals, a veterinary hospital with 190 stalls and a station hospital with 676 beds.[321] Appurtenant military housing included unit guardhouses for 132 guards, stockade guard facilities for 74 guards, stable guardrooms for 140 guards and a prison for 162 prisoners. Storage facilities at Camp Hale had to be modified because of the limited space, so battalion storehouses were used by two companies each. Other warehouses provided 9.43 square feet of storage space per enlisted man, grain storage of twenty-five bushels per animal, hay storage facilities for 1,500 pounds per animal, one year's worth of coal storage, twenty-two hours' supply of water and housing for 655 vehicles.[322] General warehousing for ordnance, clothing, equipment and utilities totaled 146,610 square feet with an extra 1,560 cubic feet devoted to inflammable storage. The camp also contained administrative buildings; motor repair facilities; and ski repair, blacksmith, ordnance, carpenter, utility and clothing repair shops. Service facilities included a bakery that operated sixteen hours a day,

Camp Hale viewed from the south side looking north. *Courtesy of the Denver Public Library, Western History Collection, Ralph W. Hulbert, TMD-509.*

Two incinerators at Camp Hale that operated eight hours a day. *Author's personal collection.*

cold storage, an ice-making plant and incinerators operating eight hours a day.[323] Recreational buildings consisted of multiple theaters, a field house, enlisted and officer service clubs, auditoriums, company day rooms, officer day rooms and hospital recreational rooms.[324] Multiple chapels provided worship opportunities for soldiers and civilians while multiple school districts, partially funded by the Federal Works Administration, provided educational opportunities for officers' children and civilian workers. Camp Hale even had its own post office, dental clinic, division communication school, three fire stations and nine veterinary dispensaries.[325]

The most visible specialized difference in Camp Hale from other military cantonments came from its training aids. The cantonment had four rope tows on the surrounding hills for ski training and one ski lift, 6,000 feet

Camp Hale Theater No. 2, located across 11th Street from the Service Club. *Author's personal collection.*

horizontal and 1,122 feet vertical at Tennessee Pass, at a location called Cooper Hill.[326] Initial investigative reports revealed ample opportunities for skiing around Camp Hale. However, after further consultation with the National Forest Service, the army learned that only slopes with northern exposure would suffice given the amount of snowfall, thus eliminating all sagebrush slopes, leaving only those covered in spruce.[327] On the cliffs surrounding the cantonment proper, rock-climbing opportunities were abundant, and rusted pitons can still be found bolted to the rocks today.

Cooper Hill proved to be the ideal location for skiing. The T-bar lift hauled skiers to the top of the mountain, crossing the Continental Divide three times, providing ten ski runs with ample ski opportunities for the troops.[328] In addition to these specialized lifts at Tennessee Pass, the ski area had twelve winter camp barracks, two winter camp mess halls, an infirmary,

Camp Hale tile art made by a soldier with initials "RW" (1943). The art was most likely made in the hospital "Handcraft Shop" for the All-Camp Art Exhibit. *Author's personal collection.*

a barbershop, quarters for the regimental and battalion staffs, drying rooms heated with big potbellied stoves and twelve latrines for mountain training field exercises.[329] The Camp Hale Post Exchange (PX) even provided a mobile PX for troops out in the field in this area so they could restock on essentials while out on extended bivouacs.[330] One soldier commented about Cooper Hill, saying, "This place reminds me of a big lumber camp I worked in once."[331] Also, exclusive to Camp Hale, the cantonment operated completely on coal power, rather than gas, due to the lack of a feasible source of natural gas. The only gas power found on post came from the bottles used in the dental clinic. Three coal fields located within 150 miles at Cañon City, Crested Butte, New Castle and Routt County supplied the camp via the Denver & Rio Grande Western Railroad.

Pitons in the rocks of the east cliffs at Camp Hale. The photograph was taken at Camp Hale in 2010. *Author's personal collection.*

Camp Hale even had an artificial glacier created by spraying water on a mountainside, providing technical ice climbing capabilities in the Lower Resolution Creek Valley.[332] Seracs and crevasses were artificially constructed by piling logs on a steep slope and then pouring water on top of them. However, this glacier melted under the intense sun, so engineers constructed another one on a north-facing shady slope. Corporal Hal Burton confirmed that this one also melted quickly and that mountain troops received little training at Camp

Left: T-bar lift at Cooper Hill, Tennessee Pass, Colorado. *Author's personal collection.*

Below: A view of the barracks at Cooper Hill, Tennessee Pass, Colorado (1943–44). *Courtesy of the Denver Public Library, Western History Collection, Pando Constructors, William A. Southworth, TMD-730.*

Hale in snow and ice climbing.[333] For traditional training, Camp Hale had three bayonet courses, three grenade courts, one rifle range, a machine gun range, three anti-aircraft ranges, a pistol range, a landscape target range, a combat range and a gas chamber.[334] In addition to the outdoor ranges, Camp Hale's dirt-floored, concrete-walled training halls each included a fifty-foot indoor .22-caliber rifle range for marksmanship training during the winter months when conditions did not warrant sitting on the outdoor range.[335] Finally, Camp Hale boasted a Mountain Obstacle Course of around ten thousand feet in elevation. This course combined the features of a regular obstacle course with added elements of advanced mountaineering.[336] The geography of the Camp Hale Military Reservation made all of this training possible. Ralph C. Meager, Camp Hale Reservation forester, commented in May 1943 that Camp Hale was "the only camp, post or station in the nation that embraces such a vast area of primitive wilderness and forest land."[337] These differences set it apart from other military cantonments. No other cantonment constructed before or during World War II compared with the sophistication, planning and complexity of Camp Hale, making it one of the most respectable military engineering feats during World War II.

The special nature of Camp Hale helps explain how attached many workers became to the construction project and their mixed feelings upon

View of the south end of Camp Hale, including the Ordinance Ranges. *Courtesy of the Denver Public Library, Western History Collection, Ralph W. Hulbert, TMD-512.*

Two mountain troopers free climbing a rock wall as part of Camp Hale's obstacle course in 1943. *Courtesy of the Denver Public Library, Western History Collection, U.S. Army Signal Corps, TMD-603.*

leaving their work. Though many civilians did stay and work in support of the newly arriving ski troopers, many packed up their belongings and headed off to other construction jobs and war industry plants.[338] Max Hardy, writer for the camp's construction paper, the *Pando Echo*, wrote in the last edition of the paper an article titled "The Time Has Come." The article stated:

> *The men and women who have had a part in the building of Camp Hale can look back as they leave the Pando Valley with a feeling of pride in a job well done. Each one has made a contribution toward the building of a powerful war machine. That, in itself, should be compensation for inconveniences or*

minor hardships. Most of us Pandoites will soon forget the dust, the mud, the coughs and colds. The time we spent standing in line won't seem so long in the months to come. We'll spend the money we made here and wonder where it went. Many of us will have poorer jobs, worse living accommodations and more justifiable "beefs" than we had at Pando. But all of us will be able to take some worthwhile possessions with us when we leave the valley—the memory of a summer spent in one of the most beautiful spots anywhere—the association with new friends found at the job—and most important of all, the knowledge that each of us has a part in doing a huge job, an important job, a job that had to be done and was done, in an unbelievably short space of time.[339]

In addition to Hardy's article, another *Pando Echo* writer expressed similar sentiments in the last issue, writing, "This is the last issue of the *Pando Echo*! We say this with regret because it has been a lot of fun working with all of you. We have tried hard to make this paper interesting to everyone living at the camp."[340] The writer then proceeded to remind workers of all the good times they had at Camp Hale, including the sunrises and sunsets in the valley and their first impressions upon getting off the train, walking through the mud and slush to the barracks and seeing the empty, cell-like walls of the barracks. He reminisced about the good times, including picnics, singing around campfires, horseback riding, fishing and parties in the barracks and in Leadville and Glenwood Springs. He expressed sadness that he might never again see the snowcapped mountains of the valley and their illustrious glory. Nevertheless, in his final statement, he wrote, "Then compare that day to the present day when we can drive up the hill toward Leadville and look down on a completed camp—don't you get a thrill out of it? Don't you feel—'THAT'S <u>MY</u> CAMP!'"[341] Many of the workers took ownership in the camp because of the sacrifice they made in working in the harsh conditions and for long hours a day. This patriotic appreciation for their work and nostalgic sadness upon leaving exemplified the uniqueness and fascination of Camp Hale. Similarly, a woman named Lorraine wrote an editorial in the last edition of the *Pando Echo*, stating, "After seven months of watching the camp take form, it will be hard for us to leave it."[342] The final sentiments of exiting workers expressed both sadness and happiness, as well as a genuine appreciation for the work they had accomplished.

Though engineers and workers had finished most of the buildings by the middle of November 1942, finishing touches continued into December, when the army finally took down the engineers' flag and raised the "banner of Uncle Sam's mountain infantry."[343] By the time of completion in mid-December, eight months after it started, the cantonment consisted of buildings totaling

The view in this press photograph of Camp Hale in 1943 looks from the northwest to the southeast. *Author's personal collection.*

The image in this circa 1944 original period postcard shows Camp Hale from the southwest to the northeast. *Author's personal collection.*

3,650,000 square feet, or eighty-four acres of floor space, built for about $262,000 per acre of floor.[344] Total costs, originally estimated at $29,641,016, ended up slightly more at around $31,148,964.[345] Engineers had constructed an entire workers' city in addition to the cantonment itself, under twenty-one different government directives and authorizations. One of the final finishing touches to Camp Hale that was excluded from the initial budget did not come until the fall of 1943, when Ralph C. Meager, Camp Hale Reservation Forester, helped purchase and acquire grass seed to be planted in the cantonment ground after grading and drainage was complete.[346] Due to the fact that the ground that made up Camp Hale had primarily been backfilled with subsoil from borrow pits, organic salts had to be added in order to support vegetation.[347] Meager emphasized that the state had equipment and machinery necessary for seeding the ground and that Camp Hale simply needed to act. Camp Hale continued to develop and improve even after officials accomplished this task and while the ski troopers trained.

A poem written by a construction worker at Camp Hale named H.E. Robinson on December 22, 1942, sums up the general feelings, both happy and sad, at the completion of the cantonment. Robinson wrote:

High on the slope of the Rockies
Nestled among the pines,
Was located the town of Pando,
Some cabins, a depot, some mines.
Know far and wide for its fishing,
For the last "Frontier of the West,"
They came from all over the country,
For pleasure, for fishing and rest.

Then came the scouts for the army,
Seeking a suitable site
To build a camp for our soldiers,
Some place to teach them to fight.
A snow-covered country for skiing,
A rifle range on the hill,
Trails thru the pines for the pack mules,
Space on the flats to drill.

Next on the job came the engineers
While snow was still on the ground,
They topoged the place from end to end,
Ran levels up and down.
They located the trails and the ski course,
An igloo here and there,
The hundreds of buildings that line the streets,
And a barn for the "Old Gray Mare."

Then the diesel "cats" came rolling in,
With ten-yard "carry all,"
They dug it here and piled it there
From spring 'til early fall.
The "back-hoes" made a mess of things,
The draglines did as bad,
The 'dozers tried to cover up
These holes that made us mad.

They changed the Eagle River,
They ran the beavers out.
They just raised hell with everything,
They even killed our trout.
The playtime will soon be over
The slackers will soon be gone
May the loafers, the cheaters and saboteurs
Snow in a brine that's strong
But the men and the women who labored,
Who gave everything from the start,
May they ever rejoice in the knowledge
That they honestly did their part.

The equipment is down for the winter.
The crew has stacked up their tools.
The PX is crowded with soldiers,
And the corrals are crowded with mules
The pack trains wind up thru the "quakers,"
Loaded with cannons and guns,
The ski men shoot down through the pine trees
Some surprise for the Japs and the Huns.

If we go to another Defense job,
Let's start from the first to be true
To the flag that's the emblem of freedom,
The red, the white and the blue.
Three days more until Xmas,
Ten left in forty-two.
May the Axis get what they have coming,
From the efforts of you & you.[348]

5

THE SKI TROOPS ARRIVE

Nowhere, with the possible exception of the jungle, are military operations more difficult than in winter and mountain warfare. Variable weather conditions, incredibly difficult terrain, and a determined enemy will test the soldier to the utmost.[349]
—*Whitman M. Reynolds, medical director of the National Ski Patrol System*

After May 28, 1942, mountain troops never stepped foot again in Mount Rainier National Park on a battalion level for official training. The contract had ended, and all returned to Fort Lewis. As one mountain trooper regretfully put it, "the days of the ski club were over."[350] Despite this closure, training continued at Fort Lewis even with its geographical limitations. Captain John Woodward, ski officer in charge of Company B of the 87th, came up with the idea to build three thirty-foot wooden walls on which soldiers could practice technical climbing skills, including rappelling, at Fort Lewis.[351] This worked well in training one area of mountain warfare, but it could not make up for the fact that Fort Lewis, in the summer, offered little hope for training in snow, ice and other cold-weather conditions. Various groups returned to Mount Rainier National Park on a limited basis to train, but nothing ever materialized. From this point on, attention began to switch from Fort Lewis to the newly constructed Camp Hale. In August 1942, an Aspen detachment of the 87th Mountain Infantry began training with the Army Corps of Engineers in building aerial tramways and suspension bridges near the ghost town of Ashcroft.[352] Upon completion of this training in November, the detachment began to hike forty-five miles with its mules from Aspen to Camp Hale. Nearly the entire town, including seven hundred individuals and a brass band, sent it off on its way. However, less than twenty-four hours out of Aspen, the detachment turned around due to significant amounts of snow and impassible conditions for its mules.[353] These soldiers did not reach Camp Hale that day, but others soon arrived in their place.

The first five hundred troops to arrive at Camp Hale, excluding those in the Army Corps of Engineers involved in the construction process, came on October 5, 1942. Around this same time, the army began its orders to begin moving other units into the cantonment. On October 15, 1942, the army sent orders to the Service Command Unit No. 1758, activated on August 10, 1942, at Glenwood Springs, Colorado, to proceed to a new station at Pando, Colorado.[354] These troops made up one of the first military contingents stationed at Camp Hale and began preparations for the arrival of others. Next, on November 15, 1942, the 1st and 2nd Battalions of the 87th moved from Fort Lewis to Hunter Liggett Military Reservation in Jolon, California, for training. These two battalions did not join the command until December 31, 1942, when they arrived at Camp Hale. The 3rd Battalion moved directly from Fort Lewis to Camp Hale on November 18–21, 1942.[355]

The Mountain Training Center that the army established on September 3, 1942, at Camp Carson under the command of Colonel Rolfe worked for a short time at this location in its preparations for mountain training.[356] Shortly thereafter, the entire organization moved its command staff to Camp Hale on November 16, 1942.[357] The entire MTC packed up and left Camp Carson via a combination of rail, truck and private car convoy to Camp Hale.[358] Upon arriving at the 9,250-foot cantonment, the MTC found a light snow covering the ground and plenty of leftover trash and equipment from the summer and fall construction. The snow also covered the "quagmire of slush" that concealed leftover nails that penetrated jeep and truck tires.[359] *Denver Post* correspondent Jack Carberry wrote that the streets and the parade grounds were "rivers of black, gummy, thick mud, with sticking qualities like glue."[360] Construction crews had not yet completed any of the camp's sources of entertainment, including clubs, theaters and other recreational halls. Leadville was off-limits except for special passes. Those were restricted to twice a month, and sometimes none at all were allowed unless an emergency arose.[361] Camp Hale greeted soldiers of the MTC with an uneasy sense of the future and a perplexing combination of challenges. It soon obtained the nickname "Camp Hell" for some as the MTC began to reorganize itself, along with the newly arriving battalions from across the country. The arrival of the MTC at

Camp Hale marked the beginning of operations in mountain training on a larger scale than any previous efforts.

One day after the arrival of the Mountain Training Center command on the sixteenth, the 601st Field Artillery Battalion (Pack) arrived at Camp Hale from Camp Carson. The *Denver Post* wrote an article about its arrival, identifying the unique nature of this field artillery battalion given the terrain it worked in at Camp Hale. The writer identified that the pack artillery arrived well equipped with jeeps, mules and toboggans to move artillery pieces across snow.[362] Colonel David Ruffner, the pack commander of the 601st, commented to the paper that after twenty-six years of service in army mule outfits, his unit faced "the hardest they [had] yet encountered" at Camp Hale.[363] The field artillery relied primarily on jeeps and mules but, occasionally, turned to toboggans when the terrain became harsh enough to require soldiers on snowshoes to move the six different parts of the 75mm pack howitzer M1A1 and M8 carriage up and down mountain slopes without the help of mules.[364] One ski trooper described the character of a mule by writing that they are "tough, smart, and maybe a bit ornery...and an expert kicker."[365] Mules could handle narrow paths, steep slopes and heavy loads but not deep

Early training at Camp Hale included mules, men and munitions. Image taken on December 23, 1942. *Author's personal collection.*

Mule trenches, Camp Hale, Colorado (circa 1943). *Courtesy of the Denver Public Library, Western History Collection, Molenaar, C.M. (Cornelius M.), TMD-703.*

K Company, Field Artillery Battalion (Pack), getting ready for maneuvers in February 1943. *Courtesy of the Denver Public Library, Western History Collection, Molenaar, C.M. (Cornelius M.), TMD-484.*

snow. Most soldiers in the pack artillery appreciated the role of the mule while realizing that it did have limitations.

Wherever the mountain infantry went, the pack artillery followed as support, with what they affectionately called their "Pack hows."[366] Colonel Ruffner had no qualms about calling his unit the "Jackass Artillery," as it seemed to be the nickname everyone at Camp Hale assigned them. His men trained hard, and he assured all people with reservations that his 75mm howitzers, some of the most effective artillery pieces for mountain warfare, stood ready to be deployed at any moment in support of the mountain infantry.[367]

Major James F. Donovan, artillery officer in the 601st, designated several hills around Camp Hale for use by the pack artillery for howitzer practice and provided a demonstration for a *Denver Post* reporter.[368] After Major Donovan's men fired a few rounds into precisely the location at which he pointed, Colonel Ruffner concluded his conversation with the reporter by setting apart his "heroes" from the regular mountain infantry regiments, saying, "They're just run-of-the-mill boys," not hand-picked like the ski experts and professional mountain men of the 87th.[369] About six weeks after the arrival of the 601st, the 602nd Field Artillery Battalion arrived at Camp Hale from Camp Carson. Now there were two artillery battalions in the Mountain Training Center. Around this same time, elements of the 4th Cavalry Regiment from Fort Meade, South Dakota, redesignated the 10th Cavalry Reconnaissance Troop, arrived at Camp Hale with its horses.[370] Unaccustomed to the cold climate and deep snow, the horses were eventually swapped out for mechanized equipment while the remaining soldiers were integrated into existing companies within the Mountain Training Center primarily because they refused to learn how to ski and rock climb once their horses were proven ineffective.[371] One member of the 10th Cavalry Reconnaissance Troop wrote, "We've spent our lives breaking horses, now if we don't break these boards they may break us!"[372]

A week and a half after the arrival of the 601st, the army activated the 1st Battalion of the 86th Infantry Regiment at Camp Hale on November 26, 1942. Though the 87th included three battalions, the 86th lacked financial authorization initially and subsequently formed two provisional battalions until funding came through. The 86th quickly filled up its ranks with new handpicked recruits from the National Ski Association. Lieutenant Colonel Robert L. Cook took command of the regiment while the training leadership consisted of 87th veterans from Mount Rainier. The battalion started off on rough footing as it figured out how to best train in the mountains, but it

A 75mm howitzer in action on Homestake Creek near Camp Hale on April 6, 1943. *Author's personal collection.*

soon impressed the leadership of the Mountain Training Center, including Colonel Rolfe. Morale began to build up, and the 86th quickly gained recognition as a "crack outfit."[373]

As November came to an end and the winter snow picked up at Camp Hale, the army brought in yet another unit to train. The 99th Infantry Battalion (Separate), composed of 770 first- and second-generation Norwegians, arrived from Camp Snelling, Minnesota, via train for mountain warfare training on December 19, 1942.[374] For many of the Norwegians, Camp Hale felt like their ancestral home in Norway. The snow, the cold and a chapel in which to worship on Christmas made them feel right at home despite the lonely nature of a military cantonment. Most were devout Christians who attended worship, conducted in Norwegian, in the post chapel on Christmas Day, far outnumbering the attendance of any other service at Camp Hale.[375] Also, around this same time, members of the 126th Engineer Mountain Battalion arrived at Camp Hale from Camp Carson. The 126th, activated under the command of Lieutenant Colonel John

Parker, became another unit under the direction of the Mountain Training Center.[376] Initially, the army established two companies within the 126th. They delegated to Company A experimental work on the construction of aerial tramways. To Company B, the army delegated experimental work on the construction of suspension bridges in mountainous terrain.[377] Many of the engineers envisioned their new assignment to Camp Hale to include building the standard pontoon bridges across swift streams and negotiating terrain across which tanks, guns and men might blitz. However, these engineers soon understood the reality: their time was to be consumed by building tramways and mountain roads at high altitude.[378] By the end of December 1942, Camp Hale had soldiers from the 86th and 87th Infantry Regiments, the 99th Infantry Battalion, the 601st and 602nd Field Artillery Battalions (Pack) and the 126th Engineer Mountain Battalion, all training under the command of the Mountain Training Center. "During the summer and early fall of 1942 Camp Hale was a hodge-podge of feverish construction, seas of mud, thousands of hard-living, hard-working civilians. On this scene came the vanguard of officers and men."[379]

The arrival of troops continued into 1943 as several unprepared and misfit units came to Camp Hale. Troop B of the 4th Cavalry Regiment (Mechanized), from Fort Meade, South Dakota, and members of the 31st (Dixie) Division from Leesville, Louisiana, arrived and soon realized that their lives were about to change significantly. Private First Class Henry J. Perkins, ski instructor at Cooper Hill and member of Company A, 10th Mountain Quartermaster Battalion, wrote that the 10th Cavalry Reconnaissance Troops (10th Recon, newly converted from the 4th Cavalry) were composed largely of "cowboy and Indians."[380] In addition to this assessment, *The History of the Mountain Training Center* critiqued Leesville, Louisiana, as "one of the hottest, flattest, and lowest spots in the United States."[381] None of the soldiers in these units had any experience in skiing or any other outdoor sport necessary for training at Camp Hale. However, the 10th Recon's makeup soon changed rapidly as more experienced soldiers joined the ranks and helped educate those in need of assistance.

The 10th Recon first made a name for itself while being assigned to instruct different army units in rock climbing at Seneca Rocks, West Virginia. A detachment of twenty soldiers and three officers left Camp Hale to go to Seneca Rocks for a yearlong stateside deployment. While training soldiers in many different mountain problems, including rough terrain, supply acquisition, movement and evacuating casualties, the instructors saw twenty different divisions, most right before deploying overseas.[382]

One soldier, Corporal Woody Waldrip of the 10th Recon in the middle of August 1943 in Seneca, joked about the low elevation of the Appalachian Mountains after being asked by a native West Virginian, "'How do you like our mountains?' 'What mountains?' countered Woody."[383] Soldiers from other units that remained back at Camp Hale joked that the 10th Recon might return to Colorado with a mysterious new disease called "low-altitude melancholia."[384] Some of the soldiers from the 10th Recon agreed as they made their way back to Camp Hale, muttering about how the air was too heavy for them to breathe well in West Virginia.

In July 1943, soldiers of the 10th Recon joined with members of the Mountain Training Center at Seneca Rocks, West Virginia, in order to better prepare themselves and others for technical rock climbing in the Alps. The army chose these cliffs because they best resembled those that the soldiers would potentially face in the Apennines and the lower Alps.[385] However, Seneca Rocks and the surrounding area eventually became more than a training site for the Camp Hale men, as it began to take on units from around the country for training in pack animals, improvised river crossings, mountain medicine and evacuation. Most importantly, however, it became an established rock-climbing school for the army.

Prior to their arrival at Seneca Rocks, West Virginia, members of the Mountain Training Center served as instructors for the 36th and 45th Infantry Divisions at an established training area in Buena Vista, Virginia.[386] Here they taught operations in mountainous terrain to the two divisions in order to prepare them for their coming invasion of Sicily. Their training proved so successful during the invasion that the army wanted to train the other units of the 8th Corps in a similar manner, this time at another new training site in Elkins, West Virginia.[387] The training area expanded across three counties and contained 3,000 to 4,000 soldiers each month, with its headquarters in Elkins.[388] Soldiers worked on physical conditioning, topography, stream crossings, aid climbing, the use of hand signals and experimentation with muffled piton hammers.[389] The members of the 10th Recon, however, put a special emphasis on the rock-climbing school located at Kaisermore Pig Ranch in the North Fork Valley at the foot of Seneca Rock. Every two weeks, around 150 soldiers spidered over the rocks at Seneca for an intense bout of training. By the end of their training at Seneca Rocks, Champe and other surrounding rocks, they had hammered around seventy-five thousand pitons into the cliffs, many of which still remain there today.[390] Seneca Rocks proved to be a cheaper, more efficient and closer location to the East Coast to train soldiers in rock climbing before deploying. The location grew substantially as Camp Hale men taught soldiers from many different units the skills necessary to rock climb. However, the location never became one that could train soldiers in any other type of mountain warfare and thus training continued to be limited to rock climbing.

In the late spring of 1943, a majority of the troops staffing the Mountain Training Center came from the 31st (Dixie) Division; the 33rd Infantry Division out of Camp Forrest, Tennessee; and the 30th Infantry Division from Memphis, Tennessee.[391] Many of these southerners at Camp Hale called their ski's "Mah to-chuah (torture) boards" or "Suicide Slats" as a reflection of their true feelings about ski training.[392] Even some of the most experienced skiers, including instructors, never felt an attachment to Camp Hale and its high Colorado altitude. One instructor, Private First Class Clarence E. Gilbert, commented about this in a letter sent back home, writing, "I have been across the country 2 times and so far I've seen know [sic] state that will compare or begin to compare with good old Vermont. One doesn't realize what a lovely state he lives in until he has two [sic] live somewhere else."[393] Another soldier commented about the conditions, writing, "I haven't seen the sun for two days now and I'm getting mighty tired of this cold miserable weather."[394]

With the influx of new recruits to Camp Hale, the MTC ran into an unforeseen problem. The command quickly realized that soldiers not used to functioning at an elevation of around 9,250 feet needed up to six weeks to acclimate to be able to fully function.[395] One soldier balked, "How can they expect us to get along up here if even the aviators turn on their oxygen at 10,000 feet?"[396] Additionally, some soldiers upon arrival at Camp Hale were put to work unloading heavy crates from boxcars and shoveling thousands of pounds of coal in order to feed the boilers of the camp.[397] This strenuous work put some newly recruited, white-collar workers from the East in positions that they could not handle. One soldier by the name of Private Edwin Gibson, of Company F, 86th Mountain Infantry, commented, "When I stepped off the train, the air was so thin and light I almost fell flat on my face. It was clear and sparkling—like champagne. Only just then it felt like too much champagne."[398] Claus Høie of the 99th Infantry Battalion (Separate) remembered testing a radio transmitter one day, when a voice came out of the loudspeaker, "Will you get off my wavelength; I'm trying to land at Denver Airport. I'm at an altitude of 7,000 feet."[399] Høie operated at an elevation around 14,000 feet in the snow at the time, twice as high as the landing plane. For some, life at 9,250 feet came naturally, but for others it became an experience unlike any other in their lives.[400] One newly arrived

Camp Hale hospital boiler plant, November 1942. *Author's personal collection.*

soldier with the 85th Mountain Infantry commented, "This is the first time I've ever been intimate with heaven and hell at the same time."[401]

Also, among the first individuals to arrive at Camp Hale included pastors and chaplains from around the country. One pastor, named Reverend Milo Beran of Mount Washington Presbyterian Church in Cincinnati, Ohio, agreed to serve for three weeks at the army's winter troops training center upon learning that Camp Hale did not have a regular chaplain. Beran, who learned how to ski in Muscoda, Wisconsin, wanted a chance to ski with the troops in addition to his spiritual work. Beran became quite popular among ski troopers as he tweaked a line from one of the most famous songs of the time, written by a fellow chaplain at Pearl Harbor, called "Praise the Lord and Pass the Ammunition." Ski troopers marveled at his change of words to "praise the Lord and pass me those skis!"[402] Beran—along with Reverend Edward L. Horgan, pastor of the Annunciation Church in Leadville, and his assistant, Reverend Robert Banigan—worked hard to raise the morale of the newly arrived troops who faced a unique, often unbearable environment during the winter of 1942. There was no break-in period for the newly arriving ski troopers, as November and December brought some of the heaviest snowfall and the coldest temperatures Pando saw all winter. The first two military chaplains, First Lieutenants Otto Kohn and W.R. Carner, arrived in time to hold the first Roman Catholic Mass on Armistice Day in 1942.[403] The encouraging words of chaplains helped ski troopers both mentally and spiritually as they adjusted to their new home and lifestyle in Pando Valley.[404]

By January 1943, the camp had a population of around sixteen thousand troops and 2,500 mules. The camp came alive. By the middle of the month, all of the electrical engineering was complete and most of the construction was finished. A majority of the construction workers had already left, and now many of the engineers and directors of construction packed up their families and temporary living quarters and left Camp Hale for good. J.R. Smith, chief electrical engineer, reminisced about leaving Camp Hale on January 16, 1943, in his memoirs, writing, "The Smith family packed up the old trusty Dodge at Redcliff, headed south and east to Pando Valley that had so recently become Camp Hale—through the camp—out the southeast gate and up on the overlook where we stopped and with pride looked upon a job well done."[405] As workers exited Camp Hale, they made use of the newly completed section of Highway 24 that cut off three miles of travel between Leadville and Red Cliff.[406] Though this time marked a phase of departure at Camp Hale, a new phase of life and excitement entered with the entrance of ski troopers.

The *Pando Echo* published its last issue on November 18, 1942, ending its mission of providing news and stories to the workers of Camp Hale. After its completion, a new paper developed exactly one month later. In the December 18, 1942 issue of the new paper, published three days after the official completion of Camp Hale, the editors printed it without a title. In place of the title, they wrote, "What's My Name?"[407] The editors of the paper recognized that the camp had entered into a new phase of its history, and its title and message needed to reflect the arrival of the ski troopers, their expectations and their interests at the camp. Thus, after taking suggestions from soldiers and workers at Camp Hale, the camp's chaplains chose the title the *Camp Hale Ski-Zette*, allowing the editors to publish the following issue with the new name.[408]

One of the first major events recorded in the *Camp Hale Ski-Zette* that opened up the chapter of ski troopers at Camp Hale was a Christmas gala at the new enlisted Service Club, located on 11th and B Streets, on

Monday, December 21, 1942. Camp commander Colonel L.D. Bogan and commanding general of the Mountain Training Center Brigadier General Onslow S. Rolfe spoke briefly to the troops, welcoming them to Camp Hale and thanking them for their choice of the mountain infantry.[409] Since men significantly outnumbered women in the camp, about one hundred women came in from Leadville, Gilman, Red Cliff and the Pando Construction Company to provide dancing partners for the enlisted men who did not have their wives and family with them during training.[410] The festivities continued Tuesday with a game night, Wednesday with a talent show, Thursday with a Christmas carol performance on Christmas Eve and finally another formal dance on Friday, December 25, Christmas Day. Four chaplains also conducted Christmas Day services, with post chaplain Otto E. Kohn giving the main message. A twenty-five-man choir made up of soldiers from the 99th Infantry Battalion and 601st Field Artillery Battalions provided the music.[411] If there was any positive for the soldiers being at Camp Hale over Christmas, it may have come from the fact that Christmas trees were abundant and issued to units while the rest of the country faced rationing and strict regulations on obtaining a Christmas tree.[412] Camp Hale civilians were also given an opportunity to obtain a tree as long as they lived within "pass" distance of the cantonment.[413] Living within a National Forest did prove to have some advantages for the soldiers and civilians of Camp Hale.

As more soldiers started to arrive at Camp Hale during the months of November and December, the surrounding community started to once again open their hearts and pocketbooks in support of the troops. On Thanksgiving Day, November 26, 1942, a group of entertainers—including a singing trio from Glenwood Springs called the Dawson Sisters and a seven-piece orchestra from Red Cliff—performed at the newly finished post theater.[414] A month later, several townspeople and merchants of Salida, Colorado, through the Salida Chamber of Commerce, extended invitations to troops for a home-cooked Christmas Day dinner. The army declared a Christmas holiday, allowing troops with transportation to leave post and take advantage of the invitations. Many of the troops chose to stay on post for the exceptional meal—which included thirty thousand pounds of food, equaling about five pounds per person—served by the cooks for Christmas dinner. In addition to this gesture, A.S. Barnes and Company of New York City sponsored a poetry contest with the help of the Camp Hale Red Cross Office. Prizes awarded to contestants ranged from $5 to $250, depending on the quality of writing. Finally, Denver residents, at the request of the *Rocky Mountain News* and the American Legion, donated money to provide Christmas gifts to the troops at Camp Hale, expecting that they otherwise would receive little, if anything.[415] With all this local support, ski troopers slowly started to appreciate Camp Hale and everything the area had to offer them.[416]

While the welcoming and holiday festivities engulfed Camp Hale in a media frenzy, the ski troopers settled themselves in and training began. Many soldiers who were new to Camp Hale had never touched a pair of skis before and needed to be introduced to this new way of living. The army introduced them not only to skiing but also to carrying skis on their rucksack. Soldiers oftentimes made the ten-mile march from Camp Hale to Cooper Hill, carrying rucksacks with skis and a rifle attached, weighing about eighty-two pounds.[417] Some soldiers dropped out of the march before the end of the first five miles.[418] However, for those who completed the march, their day was only beginning, as they then often constructed snow huts upon arrival so they had a place to sleep that night.[419] Cooper Hill had permanent barracks, but these were mostly used only for serving meals. Once the soldiers settled in, the skiing began.

Hal Burton, author of *The Ski Troops*, wrote as a corporal in the Headquarters Company of the 10th Light Division (Alpine) in the December 18, 1942 edition of the camp's newspaper that ski instructors took soldiers in groups of eight to ten through intense ski training at Cooper Hill, which involved snowplowing, stem turning, cross-country skiing and downhill skiing.[420] Official training began under a directive issued by Colonel Rolfe on January 2, 1943, for forty half days of ski instruction with every new class that entered the camp. Within these half days of ski instruction, soldiers first learned via a training film about proper care of equipment, proper methods of waxing, skiing first aid, proper ways of fixing bindings, skiing nomenclature, ski drills on level ground, uphill techniques, cross-country skiing techniques and various other downhill skills.[421] Next, training commenced with daily calisthenics to strengthen muscles used significantly while skiing. Practical ski classes then began with skiing on the level, sidestepping up a hill and herringboning. Once a skier mastered these skills, he began learning the snowplow and shoulder and knee motion with the ninety-pound rucksack on his back. Finally, during the last half of the program, soldiers took to the main slope of Cooper Hill and learned how to ride the world's longest T-bar up the hill.[422] They went on cross-country ski treks and even joined companies and regiments on daylong ski trips while learning the proper ways to fall down and jump over small trees sticking through the snow using their poles.[423] Some soldiers endured a more expedited program that lasted for six to eight hours of drilling daily with six to ten men in a class.[424] Instructors considered this a full-day program and cut the total ski training in half to a total of twenty days to make an ordinary soldier a combat skier.[425]

After weeks of drill, ski instructors tested the men on a course located at Cooper Hill. Flags marked the course, and numerous strategically placed obstacles created a hazardous run that was physically exhausting as well.[426] These soldiers also endured 160 hours of training in Rolfe's "rigid snow program," which sometimes sent "soldiers in white" thirty miles a day with rifle and rucksack over the tricky Rocky Mountain terrain.[427] This type of skiing was not always appreciated by soldiers with a background in the sport before coming to Camp Hale. Private Victor J. Sievers commented in a letter to his sister, "It's swell skiing but I can't enjoy it because we can only ski the army way and that's mostly snow plowing for the first week."[428] He further commented about skiing with a heavy rucksack, writing, "When your skiing with a pack it turns into work if your [sic] not use to it…this army skiing is mostly cross country and skiing in the deep snow, which makes it hard to keep control of yourself."[429] For some, skiing became a humiliating act in front of their peers who already had the skills. One soldier who did demonstrations for a ski class commented to the class, "If anyone laughs, I'll ram these ski poles down your throat!"[430] Other soldiers, such as Merrill J. Clark III of K Company in the 85th, commented that it was "obvious the officers and men were learning on the fly as the Division became more and more prepared for the duty ahead."[431]

In order to increase the efficiency of the training, members of the 110th Mountain Signal Company worked tirelessly at the end of December clearing trees, stumps and rocks from the ski runs at Cooper Hill as training progressed.[432] In addition to training on skis, combat engineers trained on the nearby cliffs building aerial tramways and bridges. Other soldiers began training in rock climbing, mountaineering and camping essentials.[433] Evening classes conducted by the G-3 indoors included proper use of the rucksack, mountain tent and snowshoes. A school even opened for the proper maintenance and use of the T-15 Weasel, which was led by civilian instructors from the Studebaker Corporation.[434] Another minor school included a two-week course in firefighting, conducted by the district forest ranger in the spring of 1943.[435] Finally, a school opened for mule packing to ensure efficient loads could be placed quickly and securely on mules.[436] Camp Hale moved into full operation as it welcomed in the New Year of 1943. After seven months of official construction, plus two months of finishing touches and transitions with the arrival of soldiers, ski troopers became the primary focus of the army cantonment. Specifically, the instruction of soldiers in

Mule packing school, circa 1943. *Courtesy of the Denver Public Library, Western History Collection, Phil O'Rourke, TMD-798.*

how to fight and survive in any type of mountainous terrain under any cold-climate conditions became the mission of Camp Hale.[437]

The complete story of Camp Hale does not end with the arrival of the ski troops, but it does bring to a close the account of the days of preparation, planning and construction for the most unique training camp in American military history. The cantonment challenged architects, army engineers, constructors and even the lowest-level workers who labored for months on end. Advancements in the camp led engineers to develop new ideas in cantonment construction and to create special ways to manipulate existing plans to suit an inconsistent and unyielding environment. The need for exclusive training aids for mountain troops invigorated the army to write new training manuals and to establish uniquely suited training grounds requiring skills never before taught in the army. The construction of the cantonment challenged not only the army in all of its preparation for its first mountain division but also the American people. Citizens from the around the country made the trip to Camp Hale to work on a job that might have paid more than most around the country during the war but also required more human strength, endurance and determination to complete. Faced with basic human struggles, workers prepared themselves well both mentally and physically for a journey to the finish line in November 1942. Whether out of patriotic duty or a steady paycheck, workers finished the Pando cantonment nearly on schedule, bringing it to life and beating the odds stacked against it due to its elevation, weather and limited space from the beginning.

The Growth of Camp Hale and the Intensification of Training

It was becoming evident that mountaineers were not to be made overnight.[438]
—*Major John C. Jay*

As training commenced for mountain troops at Camp Hale, the cantonment continued to grow and specialize to meet the needs of its inhabitants. On December 29, 1942, the Mountain Training Center activated a sub-school for cooks and bakers located within the camp's boundary to start training eighty cooks under the leadership of Lieutenant Daniel C. Ring of the army's parent cooking and baking school at Fort Riley, Kansas.[439] The cooks utilized seven different mess halls scattered around the camp. Shortly thereafter, the Mountain Training Center began training an antitank and antiaircraft company. The company received a 37mm gun mounted on a three-quarter-ton truck along with all of their winter clothing in the first week of 1943. The men immediately set out behind their quarters on 11th Street, firing into the hills for training and roaring their guns throughout the valley.[440] On the same day that the MTC established the school for cooks and bakers, it sent out a notice to the National Ski Patrol System (NSPS) to once again begin recruiting men with winter and mountain experience.[441] The 87th had filled its ranks, and now it was time for the 86th Mountain Infantry Regiment to strengthen its force. The Army Ground Forces gave the NSPS ninety days to recruit two thousand soldiers.[442] As a result, notices went out around the country, and recruits began to sign up for the mountain troops. With Camp Hale close to being completed and in full operation, the army brought new recruits in within ten days from the time they filled out their initial application.[443] Thus, the 86th soon contained some of the most experienced and knowledgeable outdoorsmen of any unit in the U.S. Army in World War II.[444]

Brigadier General Onslow F. Rolfe described other types of specialized training that occurred at Camp Hale in the middle of January 1943 when he commented to the *Denver Post* that Camp Hale was training "triple-threat soldiers."[445] He said that triple-threat soldiers must "(1) ski, (2) ride mules and (3) use mountain motorized equipment—besides fight with special mountain guns."[446] The high expectations of soldiers at Camp Hale did not come unfounded. Among the soldiers who had made their way to Camp Hale included former professors and scholars, including a former assistant to Albert Einstein. In addition, the average IQ of the soldiers who joined the ranks of the mountain troops, including enlisted men down to privates, was reported to be much higher than other divisions.[447] Major John Jay wrote that for every three mountain soldiers, two had commissioned officer potential and one had noncommissioned officer potential. This higher intellect might have been due to the fact that the soldiers who could not hack it at Camp Hale were transferred or reassigned. Former senator, presidential candidate and 10th Mountain veteran Bob Dole commented in his memoir that the soldiers of the 10th Mountain Division were "anything but a bunch of rich softies trying to ski their way through World War II. Quite the contrary: its ranks contained some of the toughest, best trained, most highly conditioned fighting men in the world."[448] However, this still did not stop some of the toughest mountain troopers from asking, "When is the next paratroop examination?"[449]

The paratroopers received an extra fifty dollars per month as "jump pay." The army considered their training and mission to be extra hazardous and thus honored them with extra pay. The irony behind ski troops asking for a transfer to the paratroopers was that some considered life at Camp Hale and the training that ensued as tougher than life as a paratrooper, without the extra pay. One soldier commented, "We are coming to the conclusion that the paratroopers have nothing on us, except parachutes to ease the sudden stops, and we are applying for wages commensurate with the risks we take. It isn't the money we're after, of course, just recognition of the superiority of our achievement under exceptionally hazardous condition, a-hem."[450]

Camp Hale was one of the only training sites during World War II where human beings faced physical and mental obstacles that sometimes literally overtook them.[451] Falling out of a long distance run during normal training at any other basic combat training site differed from freezing to death at Camp Hale. Not everyone had the determination, expertise and raw strength to persevere at 9,250 feet. Interestingly, only about 20 percent of the soldiers who came through Camp Hale to join the mountain troops had a background in mountaineering, skiing or outdoor work and survival.[452] This meant that the MTC had to train 80 percent of its soldiers in the basics of cold-weather survival and pray that they took their training seriously. Major John C. Jay commented, "Men either loved the life of a mountain trooper and strove hard to perfect themselves in its difficult skills, or hated the entire setup violently and took no interest in the training whatsoever."[453] For some, Camp Hale was a concentration camp from which they could not escape. For others, it was a paid adventure into the mountains with rifles strapped to their backs. Colonel Bogan, camp commander in April 1943, commonly referred to Camp Hale with endearing affection as the "camp nearest Heaven."[454] Another soldier, who left Camp Hale for a unit south of the Mason-Dixon line, commented in a letter back to friends, "Here I sit in a hot whole [sic] which is a (censored) tent, but I can take it. If you feel sorry for me just bottle up a quart of Camp Hale water. I sure could go for a little. Take me back to Colorado to stay. Tell the whole (censored) bunch they are lucky to be there."[455] Finally, another soldier wrote, "We seem to have the 'cream of the crop.' Loafers, or halfhearted spiritless recruits are not likely to apply for a mountain camp, with its high altitude, cold weather, and isolation. Most skiers are one-time sportsmen. What a wealth of manpower of diversified talents at Hale."[456]

One of the other major areas of training at Camp Hale was rock climbing. As part of General Rolfe's desire for triple-threat soldiers capable of skiing, utilizing mules and adapting to the unique nature of the mountains and winter warfare, rock climbing undoubtedly fell within the third aspect. This skill proved to be valuable during the division's combat in Italy. During one training exercise, an entire battalion watched and waited at the bottom of a two-hundred-foot cliff while two climbers demonstrated what distracted climbing could result in. While the two climbers overtook the top of the cliff, an element of two German soldiers attacked them. Shortly thereafter a hidden soldier at the top threw a dummy over the cliff, petrifying many of the soldiers below as it smashed to the ground.[457] The training proved to be harsh but also effective in preparing the soldiers for the reality of what they faced.

Much of the initial training going into 1943 occurred before an audience or while reporters and other media visited Camp Hale to show the country what was going on at the army's new training center. The first notable event took place before a large audience at Winter Park, Colorado. As much as

Rock climbing at Camp Hale, Colorado, circa 1943. *Courtesy of the Denver Public Library, Western History Collection, Molenaar, C.M. (Cornelius M.) TMD-576.*

Opposite: Rock climbing at Camp Hale with full gear, circa 1943. *Author's personal collection.*

the natural conditions of the high elevation often made training difficult for soldiers, they also provided some opportunities for enjoyment while learning the skills of a ski trooper. Over the weekend of January 2–3, 1943, the best of the Camp Hale ski troopers formed a fifteen-man team to compete against the best civilian skiers in Colorado in the downhill and slalom events at Winter Park. The Southern Rocky Mountain Ski Association sponsored the event, which awarded individual and team winners. Though civilian Colorado native Barney McLean won every event as an individual skier, the Camp Hale fifteen-man team prevailed in the end with a decisive team victory over the civilians.[458]

Other notable training occurred from January 12 to January 14 when the 601st Field Artillery Battalion (Pack), the 87th Mountain Infantry Regiment, the 10th Cavalry Reconnaissance Troop and the Cooper Hill detachment of instructors and students performed various phases of training before an audience of the Associated Press, International News Service and Time, Inc. The artillery men of the 601st moved their pack howitzers on sleds, assembled them to fire, disassembled them and then packed them up to move again. At Cooper Hill, eighty skiers in white parkas and ski clothes flowed down the mountain before movie cameras. The army also unveiled its "motorized toboggan" for the first time at Camp Hale on the twelfth and revealed to the press that this was the "gravy train" assignment for soldiers.[459] Brigadier General Rolfe also proudly told the media about his "good soldier" dogs that he recruited from police units from across the nation and how "many lives" would be saved by the dog companions.[460] Rolfe identified three different types of dogs at Camp Hale: "sentry dogs, messenger dogs and huskies."[461] He further explained that sentry dogs were trained as guardian and attack dogs for soldiers on guard. These dogs obeyed only one individual's commands. Messenger dogs were trained to obey two individuals. They were used to carry messages from headquarters to commanders on the front line by traveling long distances by scent, trail and instinct. Rolfe concluded that the husky dogs were used to convey injured soldiers and to carry supplies with great speed through deep snow faster than any other form of transportation.[462] Men and dogs worked together by pulling equipment across the snow, leading General Rolfe to declare that his ski troops were the "best equipped in the world."[463] Dogs and mules were not the only animals utilized by soldiers at Camp Hale. The 110th Signal Company had the 282nd Pigeon Detachment as part of its ranks, which consisted of a few hundred pigeons at any one time.[464] In World War I, the army used pigeons for communication purposes when radio and other means were impractical. This same thought crossed the minds of the army once again in World War II. At a lower altitude, pigeons could fly about sixty miles an hour and five hundred miles a day in distance. At higher altitudes, they could only fly about forty-five miles an hour. As much as the Denver Pigeon Racing Club desired to help the war effort by supplying pigeons to Camp Hale, the mountain troops quickly realized that they were not practical and efficient at 9,250 feet. The MTC eventually scrapped the entire pigeon program.

Finally, on the last day of the media spectacle, 400 skiers of the 87th Mountain Infantry Regiment went through the manual of skis on the

Mountain troops on motorized sleds at Mount Rainier on March 23, 1942. *Author's personal collection.*

parade grounds at the south end of the camp in one mass formation.[465] The sea of men sporting white mittens, parkas, pack covers and skis moved in one graceful motion, showing off their approximate $1,000 worth of the "best [equipment] in the world."[466]

On Sunday, January 17, 1943, the camp made its radio debut as a featured location on the *Army Hour*. The *Army Hour* was an hour-long broadcast every Sunday from 1:30 p.m. to 2:30 p.m. Rocky Mountain Time. The National Broadcasting Company featured the program around the country and specifically on Denver's own KOA during World War II.[467] For Camp Hale's debut, soldiers took the event seriously and prepared three locations for the twelve-minute broadcast to take place. The first location was Cooper Hill, where soldiers demonstrated machine gun fire, artillery fire and skiing techniques. The stage then shifted to a different mountain pass where the 601st Field Artillery Battalion (Pack) demonstrated firing tactics using its 75mm pack artillery and marched by reporters with their mules, sleds and dog teams. Finally, the broadcast ended at the headquarters of the Mountain Training Center, where General Onslow S. Rolfe and Lieutenant Paul Townsend discussed various aspects of mountain training.[468]

By the end of January 1943, Camp Hale and the ski troopers had become quite popular around America. This popularity grew not only out of the media attention given to Camp Hale and the ski trooper training but also from a popular filmmaker and 10th Mountain Division soldier named John Jay. Jay began making films about skiing during the Great Depression while attending Williams College in Williamstown, Massachusetts. His interest in skiing and filmmaking took him to Woodstock, Vermont, where the first rope tow in the United States was located. During the next few years, Jay filmed several local ski events and even traveled to South America to film at Farellones, Chile. His first epic film, *Ski the Americas, North and South* (1940), caught the attention of many Americans and increased their awareness of his filmmaking capabilities. However, in April 1941, while filming in the northwestern United States, Jay received his draft notification and left for Fort Dix, New Jersey, with the army.[469]

Meanwhile, the army commissioned the most famous ski film producer of the time, Otto Lang, to produce a film on official skiing techniques called *Basic Principles of Skiing* (May 1941). Private Jay began working at this point as a Signal Corps photographer and training film cameraman on this project for Otto Lang. Jay learned techniques and skills from Lang that eventually helped him in his own filmmaking endeavors. In the spring of 1941, Jay signed up for Officer Candidate School and, three months later, was commissioned as a second lieutenant. He then received orders to report to 1st Battalion, 87th Mountain Infantry Regiment at Fort Lewis, Washington. Jay soon became one of the regiment's Winter Warfare Board photographers, field testers and evaluators of equipment on Mount Rainier while also serving as the battalion publicity officer. Jay became instrumental in tripling the size of the 87th after the bombing at Pearl Harbor on December 7, 1941, by garnering media attention for recruitment purposes. Lieutenant Jay soon became Mountain Training Center intelligence officer Captain Jay, who spread the mountain troop's story to papers, magazines and radio stations to help recruit two thousand men in three months.[470] One of the ways he accomplished this task was through the production of his own film about the 87th Mountain Infantry Regiment skiers at Fort Lewis, Washington. Jay produced a film in the spring of 1942 called *They Climb to Conquer*. The all-color motion picture became a hit among the American people and especially the soldiers of the 87th. In the January 22, 1943 edition of the *Camp Hale Ski-Zette*, one writer noted that camp theaters showed the movie to mountain training units, many of whom were in the two-hour film produced mostly while skiing on Mount Rainier.[471] Not only did the movie bring a new life of excitement to Camp Hale, but it also boosted morale among soldiers who began to have doubts about their choice of becoming a ski trooper and training at 9,250 feet.

Jay's public relations efforts were only beginning at the end of 1942. The army pressured him to bring more public attention to Camp Hale with the

Camp Hale matchbooks (1942–44) from the Post Exchange, the Service Club and the Thomas and Green Barber Shop. *Author's personal collection.*

Various Camp Hale memorabilia that could be purchased from the Camp Hale Post Exchange. *Author's personal collection.*

Camp Hale pillow covers that could be purchased from the Camp Hale Post Exchange. *Author's personal collection.*

continued growth of the camp physically, including buildings, and numerically, with soldiers.[472] As a result, in December 1942, Jay began shooting his second film focusing on the army's ski troopers. This time Jay shot the film almost exclusively at Camp Hale and the surrounding mountains but did include footage taken from the 87th on Mount Rainier.[473] Jay named this film *Ski Patrol* and completed it in the fall of 1943. This recruiting video became an even larger hit in America than *They Climb to Conquer* ever did. Since Jay had military responsibilities to take care of at Camp Hale, Debbie Bankhart, head of the Hanover Ski School at Oak Hill in Hanover, New Hampshire, worked with Jay and took the lead on making a coast-to-coast tour with the film to ski clubs and civic organizations.[474] Bankhart helped spread the recruiting film to over seventy-five thousand viewers from across America during the fall of 1943 and the winter of 1944 and handed out applications for volunteers at the end of each viewing.[475]

Jay's influence even stretched beyond motion picture media. Newspapers from across the nation, including the *Boston Globe*, *New York Sun*, *Denver Post* and *Leadville Herald Democrat*, published articles or portions of articles written by Jay. Even the army's newspaper, *Yank*, published a two-page spread in its February 17, 1943 issue, which *Ski-Zette* writers described as "one of the most complete to have appeared in any periodical" on Camp Hale.[476] The combined efforts of John Jay and Debbie Bankhart made the name Camp Hale common verbiage among many Americans across the country during the heart of World War II. One writer for the *Camp Hale Ski-Zette* affirmed this notion in the February 15, 1943 paper, where he wrote, "Camp Hale is becoming one of the most publicized camps in the nation."[477] This publicity was not always the case for the ski troops.

Knowledge of the mountain troops did not significantly reach the general public in the United States until the late fall of 1942, when the army established the Mountain Training Center at Camp Carson, Colorado.[478] The only previous publicity came from a small, limited and controlled group of reporters and photographers who had brief access to the training at Mount Rainer in the spring of 1942. Nevertheless, when the mountain troops began occupying Camp Hale during the winter of 1942, the secret was out about the importance of the camp and the unique nature of training that occurred there.

In addition to the work of John Jay and Debbie Bankhart in getting the word out about Camp Hale, the National Ski Patrol System still worked diligently in its recruiting efforts during the first few months of 1943. Whereas Jay and Bankhart sought candidates with a broad stroke of advertisements, the Ski Patrol initially sought only skiers and mountaineers, though it eventually changed its selection criteria to include mountaineers, north woodsmen, trappers, lumberjacks, skiers, packers, geologists, horseshoers, hunting guides, geographers, saddler aids, harness makers, teamsters, stablers, axemen, prospectors, hard-rock miners, timber cruisers and physically fit individuals for the mountain troops.[479] The Ski Patrol, as a consultant to the War Department, had the advantage of being able to recommend special assignments to the army for men who had the necessary qualifications.[480] Its regional representatives presented opportunities to individuals and interviewed subsequent candidates using questionnaires to find relevant information about them for mountain troop recruitment.[481] The NSPS used fifteen full sets of mountain troop equipment on loan from the Quartermaster Depot (Q.M.D.) in Ogden, Utah, to set up window displays.[482] It also purchased one thousand blown-up covers of the March 27, 1943 *Saturday Evening Post* featuring a ski trooper in full white camouflage on skis, holding an M1 Garand rifle.[483] Dole's recruiting effort proved to be so effective that the army later regretted freezing the process during the summer of 1942. Rumors spread across the country over the summer that the ranks of the mountain troops were full and that individuals had to look elsewhere to find a spot in the military.[484] Unfortunately, this resulted in many qualified, experienced and knowledgeable mountain men joining the ranks of the navy and air force as commissioned officers and the regular army as standard infantrymen.[485]

Additionally, in the beginning of 1943, avid outdoorsman and skier Frank Harper published *Military Ski Manual: A Handbook for Ski and Mountain Troops*, which he intended to use as a recruiting tool for military ski troopers. He believed firmly in the necessity and effectiveness of ski troopers, writing, "Perhaps this book may help in a small way to inspire many more skiers to join up with the ski troops—the one place where all of us belong today."[486] All of the recruiting efforts started to pay off for the army as it filled its ranks at Camp Hale and continued to dive deeper into training.

The popularity of the mountain troops in America reached a pinnacle in April 1943. President Franklin Roosevelt made a trip to Camp Carson, Colorado, and Camp Hale sent the 99th Infantry Battalion (Separate) to represent the camp in all its glory. As President Roosevelt sat in his open white car, the 99th "paraded in ski boots and wind breakers" past the president.[487] Rarely did a unit as small as the 99th Infantry Battalion (Separate) become the center of an inspection by the president of the United States. The Norwegians of the 99th made the president proud of his ski troopers at Camp Hale.

NATIONAL SKI ASSOCIATION OF AMERICA

THE NATIONAL SKI PATROL SYSTEM
CONSULTANT TO THE WAR DEPARTMENT
FOR THE SELECTION OF
SPECIALIZED PERSONNEL FOR MOUNTAIN TROOPS

CHARLES M. DOLE
Chairman
JOHN E. P. MORGAN
Treasurer
STEPHEN HURLBUT
Director of
Personnel Selection

415 LEXINGTON AVE.
NEW YORK 17, N. Y.

BULLETIN No. 10E7 (Revised 12.6.43-
Previous issues should be destroyed)

THE ARMY WANTS SKIERS AND CLIMBERS WHO ARE PHYSICALLY FIT FOR RIGOROUS
MOUNTAIN TRAINING. THOSE WHO HAVE LIVED AND WORKED IN THE MOUNTAINS ARE
PARTICULARLY DESIRED.

No candidate need be a member of the National Ski Patrol System, or of any
ski or mountain club in order to apply for such assignment.

Men are recommended for assignment to mountain units based on the information
submitted to National Ski Association on the attached questionnaire. Personal interviews are not necessary.

The assignment procedure for applicants is simple and direct and involves
no uncertainty or delay. Applicants who may apply are grouped as follows:
inductees prior to arrival at reception centers, trainees at replacement
training centers under Replacement and School Command, and other military
personnel. Individual procedure for men in each of these groups is indicated
in Section I to IV below.

NATIONAL SKI PATROL SYSTEM

SECTION I.   GENERAL PROCEDURE FOR MEN WISHING TO JOIN MOUNTAIN TROOPS:

Men desiring to join mountain troops may submit application by filling out
attached questionnaire and forwarding to the National Ski Patrol System,
415 Lexington Avenue, New York. Do not fail to provide letters of recommendation from responsible persons who can testify to your qualifications
for service with mountain units - qualifications which should include exceptional stamina and the ability to live and take care of yourself in the
mountains. Character references, as such, are not required. The National
Ski Patrol System will use its best judgment in considering applications
and its decisions are subject to review only by the War Department.

Note

SECTION II.   PROCEDURE FOR INDUCTEES:

(a) Men about to be inducted should submit their applications in accordance with procedure outlined in Section I above at least two weeks prior to
induction. Every applicant will be notified promptly as to whether his
application is acceptable or not.

(b) An approved inductee is informed that, as soon as he is inducted, he
must let us know at once (preferably by wire) his ASN (Army Serial Number)
and where and when he is to report for active duty at the end of his furlough.
As soon as we have this information, we issue him a letter (Form ALRO) addressed to the assignment officer at the reception center to which he is to
report, requesting his assignment to an infantry or field artillery replace-

Original National Ski Patrol System recruitment letter dated December 6,
1943. *Author's personal collection.*

Camp Hale bustled with activity going into its first large-scale training
exercise labeled the Homestake Peak Maneuvers. The headquarters
of the Army Ground Forces required a test of a battalion in the field at
Camp Hale.[488] The exercise drew national attention and the interest of
Minnie Dole and John E.P. Morgan. They arrived for their first visit to
an occupied Camp Hale, marveling at the occasion as they drove over
Tennessee Pass. Morgan wrote that the journey over the pass "is quite an

impressive spectacle. You get a real bird's eye view of the whole show before dropping down into the valley."[489] As a result of the media attention and that of Dole and his entourage, the Mountain Training Center mobilized a reinforced detachment of one thousand men comprising the headquarters and headquarters company, 2nd Battalion of the 87th, the 99th Field Artillery Battalion and various other attachments of medical, quartermaster, signal, antitank-antiaircraft and engineer units and dispatched them on maneuvers around 13,212-foot Homestake Peak, twelve miles southwest of Camp Hale from February 4 to February 12, 1943.[490] Their ultimate objective was to hold a defensive position just below the peak of Homestake Mountain and repel enemy attacks by ski troopers. The soldiers and mules began the mission by marching five miles from near the top of Tennessee Pass to Homestake Lake at 11,300 feet.[491] Soldiers waited around standing for almost two hours before the march, literally freezing in their boots. From the beginning of the five-mile march, commanders ordered 106 steps per minute, a grueling pace for many of the newly arrived soldiers from sea level who had not even acclimated to Camp Hale, let alone higher elevations. Also, many of these troops did not receive any training in how to wax skis, how to operate their new Model-1942 (M-1942) portable stoves or how to utilize their newly issued ski skins for traction going uphill. For every two feet up the trail, they slid back one and exerted more effort to regain their footing."[492] Men began to fall out under the blazing mountain sun, which reflected off the snow and scorched their unprotected faces. Rucksacks in excess of 90 pounds for some troops and gear totaling almost 125 pounds for mortar and machine gunners led to many cases of exhaustion.[493] Even some mules suffered as they got stuck in the multiple feet of snow, which forced their equipment and howitzers onto sleds with soldiers utilizing their one- and two-man harnesses for towing the equipment. Some of the troops, including Art Delaney, fell out of the march and got lost in the woods. Delaney ended up lost for two days before he wandered back into camp.[494] By the end of the first day, 25 percent of the troops became casualties, which resulted in a "continual procession of stragglers" to the rear of the formation.[495]

Upon arrival at Homestake Lake, perspiration froze on the soldiers as daytime temperatures hovered around zero.[496] Whenever opportunity arose, soldiers took off their boots and rubbed their feet to increase circulation in fear of frostbite. About 260 men fell out on the first day, resulting in about 30 percent of the entire force being eliminated from the rest of the training.[497] As a result of these conditions, the command cancelled the tactical exercise and devoted the rest of the time to snow camping, reconnaissance, maneuvering

Identified as (left to right) Roger Langley, Minnie Dole and Paul Lafferty at Camp Hale sometime between 1942 and 1944. *Courtesy of the Denver Public Library, Western History Collection, Paul Lafferty Scrapbooks, TMD-436.*

Mountain troops on skis above Camp Hale, Colorado. *Author's personal collection.*

Camp Hale artillery soldiers pull 75mm howitzers in the snow on December 23, 1942. *Author's personal collection.*

in snow conditions and testing the soldiers' training, equipment, clothing, methods of supply and mostly their will to survive. As the troops settled themselves in around Homestake Lake, they assembled their tents and built snow caves. Shortly thereafter, the army organized a resupply effort via an army air corps drop. The mules had proven ineffective in hauling supplies through deep snow, so the army relied on its planes to bring them in. Two C-47 planes from the 50th Wing, 1st Troop Carrier Command out of Peterson Field, Colorado Springs, made three supply drops of rations, ammunition, skis and rifles.[498] One drop landed on the east face of Homestake Peak, and a retrieval group was ordered out to pick it up. While en route, Major Wood, one of the observers and an expert mountaineer and leader of two expeditions into Alaska for the American Geographical Society, ordered the group back because there was a risk of an avalanche and due to the fact that the east face was an artillery target for the 601st Pack and was about to be fired on.[499] Artillery commander Colonel David Ruffner decided to fire a few 75mm rounds into the face of the hill to see if he could dislodge the snow cornice and create an avalanche. The artillery rounds worked, and the snow came crashing down the mountainside, causing Homestake Lake to "leap into the air like a geyser," basically draining the entire lake.[500] One infantryman recalled that the crashing snow created a six-foot-thick wall of ice off the top of the lake that washed up on shore a few feet from the brass.[501] Robert W. Parker of the 87th Mountain Infantry additionally remembered how the officers, visitors and dignitaries scrambled in embarrassment for safety while the snow cloud and ice blocks came right at them.[502] Fortunately, nobody was injured. To the detriment of the command and the well-being of the troops, four important individuals with connections to Washington witnessed the entire event.

The observers included Minnie Dole; Major Walter A. Wood, G-4 (Logistics); Captain Jack Tappin, G-3 of the Army Ground Forces; and William P. House, a member of the first American expedition to K2 in the Himalayan Mountains and War Department consultant of the National Ski Patrol System.[503] Wood and House combined their observations in a report to General Leslie James McNair, chief of the Army Ground Forces, which detailed how officers slept in tents while soldiers froze outside and carried excessively heavy rucksacks.[504] Of the four, Minnie Dole probably wrote the most scathing report to Washington that criticized the Camp Hale brass. In the report, he identified that the staff was "rank happy, with rank at the top and brains at the bottom."[505] In response to these complaints, McNair sent a letter back to General Rolfe at Camp Hale that identified that the soldiers were given inadequate equipment and training for the level of intensity that they experienced. About half the soldiers received specialized equipment, including the mountain tent, M-1942 stove and mountain sleeping bag, only a day before the exercise.[506] He also said in the letter that a significant number of soldiers fell out of the training due to sickness, fatigue, frostbite and fear and warned against officers neglecting the pool of expertise prevalent among the enlisted men.[507] Multiple accounts now reveal that the maneuvers were for the most part a disaster that resulted from inexperienced leadership, lack of training and unexpected blizzard conditions blowing horizontal snow and temperatures breaking thirty degrees below zero, the coldest of the season.[508] Officers at the Mountain Training Center, including General Rolfe, later admitted that numerous errors and hardships occurred due to the fact that many of the enlisted men had not completed their basic training but were still used in the exercise because of impracticalities in organizing a force of only experienced mountain troops for the exercise.[509] By the end of the training, about 260 men, making up 30 percent of the command, obtained frostbite or suffered from exhaustion and prematurely retreated back to Camp Hale in what became known as "the Retreat from Moscow."[510] Floods of white-clad soldiers stumbled back to Camp Hale from Homestake Lake, unable to bear the harsh conditions.

Mountain tents in the spring of 1944. *Courtesy of the Denver Public Library, Western History Collection, Duryea Morton, TMD-539.*

During the early days of training at Mount Rainier, the brass continually ran into issues by often being unwilling to learn and take advice from the enlisted men among whom most of the experts in skiing and mountaineering resided. This became apparent also at Camp Hale during exercises like the one at Homestake Peak and later during the "D" series maneuvers. Many enlisted men lost confidence in the training program due to the floundering of officers in outdoor matters.[511] Private Viktor J. Sievers commented about this reality in a letter to his sister in which he wrote, "You can ski as well as the Lieutenant that were with us yesterday, there [*sic*] good but your [*sic*] better."[512] As a result, General Rolfe attempted to solve this problem by sending ski veterans of the 87th to officer candidate school during the first half of 1942.[513] He then acquired these soldiers back as commissioned officers, second lieutenants so that they could instruct other officers at Camp Hale's ski school. However, during the most intense days of training in 1943, enlisted soldiers, still stuck at the rank of private first class, continued to instruct at Cooper Hill.[514] Regardless of rank, Camp Hale and the wilderness surrounding it were unforgiving to soldiers when it came to survival in extreme cold-weather conditions. The construction crews learned this first when they built Camp Hale, while the Mountain Training Center learned it going through initial training in 1943. Consequently, the Mountain Training Center soon made extensive changes to the mission and scope of training, learning and instructing at Camp Hale.

As training modifications commenced after the Homestake Peak Maneuvers, the infrastructure of Camp Hale suffered a minor setback on February 19, 1943. A fire broke out between three and four o'clock in the afternoon in the Ordnance Service Command Shop, sending exploding ordnance and flames to the two-story frame building of the Automotive Maintenance Shop. In forty-five minutes, the fire destroyed machinery and equipment valued at about $100,000 and the building at an additional $150,000.[515] The largest bursts of fire came from exploding gas tanks from fifteen to twenty vehicles parked in the maintenance shop. Firemen, aided by the help of favorable winds, kept the fire contained and put it out shortly thereafter.[516] Progress only stopped momentarily as most of the employees, along with the remaining trucks and equipment, moved to the Ordnance Weapons Shop at the north end of the camp. Other workers set up a temporary workstation at the warehouse near the destroyed maintenance shop.[517] Camp Hale authorities never determined the cause and precise origin of the fire. However, this did not seem to bother the command, who settled with being thankful that the fire did not destroy more than it did at a critical time in training at the camp.[518]

By the end of March 1943, renovations already had taken place in other buildings across the camp in order to repurpose them for a more developed MTC and cantonment as a whole. A noncommissioned officers' club opened south of the old icehouse and served soldiers, family and friends for three dollars a month.[519] "Noncoms," as they were commonly called, frequented the club enjoying a beer and a sandwich at 9,250 feet during leisure time. Engineers renovated the club at the end of the summer and allowed Staff Sergeant Eugene L. Kramer, a former interior decorator from Chicago, to design and decorate the inside with a tropical zebra theme.[520] In addition, the camp opened up a legal assistance office at the end of April 1943 to better meet the personal affairs and proper legal cases of soldiers, their dependents and civilians employed at the camp.[521]

The Camp Hale command also realized the continued need to take care of their civilian workforce. At the end of June 1943, the army contracted the Johnson-Lock Construction Company of Minneapolis, Minnesota, to begin construction on a new Pando hospital and to renovate existing buildings in Pando and the station hospital area into dormitories and 334 apartment units to house 360 civilian employees.[522] The existing buildings were initially used by civilian constructors in the early days of construction in 1942, but they needed to be renovated with new floors, new shingles and private baths for apartments. Additionally, Camp Hale obtained its first pressing shop in August 1943. The Zingone Brothers of Salida set up a pressing, altering and tailoring shop south of the Recreation Hall on 5th Street in order to provide two-day service for soldiers in need of taking care of their uniforms.[523] The cantonment continued to grow in size and sophistication as the command attempted to better meet soldier needs.

Finally, more construction work commenced in order to improve road conditions, drill areas, barracks areas and drainage ditches. Graders, bulldozers and draglines sloped off the yards and made them uniform while filling in hollows in drill grounds and roads.[524] Engineers knew this work needed to be done in the fall of 1942 but never found the time to get it completed before the mountain troops arrived. Thus, when the spring rain and snow hit, water pools and mud holes formed and caused problems for vehicles and drill training. Engineers even put in motion plans for blacktopping all post roads in order to improve their condition for soldiers, civilians and visitors to the high-altitude cantonment.[525]

The small and often few perks that Camp Hale offered kept the soldiers and civilians going while enduring the harsh weather and training that never ceased to add an extra level of stress and anxiety to soldiers. One example of how normal army training became exceptionally difficult at Camp Hale included going to the rifle range during April 1943. The task of lying prone on the cold ground of the range while shooting targets through the "myriad of Gremlin-like snowflakes" that danced in front of their rifle sights added an extra factor to qualification.[526] The mountain troops prided themselves in being excellent marksmen and oftentimes held competitions between battalions. As warmer spring weather started to move into Camp Hale, winter training transitioned into summer training. Both times of the year were crucial for mountain troops, as they learned to ski, snowshoe and survive in the cold during the winter and rock climb and mountaineer in the summer.

The month of May was a transitional month in accordance with the weather at 9,250 feet. Snow remained on the ground in shaded areas while more exposed areas became bare land of rock and alpine grass. The 602nd Field Artillery took advantage of this mix of mountain conditions in order to obtain some of the best training the battalion saw at Camp Hale. On May 3, 1943, men and mules of the pack battalion left Camp Hale on a ten-day, 170-mile trek to Camp Carson, Colorado.[527] No battalion had ever marched this far from Camp Hale while enduring snow, rain, sleet and hail on seven of the ten days. The command meant for the training to push the limits of the pack artillery by testing the men in their ability to maneuver mules through the mountains under harsh conditions while crossing the Continental Divide at 10,400. Soldiers carried a mixture of rucksacks and pack boards but left their tents at home, relying on lean-tos of pine boughs for shelter.[528] For the most part, the element followed Highway 24 from Camp Hale to Buena Vista and then departed cross-country east through the San Isabel National Forest and Pike National Forest to Guffey and subsequently to Cripple Creek before scaling over the Front Range mountains to Camp Carson. The battalion remained at Camp Carson until it left for Fort Ord, California, on June 12, 1943, to train with the 601st in support of the invasion of Kiska.

Meanwhile, back at Camp Hale, 45 soldiers of Company I of the 86th Mountain Infantry Regiment held a night demonstration for 2,500 soldiers of the regiment on the rifle range.[529] The demonstration taught soldiers how to orienteer in the night using the stars and a compass. It also tapped into the unique geographical nature of Camp Hale to teach soldiers about the different sounds and sights in the woods, including scraping through brush and barbed wire, flares in the forest, lighting a match, pounding tent stakes and various other common outdoor noises.[530] The command desired for the training to better prepare mountain troops for combat in a wooded, mountainous terrain so that they were aware of how far and fast simple noises and lights traveled. As a grand finale of the training, the company demonstrated an all-out attack and ambush by an enemy force with live fire and explosions.[531] Both the 602nd's 170-mile trek and the 86th's night demonstrations were types of training that made Camp Hale valuable and unique for the mountain troops because it challenged the soldiers to conduct tactical operations at high altitude through diverse terrain.

As the summer of 1943 moved into Camp Hale, training began to change to include activities never seen before during the winter months. Soldiers first arrived at Camp Hale upon its completion in November and December 1942, and therefore, they were yet to see the cantonment in the summer. The 9,250-foot cantonment never ceased to provide unique challenges and training opportunities, even during the summer months. The summer marked an expansion in personnel and reorganization of units with the addition of the 85th Mountain Infantry Regiment, the 90th Infantry Regiment and the 616th Field Artillery, all activated on July 15, 1943, as part of the 10th Light Division (Alpine)'s activation at Camp Hale.[532] On that same day, the 604th

Field Artillery Battalion arrived at Camp Hale after marching 170 miles on foot and mule from Camp Carson over a ten-day timespan.[533] Four days later, the 605th Field Artillery began the same trek as the 604th from Camp Carson, maneuvering through Cripple Creek, Hartsel, Fairplay, Leadville and Tennessee Pass, arriving at Camp Hale on July 27, 1943.[534] By this time, the 10th Light Division (Alpine) had three artillery battalions. The two original field artillery battalions (pack), the 601st and 602nd, that made up the MTC traveled with the 87th to Kiska and then came back to the States for only a brief time before being deployed overseas again.

Similarly, the army activated the 226th Engineer Motorized Company at Camp Hale on July 15, 1943, the only one of its type in the entire army.[535] The 226th was not a new company but rather was Company A of the 126th Engineer Mountain Battalion renamed and reorganized to better make a distinction for its different mission than the other company of the 126th. Its mission involved mostly working outside Camp Hale proper in the surrounding mountains building aerial tramways, cableways, sawmills, high-altitude roads, trails, suspension bridges, trestle bridges and tunnels; making maps; and constructing ski-lifts. This experimental company tested, constructed and developed whatever was necessary to facilitate transportation in mountain warfare.[536] Its command put it to a true test of its ability in the latter part of 1943 when command asked the company to construct an airport and landing strip on the ice at Turquoise Lake.[537] Shortly thereafter, the 126th constructed an aerial tramway up the slopes of Ten Mile Peak that some engineers claimed was their hardest project yet. This reorganization of the 126th Engineer Mountain Battalion better prepared its men for the coming deployment by expanding the influence and reach of the engineers in a tactical combat environment.

The addition and reorganization of these units into the 10th Light Division (Alpine) took the place of the Mountain Training Center and began a new era at Camp Hale.[538] The MTC had served its purpose of training soldiers in mountain and winter warfare, and now the focus shifted to combat readiness. In July 1943, the 87th began prepping for its deployment to Kiska, Alaska, which eventually took place when it invaded the island on August 15, 1943. As the soldiers of the 87th left for Kiska, Camp Hale finally caught up with the rest of the country in obtaining its first Women's Auxiliary Army Corps (WAAC) detachment.

7

The WAACs Take on Camp Hale

Know Your Rank? Better Check Up on Her's [sic] *as Well.*[539]
—*unknown writer, the* Camp Hale Ski-Zette, *June 2, 1943*

The history of the Women's Army Auxiliary Corps (WAACs) at Camp
Hale is one that has never been told in length. This may be due to the
fact that there is little primary source information relating to them and their
memoirs are few. However, the lack of information about their contributions
does not reflect on their impact; they brought much-needed talents and
contributions to the cantonment.

The first WAACs marched into Camp Hale in formation on Thursday,
May 27, 1943. The 12 women arrived from Fort Des Moines, Iowa, as part
of an advanced detail that prepared the way for the arrival of 140 WAACs
one week later.[540] The U.S. WAAC grew quickly during the middle of
1943 and began staffing offices across the nation. The army rapidly began
assigning detachments to posts throughout the country that needed extra
administrative and noncombat support. For the WAACs at Camp Hale,
this meant settling into an unusual, if not foreign, place for many flatland
women who had never seen the Colorado Rockies or even snow.

The WAACs who arrived at Camp Hale quickly realized the unique
nature of the cantonment, as one commented after her first week that
"it is a bit off the beaten track."[541] Another said it reminded her of "Lost
Horizon."[542] Army chow also seemed to be a step down for some women at
Camp Hale. One, Mary Stone, commented that it was "S.O.S., you know,
shit on a shingle."[543] This did not stop them from settling in and starting their

mission of serving soldiers at the country's highest military cantonment. Their devotion to the war effort easily matched that of the men, as many of the women left defense jobs or businesses that supported the war effort and said goodbye to their families to enlist in the WAAC. The enlistees faced four weeks of basic training, military specific schools, followed all military order and discipline and even had their own physical training regimen; however, they were initially not considered part of the regular army.[544]

Word quickly spread around Camp Hale that the WAACs—trained in 142 different jobs, including cooks, clerks, librarians, accountants, photographers, bandleaders, special service workers, post exchange workers and ordnance automotive workers—could begin to take over jobs long held by soldiers. The camp command attempted to calm the fears of the mountain troops by reassuring them that the WAACs would not be taking on combat roles or positions that required specific training to the mountain troops. However, this meant that noncombat-related jobs held by men could go to the women, resulting in men being freed up for overseas deployment. At that time, the WAACs had a presence on over eighty posts, camps and stations across the nation and had proven to be essential contributors to the military.[545] Soldiers at Camp Hale learned this quickly, as shown by the comments of one soldier, who wrote in the camp newspaper, "Welcome WAAC's. We are glad to have you with us here on 'Top of the World', hope you enjoy your stay as much as we enjoy having you."[546] Another soldier commented about the WAACs working at the headquarters, saying, "We think you'are [sic] tops, girls."[547] However, this mentality about women in the service did not always resonate with all the enlisted men. Some men doubted the women's ability and retained the long-held and engrained beliefs that women were still meant to serve in the home and in the family. Some even expressed that the WAACs were there only to "satisfy the men."[548] However, the women did not let this keep them from their service. WAAC member Mary Stone commented, "We knew that we had a job to do and that we were all working in the same direction."[549] The women truly believed in the words of their song, which said, "The Wac Is in Back of You."[550] The conditions at 9,250 feet did not discriminate between male and female, and thus, most of the men eventually gained a profound respect for the role women took on and for their contributions to the cantonment.

The WAACs seemed to equally enjoy the company of the mountain troops, especially those who adored them and, most importantly, dated them.[551] A newly promoted WAAC sergeant attempted to sew on her chevrons to her uniform one night and became frustrated to the point that she quit trying. A well-meaning and quick-reacting male soldier answered her call for help and took her uniform blouse back to his barracks. The next day he returned it to the female sergeant with perfectly sewn-on chevrons.[552] The mutual respect between mountain troops and WAACs grew with every marching day. Upon hearing that the field outside the administration building was filled with rocks, soldiers volunteered to help the WAACs clear it of debris so that they could practice their marching skills right outside their place of work. Another soldier wrote an article in the *Ski-Zette* titled "Dating a WAC? Here's a Tip or Two," in which he jokingly wrote, "Don't follow a WAC Platoon around waiting for a Field Strip. This applies to their equipment only."[553] The rest of his article seriously addressed soldiers in proper etiquette and treatment of the WAACs. The list of examples of mutual support between WAACs and mountain troops continued to grow throughout Camp Hale's existence.

Interaction between WAAC ladies and soldiers increased significantly in the coming weeks as the two groups not only worked together on the job but also mingled during off hours. WAACs attended their first Camp Hale dance, put on by the 123rd Ordnance Company, on Thursday, June 3, 1943.[554] Soldiers who once found the company of local Leadville and Red Cliff ladies as their only source of female attention and fraternization now turned their eyes to the newly arrived WAACs. The two groups mingled yet again at their first social event on June 7 at the engineers' weekly "beer bust," which included music and socialization.[555] The engineers considered it a blessing to be located right across the street from where the WAACs resided. This resulted in them playing many off-hours baseball games in front of the WAACs' building instead of where they usually played (behind it) so that they could interact with the women as much as possible. The men took every opportunity to show off their abilities and their interest in the WAACs, as the number of women around Camp Hale still remained limited.

The engineers were a highly respected group of soldiers given their enhanced skills in building, sustaining and solving issues in the high altitude of Colorado. However, one soldier managed to embarrass himself with the WAACs after he crossed the Eagle River on a warmer July day in order to assist in salvaging an errant truck that had taken a spill into the icy waters of the river.[556] Upon completing his portion of the salvage, he fell asleep on the railroad tracks away from everyone else on the other side of the river. Sure enough, a train came burrowing through Pando and came within forty feet of him before a soldier from the other side of the river quickly hopped in a boat, pulled himself across the river and ran toward the individual while throwing rocks at him in order to wake him up. The rocks hit the engineer

Members of the WAC Detachment–Camp Hale, Colorado. On the far right is WAC nurse Lieutenant Farel Mitchell. *Author's personal collection.*

but to no avail—he kept sleeping. Finally, the running soldier made it to him and dragged him off the tracks while abruptly waking him from his sleep.[557] The WAACs could not help but watch the entire event unfold as it happened right in front of their building. Life at Camp Hale never ceased to provide the camp newspaper with tall tales of heroism and humor at the nation's highest military cantonment.

Not only did the WAACs begin to bond with their male counterparts at Camp Hale, but they also quickly became friends with one another and supported one another like family. Mary Stone remembered how her time at Camp Crowder differed from Camp Hale because of the more "relaxed" and less "regimented" life at Camp Hale, which allowed for the females to bond and to become closer friends.[558] Camp Hale never obtained a reputation as being a very disciplined or regimented training site. To the contrary, it became an isolated army experiment in which officers and enlisted men often times comingled more than normal. This might have been due to the nature and purpose of Camp Hale in training soldiers to ski and survive in cold weather in which privates instructed officers. The WAACs took advantage of this more relaxed atmosphere to help and encourage one another during the long and grueling winter months at 9,250 feet.

With the WAAC detachment's survival of their first month at Camp Hale, previous rough spots between soldiers and the women seemed to fade away. WAAC first sergeant Hilda DiMuzio commented in the camp newspaper, "Thanks loads for the wonderful reception shown us since our arrival here. We are both glad and proud to be here and hope to prove ourselves capable of the work we are about to undertake."[559] Sadly, a few of the women found themselves in the station hospital within the first few weeks of arriving due to altitude sickness and dehydration. This, however, was not out of the ordinary, as some soldiers had similar issues after getting off the train and beginning their stay "On Top of the World."

More WAAC auxiliaries arrived at Camp Hale from Fort Des Moines on June 23. These twenty-seven women were part of the Motor Corps. Each one of them had completed four weeks of basic training and six weeks of Motor Transport Specialist Schooling so that they could drive staff vehicles and light trucks.[560] The women even serviced their own vehicles, which impressed plenty of the men who questioned their ability to run their own motor pool. Many of these questions were answered by the professionalism and knowledge of the women. One day in September 1943, on the road to Leadville, two WAACs changed a flat tire while two male sergeants stepped aside and watched.[561] The WAACs took every opportunity

Camp Hale motor repair shop. *Author's personal collection.*

to prove themselves. Though the women worked in different areas of the camp and in different types of jobs, they all stayed in one barracks, located on 1st and B Street. This allowed them to isolate themselves from the rest of the camp when on personal time.

Shortly thereafter, in the beginning of July, three Women's Ordnance Workers (WOWs) arrived at Camp Hale to assist the Motor Corps with more complex projects related to automotive maintenance. The WOWs served as mechanics in the Ordnance Maintenance Shop after completing two months of schooling at Fort Creek Annex, Plattsmouth, Nebraska.[562] Though these women were uniformed, they were not considered part of the army. Nevertheless, their sacrifice for the greater good of Camp Hale did not go unnoticed as the men increasingly saw the competency and ability of women to complete necessary jobs in support of the war effort.

Ordnance maintenance shop, Camp Hale. Notice the train cars moving nearby past the maintenance shop. The maintenance shop is the tall building in the center. *Author's personal collection.*

The women did indeed complete necessary jobs at Camp Hale working day and night, which freed up more men to take on combat positions that women could not have. The stresses of working at the highest wartime army cantonment in the entire country resulted in yet another need for recreational and leisure time for the WAACs. In the middle of July 1943, the *Ski-Zette* identified how during one week, WAACs participated in recreational opportunities during almost every evening. On Tuesday, the women played baseball with the medics. On Wednesday, they visited with soldiers and civilians in the station hospital to entertain them and lift their spirits. On Thursday, some women tried out for the Service Club Counsel's show, and finally on Friday, they attended a dance with much fanfare from the male soldiers, who enjoyed their company.[563] The Leadville USO even invited the WAACs into town for a buffet dinner in celebration of the first birthday of the WAAC when women began training at Fort Des Moines, Iowa, on July 20, 1942.[564] The WAACs enjoyed an exclusive dinner devoted entirely to them with a large two-tier birthday cake that said, "Happy

Birthday WAAC" in orange icing. They played games, listened to music and meticulously played bingo to win prizes.[565]

WAAC recreational opportunities continued to increase toward the end of July 1943 as the WAAC SHACK opened up.[566] This smaller service club provided the WAACs a place to hang out and a place to take their GI dates. Male soldiers were only allowed in when escorted by a WAAC. Dances continued to be held at the main Service Club, but when the WAACs arrived, they became invitation only because the club could not handle all of the men of Camp Hale who desired to have a dance with one of the WAACs.[567] So the club sent out invitations and began to hold more frequent dances with the hope that the WAACs would be in attendance at all of them.

WAACs also took advantage of the recreational opportunities in and around the cantonment. They enjoyed many of the same outdoor activities as the men did, including mountain climbing, fishing and even rock climbing. Some never grew accustomed to the unique high-altitude environment of Camp Hale, so while half the women went out for an alpine picnic in the mountains, the other half held an indoor picnic on their own grass, an army OD blanket, on the floor of their barracks.[568] One day in the middle of August 1943, a mountain afternoon shower hit a group of WAACs climbing just outside Camp Hale proper, causing them to return back to the camp looking as if they had gone "swimming in their slacks."[569] One WAAC by the name of Private First Class Bernice Levision intended to really go swimming when she reported for duty with a swimming suit in her suitcase, only to be informed that Camp Hale did not have a swimming pool or a beach.[570] Her fellow soldiers joked that she could get some use out of it by wearing it in the shower, where the only warm water on the cantonment could be found. In the evenings, many WAACs took advantage of the bowling alley at Camp Hale because they could wear civilian clothing, unlike in other parts of the camp.[571] This gave them a return to normalcy for at least an evening. The women enjoyed the fun and recreational opportunities that Camp Hale offered just like the men did in both the summer and winter months.

Recreation aside, the WAACs turned their attention to more serious and important matters going into August. On August 11, 1943, the women of the Women's Army Auxiliary Corps at Camp Hale became women of the Women's Army Corps (WAC) during a ceremony for which the entire WAAC detachment of three platoons lined up in formation on their parade grounds behind their barracks.[572] Each woman of the detachment raised her right hand and swore in at a retreat ceremony held at Camp Hale before the commanding officers and visitors of the camp. One of the WAACs, Emily Collinsworth, commented about this event after being asked what it meant to her, saying, "I was really glad because I didn't think we were really in the army because we were just an Auxiliary…we weren't really part of the army yet, so I was really glad to know that I was really in the regular army."[573] This officially legitimized the presence of the WACs at Camp Hale and gave them the confidence to do their job and make their presence known as an essential part of the operation of the cantonment.

By the end of August 1943, WAC officers had taken leadership and control of the Station Complement administrative positions in personnel,

Camp Hale nurse Lieutenant Farel Mitchell. *Author's personal collection.*

finance, post exchange and special service sections in the post headquarters.[574] When the army incorporated the WAAC into its ranks officially, creating the WAC, it formally recognized women who reenlisted in the WAC after the WAAC was disbanded with a unique green-and-gold ribbon.[575] By the end of the summer, the women had clearly made an impression on Camp Hale, and one Camp Hale WAC officer affirmed this in a letter to the *Ski-Zette* on November 5, 1943. She wrote:

> *The facts are that the members of the Women's Army Corps are intelligent, purposeful women who have understood better than many the magnitude of this war…the work to be done…and, more than that, have transmitted their understanding into action…Action which led them to give up comfortable, profitable civilian pursuits to accept military orders to do military jobs wherever they are needed. They are to be honored for their unselfish decision.*[576]

Her letter also revealed that some people continued to make the WAC the object of many "jokes, jibes and even jeers."[577] Some men never grew to respect the position and role that the WAC held at Camp Hale. Their preconceived notions of women in uniform and their stubbornness to change resulted in a minority of resistance against their presence. However, the WACs at Camp Hale never let this bother them in their mission. They continued to serve their country and the soldiers who needed their support. Over Thanksgiving 1943, the WACs proved their dedication to Camp Hale by volunteering to take over all KP duty.[578] They also volunteered their time in the Service Club, wrapping Christmas presents for soldiers to send home to their loved ones.

While the WACs gave of themselves to others at Camp Hale, they maintained their own strict regimen of physical training at six o'clock in the morning, for which they did calisthenics. Regardless of the season and the temperature outside, the WACs formed up in the outdoor mountain air to maintain their fitness despite those who continued to be perpetuators of "sour grape-ing."[579] Some of the ladies who grew to appreciate Camp Hale

Opposite, top: WAC at Camp Hale during Christmas 1943. *Author's personal collection.*

Opposite, bottom: Camp Hale Service Club, across 11th Street from Camp Hale Theater No. 2. at the intersection of 11th and B Streets in November 1942. *Author's personal collection.*

and the opportunities to ski were tapped by the army recruiting office to be representatives as "Ski Wacs" at various recruiting offices.[580] These women were proud to be a part of the ski troops and truly put forth their best effort to serve the soldiers of Camp Hale. Whenever an infantry regiment held a dance, the WACs were there. Whenever a battalion held a dance, the WACs were there. Their cooperation with the Special Service Division no doubt boosted the morale of the men at Camp Hale, helping them endure the tough weather and training that made them the elite fighting force they later proved to be.

As the 10th Infantry Division departed for Camp Swift, Texas, in June 1944, the WACs did not go with it. The army transferred most of them to Camp Crowder, Missouri, and others to camps throughout the country. Some of them even deployed to the South Pacific to fill positions. The WACs changed the dynamics of Camp Hale for the better, as just over two hundred of them called Camp Hale their home during the war. Their relentless devotion to the soldiers and to their country was exemplary and effective in making Camp Hale a success in its mission to train mountain troops. The history of this cantonment would not have been the same without their commitment and service.

R&R AND CAMP HALE'S PECULIAR NEIGHBOR: LEADVILLE

Leadville is whooping it up in wartime![581]
—*Leif Erickson,* Leadville Herald Democrat, *August 31, 1942*

While the relationship between Leadville and Camp Hale started off on the wrong foot in 1942, Leadville eventually proved to be an important part of the history of the cantonment and an essential provider of recreation, leisure and social support. Leadville has a long history of being a mining town that dates back primarily to 1860, when Abe Lee discovered gold in what he named California Gulch. One *Herald Democrat* writer called Leadville "a pale purple shell of Colorado's richest and rowdiest mining camp."[582] The rich and famous, varying from Horace and Augusta Tabor to the Youngers, Daltons, Texas Jack, Bat Masterson, Oscar Wilde, Doc Holliday of Tombstone, JJ and Margaret Brown and Jefferson Randolph (Soapy) Smith all at one point or another strolled the streets of Leadville and became part of its rich and fascinating history. President Teddy Roosevelt even made Leadville his headquarters during a grizzly bear hunting trip in the Pando area.[583] Leadville garnered the attention of the people of Colorado for much of its early history because of its gold, silver and social fame, which even led some to consider it for state capital instead of Denver.

By the time April 1942 came to Leadville, the town still struggled to lift itself out of the Great Depression of the 1930s and bring important industry and jobs back. The CWA, WPA and CCC all provided many young men with temporary jobs and cash to spend in Leadville, but these jobs were never meant to be permanent and did not provide a base of industry to fill the town's coffers. When the town learned for sure that ski troops would train at Pando in late March 1942, the prospects of a new olive drab (OD) green-gold soon became reality as soldiers brought cash to the economy. Just as the brothel owners, saloon owners and other managers of services to miners made a profit off the local population, business owners in Leadville were ready to make a profit off the ski troopers. In fact, in April 1942, most store owners in Leadville arranged to stay open late on Monday evenings as a gesture of goodwill to Pando workers.[584]

Nevertheless, for Leadville residents, it was not all about profit. Many citizens saw the new training camp as a means through which they could participate and fulfill their patriotic duty in serving America's finest and newest addition to the army. Residents hosted United Service Organization (USO) events, provided housing for workers and soldiers and gave them many social outlets to relax, kick back and enjoy the mountains. These outlets included free coffee and doughnuts for soldiers every Saturday and Sunday morning at the Masonic Hall and similarly at the Sodality Hall in the rear of the Annunciation Church.[585] The Leadville USO also offered a winter "Hospitality Program" for soldiers of Camp Hale in which enlisted men and women received invitations to the homes of Leadville citizens for meals and recreation.[586] By the beginning of 1944, the USO took an unprecedented step in entertaining soldiers by having its first camp show at the Cooper Hill bivouac site in the middle of the winter![587] Prior events all had taken place in either the station hospital, recreation halls or in the Service Club at Camp Hale. Finally, the Women's Society of Christian Service of the Leadville Methodist Church visited the Camp Hale Service Club every Friday in order to sew on any patches, chevrons or buttons for soldiers.[588] The relationship between Leadville and Camp Hale, though strained at times, first benefitted Leadville during the construction of the cantonment in 1942 and soon came together for the good of both groups.

Camp Hale's introduction of thousands of workers into Lake County from April to November 1942 gave Leadville a much-needed population base to boost business. These individuals gave the town a "jingling cash shot-in-the-arm" that brought back many of the signs of the mining boom days of the late nineteenth century.[589] The Pioneer Club Bar, located on State Street, once again frittered with laughter late into the night while roughly dressed men jammed five and six deep against the sixty-year-old bar.[590] Once a haven for the social delight of gold and silver miners in the late 1800s, the saloon hosted a significant prostitution house that recruited girls from Denver under the supervision of Hazel "Ma" Brown going into the 1930s and early 1940s. In a

Inside the Camp Hale Service Club lounge on December 21, 1952. *Author's personal collection.*

1998 interview with then eighty-nine-year-old Leadville resident Adolph Kuss, he recalled that the ladies who sat in the saloon's window cribs, would "call out to customers walking along the sidewalk, 'Come on in! Come on in!'"[591] Leadville obtained the nickname the "Little Paris of the Rockies" for a good reason.[592] This is the type of interaction that the army frowned on deeply, first for the workers but then, more importantly, for the ski troopers soon arriving.

By the end of August 1942, Leadville was experiencing its biggest boom since the 1880s silver rush. The town's population of five thousand in June quickly doubled to near ten thousand in August. "No Vacancy" signs soon hung in the windows of hotels and doorways leading to the second-floor rooms of apartments along Harrison Avenue. Houses and apartments that had once been abandoned were featuring signs reading "private residence," even on State Street.[593] The red-light district of State Street soon moved into nonexistence, and people were renovating buildings that had lain vacant for years during the Great Depression. One Leadville resident and piano player at the Pastime Bar commented about the arrival of hundreds of workers to Leadville, saying, "It's all right, this army camp boom, but they're not spending money like they did in the old days. These boys come to town to have a little good time, but they're careful with their money. The old mining boys, when they got started, they just didn't give a damn about how they spent their money."[594] The news of higher wages at Camp Hale spread quickly around the nation and attracted people to Leadville's hiring offices. Rumors spread around the country that Leadville once again had streets paved with gold and opportunity.[595]

As Camp Hale's popularity grew, so did its population of new recruits. By the end of February 1943, the army needed more recreational outlets for the soldiers to relax in and enjoy on weekends. Recreational opportunities outside camp were very important, as one private identified, "There isn't nothing to do accept [sic] ski."[596] As a result, the army revoked its October 1942 ban on Leadville for soldiers of Camp Hale by issuing Headquarters General Order No. 3.[597] However, this change in policy did not give soldiers complete freedom in Leadville.

Camp Hale authorities worked diligently with civil authorities in Leadville to strictly supervise soldiers and to establish policies that outlined certain limits on soldiers in town. As a result, civil authorities passed a city ordinance stating that soldiers going to Leadville must return to Camp Hale by 11:00 p.m. on weekdays and be off the streets by 2:00 a.m. if staying the night on Saturdays with a proper pass. The Camp Hale command published a daily bus schedule with times for the forty-five-minute drive between Pando and Leadville, to ensure that soldiers had every opportunity to make it back to camp.[598] In addition, bars were forced to stop selling liquor to soldiers after 10:30 p.m. on weeknights, midnight Saturdays and 8:00 p.m. Sundays. Taking matters even further in accordance with the sale of alcohol, the ordinance only allowed bottled liquor to be sold in town to commissioned officers, not enlisted men from Camp Hale.[599]

Though the opening of Leadville to soldiers did provide them a significant amount of freedom to visit the town, not all of it became available to them for enjoyment. The ban still kept present-day West 2nd Street (State Street at the time), including the Pioneer Club, Pastime Bar, the Stringtown establishments and Murphy's Bar on Harrison Avenue, off-limits to soldiers. Nevertheless, the residents of Leadville immediately began preparing entertainment and recreation facilities, including a USO-sponsored free dance every Saturday night for soldiers in the high school gymnasium.[600]

The USO became an important organizer in Leadville for the soldiers at Camp Hale. The organization initially had an information center set up in the lobby of the Vendome Hotel and had its first office at 815 Harrison

Avenue, in order to best accommodate soldiers and to inform them of their entertainment options in Leadville.[601] As USO events picked up going into April 1943, a new office opened in the newly renovated Knights of Columbus building on East Fifth Street. One of the first major events organized by the new USO location included a music and variety show put on by the 86th Mountain Infantry on May 22, 1943, at the Tabor Opera House in Leadville.[602] The soldiers put on a two-hour show for Leadville residents, marking the first time in years that this type of vaudeville came to the vacant opera house. The director of the Salida USO, present at the performance, became so delighted by the vaudeville that he asked the 86th Mountain Infantry to perform in his town for the citizens.[603] The soldiers delightfully accepted and became quite the frenzy throughout the Arkansas River Valley. In addition to putting on shows, the USO provided Friday night English classes for soldiers who may not have mastered the English language due to their urgent immigration to America at the beginning of the war.[604] Finally, the USO built a darkroom so photography enthusiasts could develop their own film after a long weekend out in the wilderness.[605] This gave soldiers a way to cheaply develop their film so they could send pictures home to their family in addition to "Letters on Record."[606]

The opening of Leadville became an exciting opportunity for soldiers at Camp Hale. Though the brothels had been officially eliminated, some still operated in different parts of the town, and this became a pleasant reality for some soldiers who desired to partake in this illegal activity. After the announcement of the opening of Leadville to Camp Hale soldiers, one first sergeant with a strong German accent was heard telling his troops, "And I vant you men to go to Leadville tonight and get schcrewed. Company dismissed."[607] Additionally, the Silver Dollar Saloon became quite popular with soldiers frequenting Leadville. Army regulations only went so far in controlling an increasingly bored and adventurous group of mountain troops. One Leadville resident named Charles H. Schlaepfer, vice-president of the Leadville Golf Club, opened up his links to both enlisted men and officers in June 1943 for soldiers to use for free.[608] As an added perk, the Western Hardware Store in Leadville offered free scorecards for the golf course. Finally, the Vocational Trade School of Leadville offered Camp Hale soldiers and civilians the opportunity to take classes Monday through Friday, from 7:00 p.m. to 10:00 p.m. in electrical, machine and sheet metal shop work.[609] The school vouched to allow any Camp Hale student to keep whatever he or she made as long as the materials came from the cantonment.[610] Camp Hale authorities even went as far as offering transportation to the school several evenings a week.

The increase in recreational opportunities did not end with Leadville.[611] Grand Junction, Colorado, volunteered its services in the beginning of January 1943. Colonel L.D. Bogan, commanding officer at Camp Hale, and Howard Beresford, regional recreation representative for the Federal Security Agency, visited Grand Junction and concluded that the city could accommodate several hundred troops each weekend, with the men reaching the city about midnight each Friday night and remaining there until Sunday afternoon.[612] Bogan added that the soldiers could ride on special cars attached to the Rio Grande No. 1 train or by bus from Camp Hale. The city and its citizens provided numerous housing options, including hotels, cottage camps and even spare rooms in homes, all at the expense of the soldier. The location, with its slightly lower elevation, accessibility and existing facilities for recreation, pleased the army.[613] Additionally, the Cañon City Chamber of Commerce sent out invitations to soldiers at Camp Hale in April 1943, inviting them to its Blossom Week. The invitation spoke of hundreds of acres of apple and cherry orchards in full bloom and entertainment that included a carnival, bands, music and free meals in the houses of local Cañon City residents.[614] Nevertheless, most soldiers chose to head for Denver when weekends allowed for leave. For some, the backwoods of Camp Hale sufficed for training, but the big-city life of Denver pleased them most.

One ski trooper who took advantage of Denver on the weekends was Private Victor J. Sievers of D Company, 86th Mountain Infantry Regiment.[615] Sievers, unlike most trainees at Camp Hale, had family in Denver. He occasionally took advantage of the opportunity and the privilege of having his sister's car at his disposal to drive from Camp Hale to Denver when weekend passes were given and his company was not scheduled to be on Cooper Hill for training. Today, Americans rarely think twice about making the two-hour trip on Interstate 70 from Camp Hale to Denver. However, during World War II, this was often a monumental task as one braved the treacherous roads (especially during the winter). On one such journey, a blizzard struck and trapped the bus on top of Loveland Pass, stranding the riders overnight in the freezing temperatures. Weather issues, compounded with a lack of available rationed fuel along the way, made any voyage in the mountains a risk. Sievers commented about this difficulty in an April 6, 1943 letter to his sister, writing, "I think I can get gas in Leadville, it's black market but all of the fellows claim they can get it."[616] The government denied Sievers the C ration book for gas on occasion because he was not married and did not meet the other requirements for it. He and his friends at Camp Hale wrote to others around the country to obtain gas coupons so they could leave the cantonment.[617]

Sievers became a good friend to other ski troopers who desired to make the trek to the city. He commented in his letters on multiple occasions about soldiers singing "Oh Yea" all the way to Denver and about how his friends appreciated the opportunity to meet and talk with his sister and her girlfriends. Life at Camp Hale was anything but normal, and the opportunities to interact with the outside world in Denver always gave ski troopers a chance to escape the military life and enjoy civilized society. Sievers often made a profit on fuel by charging his buddies anywhere between $1.50 and $3.50 for the drive to Denver and lesser amounts to go into Leadville. This was fairly substantial considering that, at one point, Sievers said he filled up his gas tank with twelve gallons of gas costing $2.08.[618]

Another soldier who took advantage of Denver was Wallace Knutsen of the 99th Infantry Battalion (Separate). In early 1943, Knutsen married his wife in Denver on a Saturday and returned to the cantonment by train around 4:00 a.m. on Sunday morning. The guard at the gate reported his late return to Colonel Harold D. Hansen, commander of the 99th Battalion, who subsequently confined the newlywed to quarters for a month. However, Knutsen defied the order and went to see his new bride every evening since she resided in a neighboring town to Camp Hale.[619]

Other ski troopers who did not have family living in the area took advantage of the weekend passes to see the different towns in Colorado. Private First Class Clarence E. Gilbert affirmed this in a letter to his folks on January 25, 1943. He wrote, "My wife and I have had two weekend passes since we got to camp. One weekend we spent at Denver, Colo, & one at 'Glenwood Springs.' We plan to go to a different town every time we get a pass, in this way we will see a lot of the good old U.S.A."[620] The Glenwood Springs USO offered soldiers opportunities to horseback ride, go bowling and attend soldier-civilian dances.[621] It also provided free housing to soldiers in the former CCC camp on Grand Avenue in town. Others took advantage of weekend passes in the summer months when there was no snow to go hunting in areas around Buena Vista.[622] Most enlisted men were not privileged enough to have a vehicle at the cantonment, so these individuals often took the train, hopped a Trailways Bus, caught a ride with a fellow ski trooper or even walked from Camp Hale to Red Cliff, Gilman, Minturn, Avon, Eagle, Gypsum and even Glenwood Springs to enjoy the evening shows the towns provided.[623] Bus trips to Denver sometimes resulted in the soldiers getting out of the bus at tight curves on Loveland Pass to push the ten-ton bus uphill past the roadside berms of snow that it sometimes caught on its side.[624] Though ski troopers did occasionally get weekend passes, they were far from the norm. Most army camps during World War II issued weekend passes to enlisted soldiers during normal training; Camp Hale started out issuing passes only every other weekend because ski training commenced even on Saturdays.

Soldiers in other parts of Colorado often became jealous of the opportunities soldiers had at Camp Hale. One soldier by the name of Corporal Donnell S. Gale wrote many letters home to his wife in Ohio while serving at Camp Carson. He longed for the opportunities to "camp in the mountains," telling his wife, "I may sound nuts the way I have been writing to you about the scenery, but really I cannot explain how beautiful it really is."[625] His comments came on November 3, 1943, after spending five days in the mountains, fifty-three miles west of Camp Carson. A month later he wrote, "We are having another of those wonderful days here. Sunshine and warm and the mountains are so beautiful with their snow trimmings. I just can't describe it. Maybe when we get our first million we can come out here and see this again as civilians."[626] Soldiers at Camp Carson often longed to do what soldiers at Camp Hale did full time. Others were happy to be away from the mountainous cold and in a well-established military post with many more amenities than what Camp Hale offered.

Visitors did occasionally come to Camp Hale in order to take part in recreational opportunities and to visit family members. The soldiers especially appreciated it when the sisters of ski troopers came for a weekend to experience the Colorado mountain life. The cantonment hosted a few guesthouses, but sometimes female visitors slept in supply rooms and ate chow in the mess halls when the mess sergeant allowed them to.[627] The mountain troops had a special bond that often led them to help one another out even when violating official army policy by using supply rooms to temporarily house females. They were proud of their uniform and proud of their training. Some soldiers even went as far as wearing their newly issued, unique white ski gaiters into Leadville when on pass. This went against the Mountain Training Center policy, which restricted the wearing of any of their distinctive mountain clothing on pass, but some took the risk as it gave them a sense of pride walking down the streets in the civilian world.

While soldiers at other military installations, such as Camp Carson, complained that "there isn't anything to do" on pass, recreational opportunities expanded greatly within Camp Hale as the Special Service

Division expanded its influence.[628] The Denver Public Library furnished about five hundred books to the Camp Hale library for the entertainment and instruction of ski troopers during their downtime.[629] A music room in the Service Club also had a donated radio-phonograph from Pro-Musica in Denver, along with many records for soldiers to listen to.[630] Also located in the Service Club was a writing room that workers filled with unique and coveted Camp Hale stationery so soldiers could write as many letters home as they wished.[631] Boxing and wrestling matches at the field house in the evenings gave soldiers from different units opportunities to compete against one another and to entertain their fellow friends.[632] Baseball and softball games were spontaneously started during free time by different units that had a bone to pick with each other and decided to take it out with a friendly game of America's pastime. One game between the intelligence section and the communications sections of the 86th Mountain Infantry, 3rd Battalion, resulted in the loser jumping in the near freezing-cold snow runoff that made up the Eagle River down the middle of Camp Hale.[633] Benny Fox's Star-Spangled Circus came to Camp Hale on June 2, 1944, entertaining soldiers in everything from the Torellis' ponies and dogs to juggling acts, skating and high-rings performances.[634] The camp newspaper even advocated for soldiers to explore the various abandoned mine shafts and tunnels on the cantonment proper and to take a backpack with them to Battle Mountain to take in some of the rich history of Colorado and pick up some Indian artifacts and relics from the historical, three-day battle in the valley between the Shoshone and Ute Indians.[635] Some members of the 90th Infantry Regiment took the newspaper suggestion literally, and while on bivouac at Homestake Creek, they panned for gold and explored the mine shafts.[636] Several soldiers came back with ore containing gold, fueling a gold bug around Camp Hale for some time after. Additionally, the Special Service Club organized tours for soldiers and WACs in which military trucks drove them from the Service Club to the Arkansas Valley Smelter, California Gulch Mill in Leadville, Resurrection Mill and the Climax Molybdenum Company.[637]

Members of the 87th established a hockey league to incorporate individuals from Europe, Canada and the United States.[638] One ski trooper named Donald G. Brown, from Company L, 86th Mountain Infantry, recalled how he and other GIs would shovel the snow from between barracks and allow the ground to flood with water.[639] When the water froze, the men turned the small pond into a skating rink to demonstrate their skating skills.[640] A twenty-five-piece Mountain Training Center band made up of soldiers entertained

Left: Camp Hale stationery. *Author's personal collection.*

Below: Camp Hale Field House, located at the intersection of 13th and B Streets in November 1942. *Author's personal collection.*

the public in conjunction with 87[641] soldiers who started variety shows at the service clubs.[641] The camp's three theaters showed productions every night of the week, alternating from one location to the next. The 99th Infantry Battalion (Separate) occasionally put on a "home-spun" musical comedy in its recreation hall to incorporate some of its culture into the camp's general entertainment.[642] Other soldiers who made up the Camp Hale Station Hospital traveled to and competed against local high school basketball teams from Red Cliff and Leadville.[643] The cantonment itself had its own basketball league made up of teams from the 87th Infantry, 86th Infantry, 10th Medical Battalion, 126th Engineer Mountain Battalion, 10th Quartermaster Battalion, 601st Field Artillery, 602nd Field Artillery and the 99th Infantry Battalion. Even the Climax Molybdenum Company formed a team that competed against the Camp Hale teams in the field house.[644] However, basketball games were not exempt from the high altitude and the necessary modifications to ensure safety. Quarters lasted for eight minutes each, but league rules required a one-minute break every four minutes, a two-minute break between quarters and a ten-minute break between halves.[645] At the end of June 1943, engineers began building a new recreation center at the west end of 5th Street, behind Theater No. 1.[646] The center included pool tables, ping-pong tables and eight bowling lanes.[647] Lastly, some soldiers were content with simply relaxing in the woods surrounding Camp Hale and enjoying nature without the stress of training. H. Robert Krear, 86th Mountain Infantry Regiment veteran, recalled that his "most pleasurable use of a weekend was to get some food from the mess hall, stick my sleeping bag and some fishing equipment in my rucksack, and hike up to some subalpine lake for the weekend."[648] He also commented that another favorite weekend activity was to travel to some of Colorado's local ski resorts, especially Aspen, and "ski the way we were not permitted to while on duty!"[649] Thus, between January and March 1943, soldiers enjoyed many opportunities to be entertained without even leaving the cantonment area.

In making the downtime more enjoyable, the War Production Board allotted Eagle County the largest tea quota increase of any county in the nation in the beginning of 1943 by giving the county a quota of 140 percent of average monthly deliveries of tea during the corresponding quarter of 1941. The 90 percent increase came primarily because of Camp Hale and its specialized snow and cold climate training high in the Rocky Mountains, and because of the large population increase in Eagle County.[650] The national spotlight never ceased to leave Camp Hale during its first few months of official operation, which continued to help boost recruitment and provide favorable army opinions about the training.

Celebrity visits to Camp Hale for general entertainment purposes were not uncommon. In the beginning of May 1943, Jinx Falkenburg, the "All-American Girl," made an appearance at the camp's Service Club and Theater No. 1 in order to entertain the soldiers.[651] Around that same time, Camp Hale held its largest entertainment enterprise since the camp opened. The camp hosted a Mardi Gras parade and celebration in which white-clad ski troopers carrying skis walked down the middle of Camp Hale with the MTC 4th Army Band in the lead.[652] Each unit put together a float and brought with it whatever unique equipment it had. The engineers, not surprisingly, constructed the best float, demonstrating bridge building, while the ski troopers marched with their skis and rifles with bayonets attached and the pack artillery with their mules and howitzers. Armored vehicles and jeeps rolled by as the crowd cheered the army's finest-looking soldiers. Brigadier General Rolfe and Lieutenant Colonel Maurice Anderson stood in a viewing stand along the main street of Camp Hale and assessed the sophistication and creativity of the floats that passed by.

Soldiers at Camp Hale did not always use leisure time to find fulfillment for themselves through the various means of entertainment. Some took the time to give back to the local community that supported them during their training. For example, Camp Hale chaplain W.R. Carner used his spiritual background to help him give a graduation speech about the "Will of God" to fourteen students at Gypsum High School in Gypsum, Colorado, at the end of May 1943.[653] Additionally, Camp Hale gave back to the young ladies of Salida toward the end of July 1943 by inviting seventy-five of them to the cantonment for a full day of entertainment, including a jeep tour, lunch in the chow halls, a matinee dance and supper at the Service Club.[654] The ladies had entertained soldiers in Salida in various ways, and Camp Hale decided to begin honoring them along with the other ladies of local towns who had supported the soldiers. Next, the 226th Engineer Motorized Company helped out National Forest Service firefighters in the middle of October 1943 by providing men, buckets, shovels and picks to fight a forest fire that broke out a few miles northeast of Dillon.[655] Finally, three of "the world's greatest ice skating stars"—Private First Class Geary Steffen, Private John Flanagan and Corporal Charlie Slagle—put on a performance at the Broadmoor Ice Palace for the residents of Colorado Springs at the Christmas Holiday Ice Revue.[656] The examples of support are numerous, as soldiers took every opportunity to help and entertain when they could.

A soldier from Camp Hale's 10th Reconnaissance Troop became nationally famous after helping clean out three barracks and finding some worthwhile scrap. He and his fellow mountain troopers acquired over five pounds of steel from collecting old sharp-edged steel razor blades that soldiers had discarded.[657] After taking this alarming fact up the chain of command, he helped establish in every barracks a collection of razor blades in half-gallon red, white and blue cans, with the story of how the collection came about posted above the can.[658] The scrap salvage of razor blades at army cantonments around the country soon took hold as soldiers began to contribute their own steel to community scrap metal drives.

Soldiers from Camp Hale also gave back to farmers in the local mountain community in several ways. Farmers often gave soldiers free opportunities to fish, hunt, swim and horseback ride on their property. In return, some mountain troops took their weekend passes and went to the farms in order to help out with the various common chores, including milking cows and to bailing hay.[659] The farmers enjoyed this sometimes free or very cheap labor and the company of soldiers so much that they began serving them good home-cooked meals with milk and ice cream and even began picking them up on Friday evenings at Camp Hale so that soldiers did not need to find transportation to get there.[660] One anonymous mountain trooper commented about this opportunity, saying, "There was work to be done, sure enough—that's what we went down there for. But it was fun at the same time and certainly did not seem tough for a hardened mountain trooper."[661]

At the end of August 1943, the U.S. Employment Office made an appeal to soldiers at Camp Hale for loggers to go to the town of Eagle, so they could then be transported to a lumber camp in the mountains.[662] Once again, soldiers answered the call coming from the local community and boarded a train, winding down the western side of the Continental Divide in the Eagle River Valley. The locals claimed that if there were a shortage of lumber, there would not be enough boards to make crates in order to pack apples for the fall harvest. The soldiers did not want to see a good crop go to waste because everything could be tied to the war effort in 1943 whether it directly impacted soldiers or not. This mentality permeated Camp Hale and drove soldiers in their free time to help out wherever they could. One soldier commented, "We were after work. We had our minds set on it, and to accept any other solution would be disappointing."[663]

More community support came from a group of soldiers who were visiting Cañon City on a weekend pass and, unbeknownst to them, became active community supporters after a fire broke out in the city.[664] The soldiers volunteered to help in whatever capacity they could and spent several hours assisting the people of the city. Relationships between soldiers and local Colorado civilians were for the most part cordial, friendly and productive. The war brought a true sense of community and camaraderie between soldiers and civilians, all with one common mission: to preserve freedom and liberty around the world, beginning at the local level.

Another way that Camp Hale attempted to build better relations with the civilian local community included the construction and renovation of buildings for civilian housing on the cantonment. Up until August 1943, civilians who worked at Camp Hale had to live off site in temporary or hastily established housing or in one of the surrounding towns like Leadville or Red Cliff.[665] Camp Hale's Civilian Housing Project, under the leadership of Lieutenant Colonel Charles Ames, began planning and constructing new housing on Camp Hale at the beginning of the summer of 1943. By the middle of August, the project had completed 40 percent of the proposed housing near the station hospital, with the other 60 percent to be completed by September 30. Lieutenant Colonel Ames did not skimp on this housing, as he believed the civilians who supported the Camp Hale war effort deserved the best possible accommodations the camp could provide given the harsh conditions at 9,250 feet. The new quarters consisted of one-, two- and three-bedroom apartments, each of which had a living room, kitchenette, bathroom, large clothes closet, refrigerator, coal range, a unit heater or oil stove, beds, mattresses, springs, a dresser, chairs, studio couch and dining table. The only household items not provided included dishes and cooking utensils. Handmade furniture, including new beds, became available for sale to civilians at Camp Hale in January 1944 so that they could replace the army cots provided for them. The accommodations continued to improve every month, and the civilians enjoyed their high-altitude stay.

In addition to the new construction near the station hospital, the project renovated all of the existing quarters located in the Pando area that were used by the construction workers who built the camp.[666] The Pando area, commonly referred to as Pando Village, also included a school, a recreation hall for children of the civilian workers, a medical clinic, a shoe repair shop, a library and a skating pond in the winter.[667] These workers began to move into the new housing in the beginning of October 1943, well pleased with the accommodations. The only complaint given by the workers recognized a need for a general store where groceries and other necessities could be purchased.[668] By the end of October 1943, the Camp Hale civilian workforce had also obtained its own mess hall, located in the Pando Headquarters.[669]

Temporary barracks area in Pando, Colorado, circa November 1942. *Author's personal collection.*

Temporary barracks in Pando, Colorado, circa November 1942. Notice the hastily constructed heating pipes running between buildings. *Author's personal collection.*

Pando Village, north end of the cantonment area. Notice the train winding through the center of the village. *Author's personal collection.*

The Office of the Post Engineer offered civilians free ski instruction and even proper ski and winter clothing at wholesale prices.[670] Similarly, Chaplain Carner began Sunday school for civilian children at nine thirty on Sunday mornings in the Recreation Room of the women's dormitory.[671] The original intent of Camp Hale becoming a self-sustainable cantonment was soon becoming even more of a reality than it ever had been.

9

RUMORS OF WAR AND
TRAINING FOR WAR

Remember that great things will be expected of you. You will be watched from high places. YOU'VE GOT TO BE GOOD![672]
—*Major Jack L. Tappin, official army ground force observer in the Aleutian theater, quoted in the* Camp Hale Ski-Zette, *November 5, 1943*

The late summer and fall of 1943 ushered in many questions from the ski troopers about their purpose and motivation for training. For many, the hope of being deployed faded with time. However, on August 24, 1943, the 99th Infantry Battalion (Separate) received orders to travel from Camp Hale to Camp Shanks, New York, via train. After being vaccinated and resupplied with new gear, the unit left Hoboken, New Jersey, on September 5 for the European Theater of Operations.[673] Before leaving Camp Hale, Ragnar Abrahamsen of the 99th remembered how all soldiers who were not yet citizens had to take the oath and swear in as American citizens before they could be sent overseas.[674] He recalled how the truckload of men needing to swear in traveled into Leadville to stand before a judge. As time dragged on, the judge ordered a recess and a few of the soldiers went across the street to a bar and got drunk. One returned only to answer the judge in Norwegian while giving his oath and was busted in rank. He returned a few days later to swear in again as an American citizen so the battalion could leave with full strength.[675]

The division had not yet been deployed in whole, with only the 87th seeing any sort of deployment action in Kiska during the summer and fall of 1943. The soldiers of the cantonment who arrived in November

1942, when Camp Hale opened, verged on a year of inhabiting the highest cantonment in the country without receiving any orders for deployment. Rumors spread quickly across the camp to include the possibility of deployment to New Guinea, New Hampshire (new training site), Kiska (again), Italy, Norway and Burma. From Europe to the Pacific, the ski troopers of the 10th Light Infantry speculated about where they would find themselves in the future. For some, the main motivation that kept them training was the imminent onset of winter and subsequently snow for skiing, while events at the cantonment began to point more and more to a coming deployment, as units changed their makeup and transformed into a new, modern infantry and artillery. The Army Ground Forces announced that its new organization of a light infantry division included fewer soldiers and vehicles but more firepower. Specifically, it would be "more compact, more flexible, surer, swifter moving—and more dangerous to the enemy."[676]

On Saturday, October 16, 1943, Camp Hale GIs participated in a special recognition of their new light infantry division, with a ceremony on the parade grounds marking the official activation of the 10th Infantry Division. Colorado governor John C. Vivian gave a welcome speech, and then the entire division passed in review. Following the ceremony, elements of the division organized an open house for visitors to see special mountain equipment, which Paul Petzoldt labeled "the best in the world."[677] This included infantry weapons, mountain tents, specialized winter clothing, climbing equipment, 75mm pack howitzers, mule-packing demonstrations and pigeon demonstrations.[678] The day concluded with a demonstrative attack on a land fortification. The division was ready for war and waited patiently for its next orders.

Veteran of the 86th Mountain Infantry Charles McLane warned his fellow soldiers in 1943 that the division had been and would continue to be "subject to vast rearrangement as time goes on."[679] One of these significant reorganizations and a sign of events to come occurred on October 23, 1943, as the army officially disbanded the Mountain Training Center. The longtime center of training, testing of equipment and influence at Camp Hale came to an end. However, the army was not about to completely eliminate any source for training in mountain and winter warfare.

The army formed the Mountain Training Group (MTG) to replace the MTC and immediately transferred all remaining personnel into this new organization. The mission of the MTG differed slightly from the MTC, as the army began to shift its focus outward from Camp Hale instead of inward for all training. The MTG consisted of "instruction teams" that traveled around the country to other camps in order to train standard units

Formation parade, Camp Hale, looking from the east side of the camp to the west. *Courtesy of the Denver Public Library, Western History Collection, David B. Allen, TMD-744.*

in mountain and winter warfare on the spot.[680] The officers and enlisted men of the MTG ceased nearly all military training and stood ready at any time of day or night as specialists in army skiing and mountaineering to mobilize in support of training standard army units.[681] The problem the army ran into at this point was that it could not find a balance between supporting the instructional staff to fill training needs and providing the necessary soldiers to fill the ranks of the 10th Infantry Division. With the elimination of the MTC and its eleven thousand positions, the 10th Infantry Division only had nine thousand and thus the army needed another unit to "provide total personnel…for mountain and winter Instructional teams," which served the thousands of nondivisional soldiers.[682] Thus, with the formation of the MTG, the army also stood up the 15th Headquarters and Headquarters Detachment, Special Troops, 2nd Army.

The 15th originally had only 5 officers and 15 enlisted men but this number quickly changed to 37 officers and 40 enlisted.[683] To make matters worse, 40 officers and 140 enlisted men from the 87th Mountain Infantry came back from Kiska and were attached unassigned to the 15th as expert ski and mountain instructors.[684] The ranks were flooded and promotions ceased to exist. Under the guidance of the 15th Headquarters and Headquarters

Detachment, the MTG and the 10[685] Reconnaissance Troop provided the entirety of instructors and mountain and winter warfare training around the country.[685] Camp Hale now served as a base of operations for all army training in mountain and winter warfare and continued to be the home for the 10th Infantry Division.

While the 10th Infantry Division continued to grow and increase in intensity of training in the fall and winter of 1943, the 10th Reconnaissance Troop faced a growing number of issues related to its purpose and mission at Camp Hale. These issues stemmed all the way to its original formation at the cantonment. Since the unit started out as cavalry from the 4th Cavalry Regiment in South Dakota, its ratings and equipment still remained that of a cavalry unit. The 2nd Army, which the 10th Recon fell under, still believed that the 10th Recon was a cavalry unit and could not understand why infantry and signal corps officers were assigned to the unit. It sent several letters to the 15th Headquarters and Headquarters Detachment demanding that officers of the 10th Recon attend the advanced course at the Cavalry School at Fort Riley, Kansas. Apparently the 15th had missed the letter dated April 25, 1943, in which the unit requested that all personnel be replaced with "skilled mountaineers and skiiers [sic]."[686] One month later in May 1943, the Mountain Training Center sent a letter to Army Ground Forces requesting that the 10th Cavalry Reconnaissance Troop name be changed to the 10th Reconnaissance Company since all personnel in the unit were essentially infantry. Army Ground Forces denied this request, stating that the 10th Recon was going to soon be part of the 10th Light Division. When this did not happen, Colonel Donald P. Spalding, commanding officer of the 15th Detachment, wrote yet another letter, through the 2nd Army, to Army Ground Forces seeking guidance as to whether it wanted the 10th Recon to be a nontactical unit with the purpose of instructing in mountain and winter warfare or an actual tactical reconnaissance company. The confusion continued, as the 2nd Army apparently did not understand the unique nature of Camp Hale and Army Ground Forces thought the matter was resolved with the 10th Recon's incorporation into the new 10th Light Infantry Division. Finally, on March 21, 1944, the matter was officially resolved when the 2nd Army transferred the 10th Reconnaissance Troop (less personnel and equipment) to Fort Knox, Kentucky. The 7 officers and 142 enlisted men were transferred to the Mountain Training Group, which in turn, five days later, transferred most of them to units within the 10th Infantry Division. For almost an entire year, the 10th Recon operated out of Camp Hale without any official guidance from higher-ups, which makes the history of the unit one of the most interesting and unique aspects of Camp Hale's story.[687] This showed how the regular army never fully understood the unique nature of Camp Hale and its unique requirements for training and sustaining units for mountain and winter warfare.

As units transformed into more combat-effective organizations, soldiers continued to arrive at Camp Hale in order to fill the ranks of the mountain troops. However, by November 1943, a War Department directive had ended the implementation of basic combat training at Camp Hale. The directive said, "No more inductees will receive their basic training at Camp Hale. They may still file their applications with the NSPS for approval but must take their basic training elsewhere. If upon completion of this training there are vacancies in the mountain troops, you may request their transfer."[688] One soldier by the name of Private Lee Thompson transferred to Camp Hale from Fort Benning, Georgia, and immediately commented that he felt like "Frozen Foods, Inc."[689] He donned every piece of clothing in his issued wardrobe, which led his first sergeant to believe that he had moved out of his bunk upon inspection and ordered his bed to be taken out to make room. Two other privates by the name of Pitman and Porter arrived from South Carolina and were caught sneaking into the ski room in order to see a pair of skis for the first time in their life.[690] Camp Hale continued to surprise and challenge soldiers as the winter of 1943 moved in. Thankfully for some of these unaccustomed soldiers, on November 29 Camp Hale obtained its first camp-wide free bus service.[691] The buses ran on fifteen-minute intervals and were free of charge for soldiers to travel from one side of the camp to another. Two terminals at Camp Headquarters in Pando and at 21st and A Streets provided bus service from 7:00 a.m. until 11:00 p.m. daily. Prior to the buses, soldiers had to walk, hike or march to the different locations on the cantonment, even during the blizzards of the winter months.

Some could not handle the stress of the high-altitude environment while others grew tired of waiting for the mountain troops to deploy and decided to transfer to the paratroopers or the air corps. The October, November and December issues of the *Ski-Zette* identified multiple cases of soldiers leaving the mountain troops for the paratroopers and air corps. All organizations had their unique aspects and elite statuses that drew in soldiers who were seeking out a challenge and the prestige of simply being the best. The unseasonable weather conditions in the winter of 1943 might have also driven some soldiers out, as Camp Hale lacked its traditional snow cover for ski training. The lack of snow in the early part of the winter prevented some much-needed training, especially in and around the Pando cantonment

Corner of A and 18th Streets, Camp Hale, Colorado. The barracks in the background were part of the 85th Mountain Infantry Regiment area. *Courtesy of the Denver Public Library, Western History Collection, David B. Allen, TMD-752.*

Pando Station, Colorado. Soldiers are leaving Camp Hale for the air corps (circa October, November, December 1943). *Courtesy of the Denver Public Library, Western History Collection, Pando Constructors, Jay Fairvalley, Z-5345.*

area. However, most members of the 10th Infantry Division were of the same opinion as 85th Mountain Infantry veteran Carl V. Cossin, who wrote, "I have soldiered in other branches of the service. I have never felt the same closeness or the strong bond of fellowship that I found in the mountain infantry. It was like a brotherhood or fraternity."[692] Another soldier in the 87th made a similar comment about the elite nature of the unit, saying, "They're only three branches of the armed forces: the Army, the Navy, and the Mountain Troops."[693]

Around the same time that more rumors of a deployment began to spread around Camp Hale, soldiers eager to see an end to the war began a forum that met every Monday night to discuss the postwar world. Topics varied from where to live to where to work and addressed issues like "What to Do with Germany After the War," "Fascism in America" and the "America to Which We Want to Come Home."[694] Discussions were oftentimes heated and obtained an intellectual nature on the level of that found at a university. Perspectives varied greatly, as there were refugees from Germany, Italy, Spain and even Japan at Camp Hale who had come to the United States to escape fascism and make a contribution to ending it.[695] Private Paul Petzoldt frequented the forums and added his perspective on international affairs given his background in world travel and climbing. This opportunity gave soldiers a chance to sound off about a life without war, something on many of their minds. These soldiers soon had another critical reason to sound off in the forums as German POWs from Africa arrived in the States.

As the Allies started to advance against Rommel's Afrika Korps, taking in German prisoners of war, the army sought places around the country to house these individuals until the war came to an end and they could be repatriated. Colorado had forty-eight prisoner of war camps around the state. The main camps were located at Colorado Springs, Greeley and Trinidad, but Camp Hale housed a limited number of prisoners for special projects.[696] The arrival of the first batch of German prisoners of war (POWs) to Camp Hale was not a welcome addition. The mere presence of Germans revealed Allied successes in the war and a diminished likelihood for the 10th Infantry to deploy. The first POWs to arrive at Camp Hale came over on the weekend of December 4–5, 1943.[697] They were sent to perform detail work on the cantonment. About three hundred German POWs arrived at the camp and stayed in separate barracks but lived among the rest of the men. This created some problems, as soldiers started to despise the enemy so close to their training site.[698] Relations at Camp Hale between soldiers and the POWs started out badly when the first POWs arrived. The only available German translator at Camp Hale, Staff Sergeant Gundisch, was on pass, and the POWs were left in the care of Sergeant Dick Schultz and an English-German dictionary.[699] The POWs were as confused as Sergeant Schultz about how he got stuck being their translator when he did not know German. Relations seemed to snowball from this point.

About two and a half months later, on February 16, 1944, an army private at Camp Hale by the name of Dale Maple assisted two German prisoners of war in escaping from the Camp Hale Internment Camp. Maple spoke fluent German and had pro-Nazi sympathies according to an FBI investigation in 1940, after he was dismissed from the Harvard University ROTC program.[700] Officers with authority over Maple at Camp Hale later revealed their suspicions of his pro-German sympathies. The Federal Bureau of Investigation, with the help of Mexican authorities, finally arrested the two German POWs and Maple in Mexico about three miles south of the border by Dedaro Martenias Mejia.[701] Maple had managed to purchase a sedan in Salida, Colorado, on the day of the escape before reporting to sick leave at Camp Hale.[702] The three drove south across the border somewhere around Columbus, New Mexico, and evaded capture for three days until their apprehension on Friday, February 18, 1944. Colonel John Chase, the commanding officer of Camp Hale, revealed on March 10, 1944, that eight additional American soldiers were involved in the escape of the two POWs.[703] However, Maple faced charges of treason for helping the two German POWs escape and remained in prison until February 1951. This event brought national negative media attention to Camp Hale.

Another fiasco at Camp Hale involving the German POWs occurred less than a month later, when Sheriff Angelo J. Travison of Leadville disclosed that military police and other army officers at Camp Hale had apprehended an "undisclosed number of crudely fashioned whisky stills and from forty to fifty gallons of apricot liquor."[704] Further evidence revealed that a number of prisoners had built and operated three or four stills that had been hidden in the walls of the prison camp. Authorities found a significant amount of liquor and learned that the prisoners had been saving apricots and similar fruits from the prison's mess hall by concealing them on their body and then taking them back to their barracks to use them in brewing schnapps.[705] As a result, several of the prisoners were arrested and taken to jails in Eagle and Lake Counties in order to segregate those involved in the construction and operation from the rest of the German POWs. Questions of how they were able to smuggle the necessary equipment into the internment camp and operate multiple stills only brought more negative attention to Camp Hale and the training that was supposed to be going on there.

Additionally, three days later, on March 10, 1944, a news story broke that military police at Camp Hale arrested five WACs on suspicion of writing romantic notes to German POWs.[706] Three of them admitted to writing the notes, and a military tribunal charged and convicted them, giving them four to six months' confinement.[707] Though the incident turned out to be an isolated case, it still brought down morale at the camp and brought criticism from outside sources. Hometown newspapers of many WACs at Camp Hale published articles about the WACs' involvement in the scandal, leading some politicians in Colorado to question the

Press photograph from March 10, 1944, of Marguerete L. Franklin, twenty-three, of Oakland, California. Marguerete was one of the three WACs who communicated with escaped Nazi prisoners at Camp Hale, Colorado. *Author's personal collection.*

necessity of having POWs at Camp Hale, where soldiers and POWs interacted so closely.

Jumping back in time to the end of 1943, when German POWs were first introduced to Camp Hale, activity at the cantonment continued to boom, and the prospect of the entire 10th Infantry Division deploying still remained a possibility. Christmas celebrations of 1943 marked the second Christmas celebrated at Camp Hale and reminded many soldiers of how long they really had been there. Major General Lloyd E. Jones, in his New Year 1944 address to all soldiers at Camp Hale, provided some promising words to those desiring to head overseas. He wrote, "This coming year promises to be a severe test for us all. A year destined to be filled with swift moving events that should lead to ultimate victory for the cause that has banded us together...let us all...find happiness in the confidence that with full completion of our training mission we are prepared and eager for any

Battery A, 616th Field Artillery Battalion (Pack) Christmas banquet program cover. (December 25, 1943.) *Author's personal collection.*

Christmas card from the 90th Infantry Regiment while stationed at Camp Hale, Colorado, Christmas 1943. *Author's personal collection.*

Mountain Troops on Mount Elbert on January 16, 1944. *Author's personal collection.*

assignment."[708] However, a Denver columnist wrote an article a few weeks later that implied that Camp Hale was going to be abandoned by the end of the winter.[709] The rumor mill was stirred, but soldiers trained on.

Three days before Major General Jones gave this speech, members of the 10th Reconnaissance Troop and the Mountain Training Group ventured out into the mountains to prove that they were indeed prepared and eager for any assignment. On Tuesday, December 28, 1943, fifty-three officers and enlisted men loaded into trucks at Camp Hale and headed out south on U.S. 24. With full packs and well dressed for winter weather conditions, the soldiers arrived at the end of the road near Herrington Creek at seven o'clock in the morning, ready to begin a three-day, thirty-two-mile journey that would take them up the contiguous United States' second- and third-highest mountains: Mount Elbert (14,433 feet) and Mount Massive (14,421 feet), respectively.[710]

They began their climb at an elevation of 9,500 feet in temperatures hovering around ten degrees Fahrenheit. All of the soldiers used skis with lambskin climbers, except for Captain Luther and seven men from the MTG, who wore snowshoes.[711] By 11:15 a.m., the group had reached its first bivouac site at an elevation of 10,400 feet, and the men dropped their heavy rucksacks in order to make their push to the summit. Skis and snowshoes were pushed to the limit and finally stashed at around 13,250 feet, where the snow became hard packed and the wind-swept ground showed exposed rock and vegetation. The expedition reached the summit at around 4:00 p.m. and enjoyed the panorama view, which included Leadville and Mount Massive to the north.[712] The group descended to the ski-and-snowshoe stash, and the skiers enjoyed a steeplechase adventure back down to the bivouac site, where they spent the night.

The next day, December 29, the soldiers began their ten-mile trek over to Mount Massive, rotating who had to break the trail so that the speed could stay constant.[713] The skiers arrived at Half Moon Creek around lunchtime and were well into their mountain rations by the time the snowshoers arrived. In good typical army fashion, the skiers jeered the snowshoers about their decision to use snowshoes, which necessitated extra work and time to keep up with the skiers. Finally, the entire group reached the second bivouac location at Willow Creek on Mount Massive at around 4:00 p.m. The weather quickly took a change for the worse as snow began to fall, and the temperature dropped.

The next day, the team started up Mount Massive, leaving its rucksacks behind, and steamed toward the summit in temperatures dropping to around five to ten degrees below zero. Balaclavas, parkas, scarfs and neckerchiefs were adorned as winds at speeds ranging from forty to sixty miles per hour blasted open exposed skin. The leadership considered the difficulties and dangers of the conditions but determined that the equipment and stamina of the soldiers warranted that they continue the ascent. The group reached the summit of Mount Massive at around 12:30 p.m. Once again, the men signed the summit register and took their pictures before heading down. The entire crew of fifty-three men arrived safely back at Camp Hale at around 5:00 p.m. on December 30 and declared the expedition a complete success. The mountain troops of the 10th Reconnaissance and the MTG proved their expertise and physical ability to handle whatever the army was going to throw at them in the coming months.

Meanwhile, the 126th Engineer Mountain Battalion trained in and around McAllister Gulch in road building and foxhole digging, fine tuning its skills in order to be ready for deployment.[714] The battalion bivouacked at the top of the gulch located north of Camp Hale, pitching tents and digging foxholes for practice.[715] However, the men realized that digging a hole with a shovel in the Rocky Mountains posed extenuating challenges: frozen ground and the abundance of rocks. To make matters even more difficult, Ralph C. Meager, Camp Hale Military Reservation forester, advocated for the soldiers to fill in their four-foot-deep foxholes after the completion of their bivouac in order to protect the natural environment and animals living in the area.[716] The topography of the land soon changed as the engineers bulldozed and cleared a path connecting the bivouac site with Resolution Creek Road, meeting the approval of the Forestry Service.[717]

Bivouacking became second nature for ski troopers, who learned to deal with claustrophobic tents and sleeping bags, freezing temperatures and cold meals. Temperatures dropped so low at night that ski boots had to be placed inside sleeping bags to keep them from being cold stiff in the morning. Water froze in canteens, and the mountain stoves became difficult to light. One soldier joked in the *Ski-Zette* when the army introduced the Expert Infantry Badge that ski troopers deserved a special badge called the "Expert Bivouacer."[718] In addition to the numerous bivouacking opportunities, soldiers of the 10th Infantry were encouraged to pass a nine-mile cross-country ski test, which forced them to put to use their skills in downhill skiing, ski waxing for uphill skiing and cross-country skiing. On February 14, 1944, members of the 2nd Battalion, 86th Mountain Infantry Regiment, competed against one another on the course that began with a ski lift ride to the starting line at the top of Cooper Hill.[719] Upon skiing down Cooper Hill in fresh powder, the mountain troops faced the brunt of the course, which traversed Highway 24 and started winding through the woods on the Homestead foothills.[720] Almost all the soldiers came in under the allotted two-hour time, including the weapons soldiers on snowshoes who competed on a seven-mile course in under an hour and a half.[721] Eventually, nearly all units—including the 576th Anti-Tank Battery, which entered the largest number of soldiers—competed on the seven- and nine-mile courses for bragging rights around the camp. But the biggest debate that came out of the competition was whether or not skis or snowshoes were faster. This debate never ceased during Camp Hale's existence.[722]

Shortly thereafter on March 6, 1944, Minnie Dole and Roger Langley made another visit to Camp Hale and Cooper Hill. After visiting with Colonel Paul R. (Pop) Goode at the headquarters for the 87th and Major General Lloyd Jones at post headquarters, the two skiers headed off to Cooper Hill in a snowstorm to partake in the fresh powder with Colonel Paul Lafferty. As the two put on their skis and made their way to the T-bar, parallel sheets of snow pelted them and froze to their ski caps.[723] The two lined up for the bar, and as it came within range, two-hundred-pound Roger Langley sat down before Dole realized what he had done.[724] Dole shot up into the air and one of his skis jammed between the upright bar and the cross bar, dragging him upside down for twenty feet until he broke free.[725] By the time Dole regained his sense of direction, he found Langley roaring with laughter and the rest of the Cooper Hill ski group similarly participating in the opportunity.

With the Cooper Hill/Homestake cross-country ski test complete, members of the 10th Reconnaissance Troop, the Mountain Training Group and the 10th Medical Battalion decided to outdo the other mountain infantry regiments by participating in and completing a fifty-mile cross-country ski trek from Malta to Aspen.[726] The thirty enlisted men and three officers loaded up on trucks at Camp Hale and drove to the Malta staging area, where they donned their skis.[727] For most, this was not just a training exercise but rather an opportunity to enjoy five days in the Colorado wilderness. Some of the most notable mountain climbers of these units, including Sergeant Paul Petzoldt from the medics, bivouacked their way across the mountain ranges, over ridges and through the valleys.

Not long after this fifty-mile trek, the MTG organized the first all-military cross-country ski competition in the history of the U.S. Armed Forces.[728] The competition began at Camp Hale on Sunday, May 14, and consisted of a twenty-mile course with a biathlon-like twist in the middle. All soldiers had to take sixteen shots at silhouette targets at a range of two hundred yards, carrying a fifteen-pound rucksack, with each hit on a target giving the competitor a deduction of one minute from his total time.[729] The MTG opened up the competition to the army, navy and Marine Corps in order to bring awareness to Camp Hale and to unite the branches in a friendly competition that also served as a training exercise for mountain warfare. The event became quite a spectacle. The MTG formed committees that organized medical teams, mess halls for the participants and visitors and staging areas with topographic maps for viewing the race along the twenty-mile course.[730] Last-minute decisions defined the course so that the best snow conditions could be utilized and so that the Camp Hale men did not have an unfair advantage over other members of the armed forces by practicing on the course ahead of time.[731] The engineers put out the progress of the race over loud speakers so all in attendance could hear. At the end of the race, fifty-, thirty- and twenty-dollar cash prizes were given out to the top three finishers, and a trophy with the inscription "Winner Annual U.S. Cross-Country Military Ski Race" from Thor Groswold of Denver became the grand prize with the understanding that it would go on permanent display at Camp Hale.[732]

Not all training came with the perks of enjoying the wilderness going into March 1944, especially for the mountain infantry regiments. The command knew that a deployment stilled loomed large for the division, so it continued to train hard for combat. This training continued with Alpha Company of the 10th Medical Battalion, which joined up with the 87th for the first time since its return from Kiska to conduct combat training in the field.[733] In the middle of March, Captain Jay took the 10th Reconnaissance Troop to the mountains above Ashcroft, an old ghost town about fifteen miles from Aspen, in order to study survival in cold weather.[734] The group primarily focused on avalanche prevention, avalanche survival, building shelters, catching animals for consumption and hiding ski tracks to obscure the number of soldiers present from land and air.[735]

Training at Camp Hale did not come without its share of unfortunate incidents. On a maneuver up near Tennessee Pass, the 86th Mountain Infantry Regiment conducted simulated combat exercises using live ammunition.[736] Veteran H. Robert Krear recalled how his Company L command post was in the direct line of fire of an 81mm mortar crew that was lobbing shells over their head to hit a target.[737] Fatally, a shell fell short and landed directly in the middle of the command post, killing Krear's good friend and company runner Russell Bayne with a mortar fragment to the back of his skull.[738] Krear, who sat farthest away from the impact, even received a shell fragment in his left calf muscle.[739] Reports later revealed that members of the 81mm mortar crew had no idea that they were firing over a company command post and that the freak accident was just that, an accident with no blame to place.

Nevertheless, training accidents did not derail the further training and reorganization of the 10th Infantry, as the 90th Infantry Regiment moved to Camp Carson on February 23. However, most of the soldiers were dispersed into the light mountain infantry regiments before the move, allowing the 10th Infantry to maintain a solid strength. The command understood that any moves made this late in the game could not affect combat readiness for the 10th Infantry and thus apportioned the soldiers from the 90th accordingly to fill gaps in the mountain infantry regiments.

Around this same time, the Camp Hale Public Relations Office, in conjunction with the Mountain States Telephone and Telegraph Company, published a small information pamphlet on Camp Hale to help orient newcomers and to provide the veterans with a source of information to help boost morale, highlighting the perks of Camp Hale. The command quickly realized it needed to keep morale up with the spreading rumors, so it began to pay extra attention and put much more effort into helping the mountain troops feel comfortable and relaxed, as times were about to change.

Left: *Camp Hale Information Handbook* published by the Camp Hale Public Relations Office and the Mountain States Telephone and Telegraph Company in March 1944. *Author's personal collection.*

Below: The inside of the *Camp Hale Information Handbook*, March 1944. *Author's personal collection.*

General Information

Camp Hale's Enlisted Men's Service Club is one of the most popular places in Camp. Located just across Eagle Creek from 11th and B Streets, it contains a Cafeteria, a large auditorium where dances are held frequently; the Camp Library, and the Music Room.

Adjoining the Service Club is the Camp Guest House, where the families of soldiers may have accommodations while visiting in camp.

14

BANKING—An office of the First National Bank of Eagle County is maintained in the Camp Headquarters at Pando. Here complete banking facilities are available from 12:00 noon to 4:30 p. m., Monday through Friday and from 10:00 a. m. to 3:00 p. m. on Saturdays. War Bonds and Stamps are available at the bank.

TRANSPORTATION—Transportation from Camp to Glenwood Springs, Grand Junction, Salida, Colorado Springs, Pueblo and Denver, is furnished by the Denver and Rio Grande Western Railway and the Rio Grande Trailways bus line. Camp bus service is available to meet bus connections at Pando. Bus and train schedules are available at the railway station at Pando.

19

The *Camp Hale Ski-Zette* around this time also began to add credence to the rumors of a deployment. Corporal A.C. Holeywell published an article in the March 10, 1944 *Ski-Zette* reminding his fellow soldiers of the significance of their training:

> *Of course some had been going along under the impression that we are a "novelty" infantry and would never see combat duty. Well, get a grip on yourself, soldier; we are plenty hot! We'll be playing for keeps before long and when that day comes we want to come out on top, and we will! We've got the stuff and we've got the training, so make the most of every day you undergo.* [740]

Another soldier included a column in the *Ski-Zette* two weeks later that boasted of the 10th Division's quality of soldier and readiness for a deployment:

> *They say that in the trip from ship to shore in landing craft the line is drawn between the boys and the men. And so it is with the 10th Division. We don't have to wait til we're "over there" and ready for the final assault. We can tell right here who can go with us—who are the boys and who are the men. We'll be the stronger for that early knowledge. We'll be able to ride into shore, confident in ourselves and in the men around us, for we have tasted what man and God can deal out; we have taken it.* [741]

The buzz continued around Camp Hale in almost every area, ranging from the *Ski-Zette* to training operations and reorganization, pointing to the reality of the 10th Infantry deploying wherever Uncle Sam had in mind into combat. However, none of the training up to this point proved to be as intense and combat oriented as the impending D-Series (Divisional-Level) Maneuvers that the 16th Corps organized for the 10th Infantry Division.

Lieutenant Colonel Lucien E. Bolduc of the 16th Corps organized the D-Series Maneuvers in cooperation with Major General Jones of the 10th Infantry to "enable the officers and men of the Tenth to tackle problems that [had] arisen in the mountain fighting of World War II." [742] He further explained that these maneuvers would be "as near the real thing as possible within the limits of safety." [743] General Jones looked forward to the challenge and especially for the opportunity to prove that his division could handle the harsh conditions better than the newly trained 87th Mountain Infantry and 99th Field Artillery did when they faltered during the Homestake Peak Maneuvers.

The men of the 10th knew from the beginning the significance of the training because never before had the entire division gone on maneuvers at the same time. D-Series kicked off on March 26, 1944, with the first week of operations enduring twenty degrees below zero in areas containing up to eight feet of snow.[744] Colonel Edwin R. Strong, commanding officer of the Camp Hale Station Hospital, commented that the physical condition of the soldiers was "very good" and that he was "well satisfied with the way the men have taken the physical rigors of mountain problems," upon completing the first week.[745] He further predicted that the number of colds and frostbite cases were expected to drop drastically as week two out of a total of three began.[746] During the first twelve days of operations, soldiers trained with their units in their respective assigned areas in order to prepare for the pinnacle event of the maneuvers, which was a three-day tactical operation. As part of the massive operations, a 10th Infantry Division dentist dragged his dental tools, including a foot-powered drill and a dismantled dental chair, up the mountains on a mule named Hitler.[747] Chaplains joined the soldiers on skis, and Weasels dragged up food supplies behind the long caravan of soldiers.[748]

Unbeknownst to the command, the mild winter of 1943–44 would change rapidly a few days before Easter Sunday into some of the coldest, most blizzard-ridden weather that Camp Hale had seen in years. Temperatures reached twenty to thirty degrees below zero, and snow blanketed the ground, causing increased problems in the transportation of ammunition, food and other materials.[749] Just as the weather turned treacherous, twelve thousand men out of the fifteen thousand at Camp Hale marched into the mountains to elevations as high as thirteen thousand feet, ready to apply the culmination of their winter training. The weather turned so cold that the plastic on glasses became so brittle it broke.[750] Bare skin stuck to metal, rifles would not fire, radio batteries froze and the soldiers had to use their ski brush to brush the snow off their parkas or it would freeze on their jackets by morning.[751] Commanders lost track of their soldiers, and the locations of entire battalions at times were lost and confused for days in the harsh weather.[752] As a result, supplies did not make it to many soldiers, who had to endure with limited or no rations. Some soldiers were even left behind. When the snow completely covered H. Robert Krear's tent one night, the regiment left without him and his tent mate.[753] It became so deep that soldiers had to cut slit trenches in the snow and into the ground just to give the men an opportunity to utilize the latrine without leaving excrement on the surface snow. Upon moving on from the bivouac location, soldiers often left a sign

D-Series Maneuvers in the spring of 1944. Pack mules graze in snowy grass as troop lines in the snow are seen on the valley floor. *Courtesy of the Denver Public Library, Western History Collection, Curt Krieser, TMD-481.*

above the covered trench that said, "Latrine, 1944," in order to warn future inhabitants of the area.[754]

During the tactical portion, the 10th faced an entire enemy battalion and at some points a full combat team that received a go from the command to use whatever tactics necessary to repel an attack and disrupt the 10th Infantry's communication and supply lines.[755] The attack unfolded from the direction of Leadville, south of the Continental Divide, and went toward Glenwood Springs. General Lloyd and his men set up defensive lines along the mountain ridges north of the Continental Divide.[756] Their mission was to drive the enemy forces from their route north from Ptarmigan Pass to Vail and Shrine Passes in order to reach a larger enemy force awaiting them north of Dillon.[757] The mission of the enemy differed in that the command tasked them to move by way of Ptarmigan Pass and Resolution Creek to destroy supplies and disrupt rail and communication facilities at Pando, eventually returning to their Vail Pass location.

The attack began with the 3rd Battalion, 86th Infantry, flanking the enemy forces by way of climbing Spruce Ridge in order to take Sugerloaf Mountain. The 2nd Battalion formed up the middle through Wearyman Creek. The enemy broke up into four forces, each set on taking Sugerloaf Mountain and Ptarmigan Hill, disrupting communication and lines of advance through Wearyman and Turkey Creeks and destroying supplies at Pando.[758] The 87th enemy troops succeeded in "blowing up" part of the Wearyman Creek Trail, including the bridge at Red Cliff, and in infiltrating Pando, where they cut communication wires and burned supply warehouses.[759] The command planted live explosives in areas that were primary targets for enemy artillery, mortars, bombs and land mines, taking all safety precautions but also making the conditions as real as possible. This gave the 126th Engineers an opportunity to practice deactivating mines and booby traps and in constructing new bridges and trails. In addition, the command gave the enemy battalion free range to take prisoners while umpires made on-the-spot rulings as to the reality of the prisoner taking and also to identify casualties.[760] In the end, enemy forces captured a division radio vehicle, which compromised communications, but Major General Jones and his troops succeeded in their mission. The war games ranged from Red Cliff to Sugarloaf Mountain and from Pando to Shrine Pass. Patrols operated within a seven-mile radius of Camp Hale, equaling a total of a fifty-square-mile battleground.[761]

The conditions were so harsh that 10th Mountain veteran Hugh Evans, while riding in a Weasel down to Camp Hale to pick up some boots, observed a line of 1,500 men in Camp Hale proper stretching from 5th Street to 15[762]th Street, hoping to make sick call.[762] Colonel Strong's prediction of a decreasing number of frostbite cases proved to be wrong. Sadly, General Jones praised the soldiers for having only 195 frostbite cases; 340 other injuries, including strains and broken bones; and 1,378 cases of sickness.[763] He stressed to General McNair that the maneuvers were a success in that there were no fatalities. What General Jones did not tell General McNair was that he made a "draconian" order that soldiers could return only to either the field or the hospital, not to their quarters. As a result, the overcrowded hospital sent soldiers back to the field who actually needed time to heal.[764] He further commented in the *Ski-Zette* that "from an increase in the AWOL rate immediately prior and during our recent field exercise period, I am forced to deduce that a certain number of individuals just don't have what it takes to perform the arduous job of a soldier of the 10th Division, fighting in the mountains."[765] This mentality proved how out of touch the command was from the actual on-the-ground conditions. While they rode around in the Weasels, the enlisted soldiers and lower-ranking officers suffered in the field. The image described by Harris Dusenbery of mountain troopers

Mountain troops march behind an M-29 cargo carrier (Weasel) on maneuvers in 1943–44. *Courtesy of the Denver Public Library, Western History Collection, United States Army Signal Corps, TMD-613.*

gathering around the muffler and exhaust pipe of a commanding officer's Weasel just to catch any bit of warmth they could symbolized once again the seriousness of the command's lack of leadership and understanding of what was happening in the field.[766]

Nevertheless, the soldiers of the 10th Infantry Division declared victory at the end of the D-Series Maneuvers. They had survived some of the toughest training any military unit had ever experienced during World War II. This declaration of victory did not come easy, as many soldiers recuperated from frostbite and other injuries. They endured the freezing cold nights without fires due to the tactical nature of the exercise. In an interview of 10th Mountain veteran Ralph Lafferty, he recalled, "Later, when we had very heavy shelling in Italy and had a real rough day with a lot of fire going on, you'd hear somebody say 'If this gets any worse, it's gonna be as bad as the D-Series.'"[767] Major General Jones publicly expressed his appreciation for the hard work and dedication of the 10th Infantry Division. He spoke to a *Ski-Zette* reporter, saying, "It gives me pleasure to express, upon returning to you, my satisfaction with the general performance of the Tenth Division, particularly during the last series of exercises. There is no doubt that these exercises were conducted under difficult conditions."[768] Colonel Goode, commander of the 87th Mountain Infantry, briefed Minnie Dole throughout the maneuvers on the successes and failures, giving Dole an informed platform to use in critiquing the final outcome of the training. Unfortunately for General Jones, the critique hammered him and his deputy commanders. Dole, an influential factor in creating the mountain division and once master of recruiting for the 10th Infantry Division, now received a warning from Luggi Foeger, who informed him in his New York office, "Don't go to Camp Hale. You'll be stoned off the company streets."[769] Dole had a direct line to Chief of Staff Marshall in Washington and was at least indirectly responsible for the relieving of two generals at Camp Hale.[770] Just like with the Homestake Peak Maneuvers, he expressed concern over the leadership. Colonel Goode made this clear to Dole and even gave a heartfelt plea for help, telling Dole, "You're the only guy in this place who can go to General Marshall and tell him what's wrong with this outfit. It's the best damned fighting crew I've ever been connected with."[771] Veteran of the 10th Mountain Division Harris Dusenbery commented at the time, "I wish some of those generals were sitting up here with us. They'd change their minds mighty quick, that's for sure."[772]

General Jones went to Washington, D.C., to discuss the maneuvers with Lieutenant General Lesley J. McNair. In their conversation, Jones made it sound like the D-Series Maneuvers were the greatest success in Camp Hale history. For the soldiers, the maneuvers might have been, but not for General Jones, who suffered throughout the entire maneuvers with a sickness that the altitude only aggravated over time. The soldiers also began to blame General Jones and the others in command for not receiving any deployment orders, believing that the War Department saw the mountain troops as undeployable and inefficient for combat. Morale reached a low point for the soldiers of Camp Hale shortly after the D-Series Maneuvers ended. Life returned to normal, and the mountain troops desired anything but normal.

Upon returning to Camp Hale in the beginning of May 1944, soldiers began once again brushing up on the basics in many indoor classes.[773] Several new schools opened up at Camp Hale in order to address deficiencies within the division. Major John B. Woodward opened up the 10th Division rock-climbing school at Camp Hale on Monday, May 29, 1944, in order to make sure that every soldier of the division received the proper training for scaling mountains.[774] Reports from Italy revealed that flatland soldiers were afraid of the vertical terrain and that only British or Canadian assault units attacked German positions on mountaintops.[775] The 10th Division command at Camp Hale was insulted by the very notion that American soldiers had to relent to British and Canadian troops in order to attack fortified mountain positions. They vowed that all soldiers regardless of specialty or unit would have knowledge of rock technique and the confidence to operate in rocky heights. This turned out to be a great success for the mountain troops, especially when they scaled Riva Ridge in the dark of night. Similarly, the 10th Division Artillery opened up a Forward Observer School for infantrymen due to reports in late 1940 from Greece that revealed that the Greeks made advances against the Italians only after artillery barrages prepared the way.[776]

Sadly, as activity continued to expand at Camp Hale during the middle of 1944, it faced a turning point that would eventually result in arguments made against its mere existence. The 10th Infantry Division had still not received a deployment order, but the War Department had its fingers on it, ready to move at a moment's notice. At this time, Minnie Dole went to Washington and challenged General Marshall on why the 10th had been kept in training at Camp Hale for so long. He then flat-out asked General Marshall, "You do believe in this type of division, don't you?"[777] As soldiers marched in formation for review before Major General Lloyd E. Jones on Infantry Day, June 15, 1944, many in attendance did not realize that four days later, the entire division would leave the cantonment on its way to Camp Swift, Texas, for further training.[778] The departure of the 10th

Infantry Division implied imminent doom for Camp Hale given that the division contributed the majority of the soldiers who trained there. Since the army no longer held basic training at the cantonment, all who remained were the WACs, the MTG and various other smaller units that sustained the life of the camp. Life at Camp Hale had slowed down tremendously by the end of June 1944 and remained this way until after the war ended. Suddenly, the highlights of the day changed from skiing and rock climbing to details that included barracks cleaning, KP and even ten-day rotations of guarding German prisoners of war and Camp Hale criminals in the stockades.[779] The *Camp Hale Ski-Zette* ceased publication at Camp Hale in the latter part of 1944 and picked up operation down at Camp Swift. In July 1942 on Mount Rainier, 87th Mountain Infantry soldier Charles McLane said, "If we are restless now, it is because it is July and we are sick of guessing at what the next few weeks will bring forth. One thing we can be sure of—it will not be flatland."[780] These words now haunted the 10th Infantry Division as it departed for flatland. The mission of the Camp Hale cantonment was complete as soldiers of the 10th Infantry Division entered their last phase of training before their departure to Italy.

EPILOGUE

Camp Hale is the only camp constructed for training mountain troops.[781]
—Colorado congressman, 1944

Three different events revealed the ultimate success of Camp Hale. The first celebration of success came at the completion of construction on November 15, 1942, when the army completed its first cantonment ever built for training mountain troops, equipped with all the amenities for skiing, rock climbing and ice climbing. The cooperation of the U.S. Army and representatives of the National Ski Association, military and civilian, became the basis for success throughout Camp Hale's existence and led to the completion of the army's most unique and specialized cantonment. Lieutenant Colonel Joseph Rockis wrote on June 30, 1948, "The training of mountain troops was from the very outset in 1940 a project requiring the combined efforts of the army and representatives of the National Ski Association. Best results were possible when the prerogatives of army command were subordinated to the superior knowledge and skills of the mountaineering experts who had come into the army from civilian life, and when at the same time the experts subordinated their enthusiasm for their specialties to army discipline." The second event came with the successful deployment of well-trained mountain troops to the Aleutian Island of Kiska on June 13, 1943, and to Italy on June 20, 1944. Finally, the third came at the end of World War II in Europe on V-E Day, May 8, 1945. The 10th Mountain Division ultimately proved its effectiveness in mountain warfare in Alaska and Italy, showing that its training at Camp Hale was truly not in vain.

Though the 87th Mountain Infantry Regiment deployed as a well-prepared fighting force to Kiska, it never actually saw combat against the Japanese. The true test of the mountain troops came in Italy. Before the 10th Light Division (Alpine) left for Italy, it endured about a month of the D-Series Maneuvers at Camp Hale. Any veteran who endured this training at Camp Hale is quick to identify how cold and ruthless the conditions were on his body. The subzero temperatures "pushed men, mules, and machines to the limit of their endurance."[782]

After these maneuvers, the 10th Light Division (Alpine), including the newly returned troops from the 87th who had invaded at Kiska, departed on June 20, 1944, for Camp Swift, Texas. Morale reached a low point for the soldiers of the division as they sweltered in the Texas heat, longing to have the mountains back. On November 6, 1944, the army renamed the 10th Light Division (Alpine) the 10th Mountain Division. Over the next two months, elements of the 10th Mountain Division moved from Camp Swift and Camp Hale to Camp Patrick Henry, Virginia, for embarkation to Italy. Combat operations in Italy commenced, and the 10th Mountain Division proved the value of its existence as a fighting force.

After the war, the soldiers dispersed across the nation, beginning the next phase of their lives that many of them discussed in the Camp Hale forums years before. Richard M. Wilson, veteran of the 85th Mountain Infantry Regiment, compiled a list of over 350 of the veterans of the division in 1992, detailing where they went and what they did related to skiing after the war.[783] His records reveal that soldiers-turned-civilians became ski instructors across the nation, U.S. Forest Service workers, ski team coaches, competitors, resort developers and managers, equipment designers and manufacturers, ski patrolmen, ski shop owners, lodge owners and operators, ski writers and skiing Olympians.[784] Their contributions to the ski industry are undeniable, and some still work in these capacities today.

These unique soldiers in American history showed how mountain warfare could be accomplished around the world. The story of Camp Hale is one that will forever remember and memorialize the sacrifices made by both civilians and soldiers. Even after the civilian construction workers left in November and December 1942 and the 10th Mountain Division soldiers in June 1944 to Camp Swift, Texas, Camp Hale continued functioning as an army training center for various units in mountain and winter warfare training. The camp did not cease military operations until July 1965, and the National Forest Service acquired the land a year later.

An original press photograph from February 1, 1955, showing ski troops in formation at Camp Hale. Major General Charles L. Dasher Jr., deputy commander of the Fifth Corps Army, reviewed the troops before their day of training. *Author's personal collection.*

Remnants of Camp Hale in June 1965, looking from the southwest to the north. *Author's personal collection.*

As of October 2015, Camp Hale remains a deserted area with only the concrete foundations of buildings remaining. The Camp Hale Memorial Campground continues to operate, and adventure-seekers still explore the surrounding hills and mountains. Various signs around the valley strategically placed and funded by the Colorado Historical Society, the Tenth Mountain Division Foundation, Camp Jeep®, the National Forest Foundation and the Forest Service provide visitors with interpretive information about the camp and the training that took place.[785] If all goes as planned for the Colorado delegation, legislation in the Senate may produce a report on the feasibility of incorporating the remnants of Camp Hale into the National Park Service. Regardless of what happens, Camp Hale will always be remembered as one of many training camps in World War II but, more importantly, as the unique camp that trained mountain troops for victory.

NOTES

INTRODUCTION

1. Coquoz, *Leadville Story*, 30.

CHAPTER 1

2. *Herald Democrat*, "Camp at Pando."
3. Harper, *Skiing for the Millions*, 18.
4. *Camp Hale Ski-Zette* 1, no. 34 (August 27, 1943).
5. Ibid.
6. Ibid.
7. Harper, *Military Ski Manual*, 14–15.
8. Ibid., 11.
9. McNeil, "Skiing and National Defense," 7.
10. Ibid.
11. Brown, *Love Letter to Americans*, 199. Werner and Rupert von Trapp put their musical talents to use at Camp Hale. Werner directed a choir as part of the 85th Mountain Infantry Regiment while Rupert, of the 86th Mountain Infantry, provided an organ accompaniment during the Christmas festivities of 1943.
12. *Camp Hale Ski-Zette* 1, no. 41 (October 15, 1943). Paul Petzoldt was drafted into the army while living in Wyoming at the age of thirty-five

and requested to be "assigned to the mountain troops, the toughest outfit in the Service."

13. Petzoldt's placement in a medical detachment allowed him to impart his vast knowledge of mountain rescues. Captain Robert S. Wade of the medical detachment took advantage of Petzoldt's experience and allowed him to help instruct fellow medics in mountain medical care. During his days of leave at Camp Hale, he climbed the peaks of Colorado, beginning with Mount of the Holy Cross (14,005 feet).

14. *Camp Hale Ski-Zette* 1, No. 44 (November 5, 1943). Petzoldt faced yet another rebuff upon reporting to Company A, 85th Mountain Infantry. A company officer told him he would be better off as a medic, telling him, "It would be tough for a fellow your age in this outfit."

15. *Lewiston Evening Journal*, "28th Infantry Ends Ski-Fighting Games." In 1951, Camp Pine became Camp Drum, which later became Fort Drum in 1974. Today, Fort Drum is home of the 10th Mountain Division. The annals of history will forever record that where the army first began training ski troopers at Camp Pine is now the present-day home of the army's 10th Mountain Division.

16. Ibid.

17. Ibid.

18. Shelton, *Climb to Conquer*, 19.

19. Ibid., 20–21.

20. Jay, "History of the Mountain Training Center," 2. Each patrol was given about $1,200 for equipment testing.

21. Ibid., 4. The 41st occupied the Ashcroft CCC Camp, three miles outside Mount Rainier National Park, in January 1941.

22. Sorensen, "Ski Patrol U.S. Army," 51.

23. On April 20, 1941, the army disbanded the 41st Division Ski Patrol.

24. Shelton, *Climb to Conquer*, 20–21.

25. Dole, *Adventures in Skiing*, 91–101; Marshall, quoted in "Skiing and National Defense," 9. General Marshall stated, "The offer of the American Ski Association to furnish informal advice and assistance in the technique of skiing and the purchase of equipment is appreciated. Please extend to Mr. Langley and to the other officials of the Association working with you my personal thanks for your patriotic support."

26. Shelton, *Climb to Conquer*, 25.

27. Adjutant General's Office, "Report of Investigation."

CHAPTER 2

28. Jay, "History of the Mountain Training Center," 8.
29. Ironically, General Rolfe (commander of the 87th and eventually the Mountain Training Center) never desired for Camp Hale to be utilized as a basic training location in addition to a mountain training site. He argued that raw recruits could not immediately enter basic training when they could barely survive in the conditions at Camp Hale. This potential problem never kept General Rolfe from pushing forward with both types of training and in being successful at it throughout the entirety of his command at Camp Hale.
30. Imbrie and Imbrie, "Chronology of the 10th Mountain Division."
31. Wolf, *Ice Crusaders*, 13–14. The army in the late 1930s initially asserted that the Great Sand Dunes in southern Colorado would provide adequate and year-round ski training on the dunes, which reached elevations as high as 750 feet.
32. Jay, "History of the Mountain Training Center," 8.
33. Ibid., 9.
34. Colonel Harry L. Twaddle, quoted in Jay, "History of the Mountain Training Center," 9.
35. Jay, "History of the Mountain Training Center," 10.
36. Ibid.
37. Ibid., 10–11.
38. Ibid.
39. Ibid.
40. Ibid.
41. Ibid.
42. Govan, "Training for Mountain and Winter Warfare Study No. 23," 4.
43. Jay, "History of the Mountain Training Center," 12. The battalion did not actually form until December 8, 1941, one day after the bombing of Pearl Harbor.
44. Imbrie and Imbrie, "Chronology of the 10th Mountain Division."
45. Laughlin, "Ski Parachute Troops," 94. In January 1942, Jack Tappin sold the War Department on experimenting with ski paratroops. This experiment took place at Alta, Utah, under the direction of Dick Durrance, director of the Alta Ski School. He taught about 150 paratroopers of the 503rd Parachute Infantry Battalion how to ski. At the time, Tappin was most concerned with seeing if ski paratroops were feasible and testing equipment, as he was an advisor to the War Department on Winter Warfare and Equipment. The experiment

largely proved to be a success, but the ski paratroops were never utilized in combat.

46. McLane, "Of Mules and Skis," 22.

47. Ibid.

48. Ibid.

49. *Camp Hale Ski-Zette* 1, no. 48 (December 3, 1943).

50. The two most important lessons learned from the ski patrol experiments related to training. The army found that men with no prior skiing experience could learn to ski the army way in two months. Also, it found that even if a man was well trained in skiing, he would most likely be among the first to fall out during training if he did not have training in winter camping and survival.

51. Govan, "History of the 10th Light Division (Alpine)," 2.

52. Jay, "History of the Mountain Training Center," 12. Fort Ethan Allen proved unsatisfactory as a permanent training location due to the inconsistent amounts of snow on the nearby mountains.

53. Ibid., 16.

54. Paradise Lodge, now commonly referred to as Paradise Inn, was built in 1916 on the slopes of Mount Rainier.

55. Around the end of February 1942 is when the army and the War Department decided on making Pando, Colorado, the location for a permanent cantonment.

56. The soldiers of the 87th occupied Paradise Lodge during the week and left it open for civilian vacationers on the weekends.

57. Lieutenant Colonel Rolfe made a point from the beginning that the soldiers of the 87th would be not just ski troopers but rather mountain troops capable of skiing and conducting mountain warfare. In addition, Lieutenant Colonel Rolfe emphasized "army skiing" instead of civilian skiing. Army skiing differed in that it involved more stamina, the carrying of a heavy rucksack and a rifle and more cross-country as opposed to downhill skiing.

58. McLane, "Of Mules and Skis," 27.

59. Ibid., 30. The choir, made up largely of soldiers from Company A in the 87th, also sang at Parent-Teacher Association meetings and the farewell gathering for General Kenyon Ashe Joyce at Fort Lewis, Washington. The pinnacle event for the glee club came at Seattle's Meaney Hall when it performed for several thousand people.

60. Bradley, "Mountain Soldier Sings," 38.

61. Lieutenant Charles C. Bradley (Company A, 87th Mountain Infantry) recounted that the ski troopers picked up the song from ski jumping

tournaments that they had attended before the war. The word *oola* most likely came from the word *ull*, a god of the ski warriors and hunters of old going back to Norway. Somehow the name Ull changed to Oola, and he became "the champion, the hero, the Paul Bunyan of the army Skier," according to Lieutenant Bradley. The lyrics changed quickly to reflect the praise and admiration the ski troopers had for skiing in the military.

62. Ibid., 39.

63. Jay, "History of the Mountain Training Center," 22. The National Park Service feared that the use of live ammunition would disturb the wildlife.

64. After the bombing at Pearl Harbor by the Japanese on December 7, 1941, Fort Lewis largely became a deserted army post, as most units moved to the West Coast for defense purposes. This provided ample space for maneuvers, but it still did not make up for the lack of mountainous conditions that the 87th desperately craved.

65. Ibid., 25.

66. By June 1, the army had already begun to take new recruits and send them to Fort Lewis to fill the ranks of the 87th. Since the original soldiers that made up the 87th primary already had previous mountaineering or skiing skills, these new recruits needed serious and extensive training in mountain warfare. As a result, the army had to make a decision about how, when and where to train these soldiers. The army eventually concluded that a larger, more extensive training site was needed, and this added to the justification for the construction of Camp Hale.

67. Burton, *Ski Troops*, 89.

68. Ibid., 90.

69. Ibid.

70. "Report of Investigation by Board of Officers."

71. Ibid.

72. Ibid.

73. Ibid.

74. Ibid.

75. West Yellowstone, Montana, sat at an elevation of about 6,667 feet.

76. Jay, "History of the Mountain Training Center," 7.

77. Burton, *Ski Troops*, 90.

78. Blair, *Leadville*, 230.

79. Jay, "History of the Mountain Training Center," 27.

80. Ibid.

81. The army actually began construction in April 1942 and completed it before the heart of the winter hit Pando in November 1942.

82. "Report of Investigation by Board of Officers." The report suggested that the noncommissioned officer housing should be located in the valley of Homestake Creek.

83. *Herald Democrat*, "Handpicked Soldiers."

84. The 179,430 acres of land that Camp Hale encompassed were part of the Holy Cross, Arapaho and Cochetopa National Forests. Beginning in 1910, the U.S. Forest Service constructed the Pando Ranger Station, which lasted about ten years, until 1920. This station served the area on which most of the Camp Hale reservation was located.

85. *Camp Hale Ski-Zette* 2, no. 22 (June 9, 1943).

86. Area Engineer, "Camp Hale Colorado," part 4, 1. The Holy Cross National Forest was established by proclamation of President Theodore Roosevelt on August 27, 1905. The Arapaho National Forest was also established by proclamation of President Theodore Roosevelt on July 1, 1908.

87. *Camp Hale Ski-Zette* 1, no. 12 (March 23, 1943).

88. The closest 14,000-foot mountain (fourteener) to Pando is Mount of the Holy Cross at an elevation of 14,005 feet. Mountain troops favored Holy Cross to climb while on weekend passes given its proximity. According to veteran Philip A. Lunday of the 126th Engineers, soldiers constructed trails from Camp Hale to the Holy Cross ghost town below the peak and also to Vail Pass. The army air corps also utilized another fourteener in Colorado for training pilots in how to survive crash landings in the arctic. In 1943, the air corps established a training area on Mount Evans along the Front Range. The Mountain Training Center assisted the air corps with this training by supplying officers and enlisted men. Also, the *Camp Hale Ski-Zette* of August 6, 1943, identifies that members of the 10th Recon trained on Quandary Peak (14,265 feet) near Breckinridge.

89. Ibid.

90. Eventually, the coal-powered heaters in the barracks also contributed to the soot in the valley, adding an extra layer of black smog. With post headquarters residing not far from the tracks, the trains running through the valley rattled the windows and made for an unpleasant noise distraction to the workday. Some soldiers joked about a get-rich-quick scheme in which they would buy up all the ear muffs in the country and sell them to the individuals at headquarters.

91. Bradley, "Mountain Soldier Sings," 39. The song lyrics came from the popular song among the ski troopers titled "The Ballad of Oola."

92. *Camp Hale Ski-Zette* 1, no. 12 (March 23, 1943).

93. Ibid.

94. Ibid.

95. Ellis, Correspondence Received, Sent (typed) October–December 1944. The geological formation of Eagle Valley, where Pando resided, resulted from a few unique events in geological history. The formation of a flat valley in the middle of the Rockies, with a river running through it, truly became a rare item and a prized location for the federal government in its search for a suitable area for ski training.

96. "Treaty with the Utah, Tabeguache Band." The Treaty with the Utah, Tabeguache Band, of October 7, 1863, officially surrendered the territory from the control of the Ute Indians. President Lincoln signed the treaty, and the Senate officially ratified it on March 25, 1864. The treaty was originally negotiated by John Evans, governor of the Colorado Territory; Michael Steck, superintendent of Indian affairs for the Territory of New Mexico; Simeon Whiteley and Lafayette Head, Indian agents, authorized and appointed as commissioners for the purpose; and the chiefs and warriots of the Tabeguache band of Utah Indians.

97. Varney and Drew, *Ghost Towns of Colorado*, 62.

98. Today, two cabins, along with the foundations and remains of several other buildings, remain at Holy Cross City. The remains constitute a true mountain ghost town in Colorado.

99. Ibid.

100. *Pando Echo* 1, no. 3 (July 11, 1942).

101. Buys, *Quick History of Leadville*, 38.

102. Ibid., 47.

103. Ibid., 48.

104. Blair, *Leadville*, 231.

105. Ibid., 233.

106. Ibid. CWA: Civil Works Administration. WPA: Works Progress Administration. CCC: Civilian Conservation Corps.

107. Ellis, Correspondence Received, Sent (typed).

108. Ibid. According to Ross R. May, worker for Platt Rogers, Inc., of Pueblo in an interview with Erl H. Ellis, well before 1925, Eggers Ice Company had contracted to supply ice to the Denver & Rio Grande Western Railroad and to use the pond. The Eggers company was operated as the Western Railway Ice Company.

109. *Denver Post*, "Ski Troops."

110. Dawson, *Colorado 10th Mountain Huts & Trails*, 38.

111. Ellis, Correspondence Received, Sent (typed August 1942). The White River National Forest headquarters confirmed with Erl H. Ellis

in his research that the Pando Ranger station did indeed have the name "Pando," which helps date the origin of the name to at least pre-1910.

112. Ibid.

113. Ellis, Correspondence Received, Sent (typed) October–December 1944.

114. Ibid.

CHAPTER 3

115. "Camp Hale Builders."

116. Mount Rainier National Park is the fifth-oldest national park in the United States. The park was established on March 2, 1899.

117. Jenkins, *Last Ridge*, 50. The Denver & Rio Grande Western Railroad Company quickly agreed to give up some of its land in and around Pando for army use.

118. Coquoz, *Invisible Men on Skis*, 10.

119. Ibid.

120. The writer of the Camp Hale Completion Report wrote that "scheduled and actual progress, based on units of work accomplished over a given time period, at this project are not comparable to similar schedules on other projects involving lighter units of work." The army clearly recognized the special nature of its mountain training camp at Pando. However, not everyone was on board with the project. The engineers were the only group that actually rejected Pando as a suitable location for the cantonment. They argued that the water supply was uncertain, that sewage disposal might pose problems and that the area was too small for the proposed number of soldiers. The final factor that tipped Pando over the top for approval came after Colonel Rolfe's February 6–9, 1942 visit. He made the same recommendation as the 8th Corps, which effectively trumped that of the engineers.

121. "Report of Investigation by Board of Officers."

122. In an interview with J.D. Craighead by Erl H. Ellis, Craighead revealed that Frank Byers was planning a cattle ranch prior to the government's acquisition of the land. He was about to start work on some buildings when news of the army cantonment reached Adrian Reynolds Jr., the publisher of the *Eagle Valley Enterprise* and father-in-law of Frank Byers. He drove to Red Cliff to stop Byers in any further plans, as Byers had talked to a carpenter and had already begun planning for the ranch. Reynolds knew government-forced acquisition of the land seemed imminent. Byers eventually took the

money he received as compensation from the government for his loss of land at Pando and purchased land near Dillon, Colorado.

123. The entire reservation of land for the cantonment itself and the surrounding training area comprised initially both private and public ownership. As stated, 1,027 of the 1,532 for the cantonment itself came from private ownership while most of the land surrounding the cantonment came from National Forest land for training purposes. Within the surrounding land, the four small villages of Mitchell, East Mitchell, Kokomo and Frisco partially resided there but never proved to be a problem in using the land for training purposes. The army concluded that their acquisition would not be necessary as long as maneuvers were granted for the ski troopers in the area. Several mining claims also resided within the reservation including Gold Park and Holy Cross City, but neither of these was active at the time and did not prove to be an issue for training. Finally, the Forest Service, under the direction of the U.S. Department of Agriculture, expressed concern over timber sale operations on the south side of Wearyman Creek near the junction with Turkey Creek. Nevertheless, the army agreed not to interfere with them while training in the area.

124. Ellis, "Camp Hale Construction." The 101 acres owned by the Denver & Rio Grande Railroad Company were rented, not sold, to the army for use at Camp Hale.

125. *Rocky Mountain News*, "Army to Start Ski Camp Construction."

126. *Camp Hale Ski-Zette* 1, no. 21 (May 26, 1943).

127. Coquoz, *Invisible Men on Skis*, 7–9.

128. Ibid., 7.

129. *Herald Democrat*, "Camp at Pando."

130. After World War II, veterans returned to Colorado to help establish Aspen, Arapaho Basin, Vail, Sugarbush, Crystal Mountain, Whiteface Mountain and the 10th Mountain Division Trail and Hut System.

131. In April 1942, the distance between Leadville and Pando on Highway 24 was about twenty-one miles. The rerouting of Highway 24 eliminated about three miles, bringing the distance down to eighteen miles apart by the time the ski troopers arrived.

132. Carroll, "Feeding the Multitudes."

133. *Pando Echo* 1, no. 5 (August 25, 1942). The *Pando Echo*, published on site at the cantonment every two weeks, was a periodical written for workers. Writers brought humor to the pioneer life of the workers and provided an escape from the daily monotonous work on the cantonment.

134. Area Engineer, "Camp Hale Colorado," part 1a, 2.
135. Coquoz, *Invisible Men on Skis*, 12.
136. "Camp Hale Builders."
137. Coquoz, *Leadville Story*, 28. In the August 25, 1942 issue of the *Pando Echo*, one writer joked that Pando had turned into the Wild West as people began to crowd every available location and carried guns everywhere they went for self-defense.
138. *Herald Democrat*, "Leadville Is Whooping." Both Price and Stevens obtained jobs from the union office in Leadville as carpenter's helpers at $1.10 an hour while agreeing to pay a $13.00 union fee and $3.00 a month in dues.
139. Ibid. The Vendome Hotel, built in 1884, later became known as the Tabor Grand Hotel located at 711 Harrison Avenue, Leadville, Colorado 80461. Today, this building has shops on the main floor and is called the Tabor Grand Apartments because of the apartments located on its upper floors. The hotel once housed many famous people throughout its existence, including Benjamin Harrison before he became president.
140. Ibid.
141. *Camp Hale Ski-Zette* 2, no. 3 (January 21, 1943).
142. Area Engineer, "Camp Hale Colorado," part 1a, 2.
143. The Architect-Engineer-Construction-Manager contract, negotiated at division headquarters in Salt Lake City, Utah, on April 6 and 7, 1942, was signed after the last meeting on the seventh, giving the go-ahead for construction on the tenth.
144. Ellis, "Camp Hale Construction."
145. *Camp Hale Ski-Zette* 1, no. 31 (August 6, 1943).
146. Ibid. Work did not officially end until December 15, 1942, one month later than their goal.
147. *Denver Post*, "Ski Troops." Typically, the higher the elevation, the more snow an area receives and stays in the mountains. The lapse rate, or change of temperature for every one thousand feet in elevation, ranges from about three and a half degrees to five and a half degrees Fahrenheit.
148. Ellis, "Camp Hale Construction."
149. "Report of Investigation by Board of Officers."
150. Civilian workers did move into the barracks right after they were completed and eventually vacated them for the soldiers when they arrived.
151. Area Engineer, "Camp Hale Colorado," part 7, 15–16.
152. In addition to Pando Constructors, four sub-contractors and thirty-eight prime contractors labored on the project.

153. Ibid., 17.
154. Ellis, "Camp Hale Construction."
155. Bolton, "Turning Point," 133.
156. Area Engineer, "Camp Hale Colorado," part 1a, 1.
157. Smith, "Camp Hale, Colorado."
158. Ibid.
159. The $1.10-an-hour wage turned out to be quite generous given the army's admission in its completion report that it had oftentimes settled for work of lower quality in order to speed completion.
160. "Camp Hale Builders." Captain Ballard came from Salt Lake City, where he had just finished supervising construction of the Utah Ordnance Plant.
161. *Herald Democrat*, "Work Starts."
162. Ibid.
163. "Camp Hale Builders."
164. Area Engineer, "Camp Hale Colorado," part 1a, 2.
165. *Herald Democrat*, "Work Starts."
166. Area Engineer, "Camp Hale Colorado," part 1a, 2.
167. "Camp Hale Builders."
168. The remnants of these miners' residences can still be seen not far away from Pando at Holy Cross City. This old mining town, now a ghost town at the top of one of Colorado's most infamous four-wheel-drive trails, became the home to miners seeking gold from 1881 to 1883.
169. Carroll, "Feeding the Multitudes."
170. Smith, "Camp Hale, Colorado," 3.
171. Ibid.
172. Ibid.
173. Ibid.
174. Ibid.
175. *Pando Echo* 1, no. 5 (August 25, 1942).
176. "Pando's Spanish-American Colony Buys War Bonds," *Pando Echo: Published on the Summit of the Nation* 1, no. 8 (September 8, 1942).
177. *Herald Democrat*, "Discharged Camp Workers."
178. Area Engineer, "Camp Hale Colorado," part 1a, 2.
179. Jenkins, *Last Ridge*, 51.
180. Ellis, "Camp Hale Construction."
181. Carroll, "Dismantling and Salvage."
182. *Muskeg* is a word from Cree origin that means "low-lying marsh." Also, this was not the first time that human beings changed the course of the

Eagle River. According to Ross R. May in an interview with Erl H. Ellis, the Eggers Ice Company wanted to improve the pond by having runways into it and to have the capability of running tractors out over the runways to gather in the ice. This meant Platt Rogers, Inc., of Pueblo had to build a dyke through the pond and change the course of the Eagle River.

183. Due to the fact that heavy machinery was at a premium because of war manufacturing around the country, Pando Constructors made use of what it had and oftentimes drove its equipment to the breaking point in order to maintain sufficient progress. Nevertheless, in the second half of September 1942, the district and division offices of the U.S. Army Corps of Engineers made available additional machinery and adequate repair parts.

184. "Camp Hale Builders." Workers cleared 1,236.5 acres of trees for the cantonment proper and another 240.0 acres of heavy spruce timber for the ski lift and runs at Tennessee Pass and the four rope tows on the sides of the mountains surrounding Camp Hale. Working conditions were oftentimes harsh during the clearing of the ski runs given that clearing went as high as 11,700 feet in elevation at times. Construction workers also cleared another 115.0 acres of spruce, pine and aspen for the relocation of U.S. Highway 24.

185. *Herald Democrat*, "Pando Construction."

186. *Pando Echo* 1, no. 13 (November 18, 1942).

187. *Herald Democrat*, "What Pando Construction Will Mean."

188. Ibid., "Camp Hale, Construction Miracle."

189. Ibid.

190. Smith, "Camp Hale, Colorado," 2.

191. Area Engineer, "Camp Hale Colorado," part 5, 1.

192. Burton, *Ski Troops*, 90.

193. Though this was the most significant move of Highway 24 in Colorado, it was not the first. Around 1925—when Pando consisted of some bunkhouses, boardinghouses, a railroad station, a school and two or three houses—engineers improved, relocated and resurfaced part of Highway 24 through Eagle Valley. The highway remained a dirt road until the beginning of August 1943, when work began to surface it in order to cut down on dust during the summer and road erosion and drainage problems during the winter and spring months.

194. Charles D. Vail's name rings prominently in Colorado today. His last name has been applied to the town located on Interstate 70 about one hundred miles from Denver, a mountain pass on the line between Eagle and Summit Counties and between the town of Vail on the west and

Dillon on the east. His name also graces a ski resort located in the town of Vail.

195. Area Engineer, "Camp Hale Colorado," part 1a, 3. The cantonment road system was composed of 3.6 miles of primary roads, 8.2 miles of secondary roads and 5.1 miles of other miscellaneous roads. Due to the low, wet, swamp and mucky soil condition of the land on which most of the roads were located in Eagle Valley, proper roadside drainage was necessary along with a bed of gravel beneath the roads. In addition to about 17.0 miles of roads in Camp Hale, engineers constructed fifteen bridges, most of which crossed the Eagle River flowing through the middle of the camp.

196. *Herald Democrat*, "Highway at Pando."

197. Area Engineer, "Camp Hale Colorado," part 1a, 3.

198. *Herald Democrat*, "What Pando Construction Will Mean."

199. "Camp Hale," *Pando Echo: Published on the Summit of the Nation* 1, no. 9 (September 15, 1942).

200. *Herald Democrat*, "Pando Construction."

201. Ibid. According to the Camp Hale Completion Report, construction workers laid 6.26 miles of new track for Camp Hale. Of this track, 0.13 miles was constructed by the Denver & Rio Grande Western Railroad for access to the camp system and 6.13 miles for internal use by the U.S. Army.

202. Platt Rogers, Inc., continued to work on ballasting the railroad well into the middle of 1943 so that trains could haul rail cars faster, stronger and safer through the Pando Valley.

203. Johnson, *Soldiers of the Mountain*, 32–33.

204. *Herald Democrat*, "What Pando Construction Will Mean."

205. Blair, *Leadville*, 235.

206. Ellis, *See Naples and Die*, 29.

207. Jay, "History of the Mountain Training Center," 37.

208. *Denver Post*, "Pando Health Record"; Baumgardner, *10th Mountain Division*, 20. The health record of Camp Hale improved with time, even with the numerous examples of the Pando hack throughout ski trooper training. In a February 4, 1943 *Denver Post* article, the Colorado surgeon general reported that he believed "the general health of the men [was] good" and that only minor ailments common to any army cantonment affected Camp Hale. He also highlighted the fact that not a single ski trooper had died during training thus far. By the end of the ski troopers' occupation of Camp Hale, twenty-eight soldiers had

died due to illnesses, injuries, training mishaps, auto accidents and a plane crash.

209. "Report of Investigation by Board of Officers."

210. Jenkins, *Last Ridge*, 51.

211. Casewit, *Mountain Troopers!*, 17. During the middle of April 1942, Generals Marshall and McNair both expressed fear that activating a mountain division during the harsh winter of December 1942 would not be a wise decision given the altitude and harsh winter conditions. Thus, the army delayed any such activation until the summer of 1943 and kept what it called a "test force" at Camp Hale during the winter.

212. Gale to Mrs. D.G. Gale, letters, November 1, 1943.

213. Putnam, *Green Cognac*, 16.

214. Robinson, "Camp Hale."

215. *Camp Hale Ski-Zette* 1, no. 37 (September 17, 1943).

216. Fine and Remington, *World War II*, 280, identifies that the Army Corps of Engineers and its workers and contractors experienced "unusual challenges and [exerted] strenuous effort" in constructing cantonments around the country during the winter of 1940–41. Fine and Remington also identify that shortages in materials plagued many construction projects. Camp Hale experienced these same issues and oftentimes to even more extremes because of its high elevation and remote location. Fine and Remington wrote that "few construction men had experienced anything like it before." If this was the case for many ordinary cantonment construction projects during World War II, Camp Hale once again must have been an extreme shock to many workers going into the winter of 1942 high in the Rocky Mountains.

217. "Camp Hale," *Pando Echo: Published on the Summit of the Nation* 1, no. 9 (September 15, 1942).

218. It was an issue for the army to keep the Eagle River flowing not only for freshwater use but also for sewage treatment and disposal. Due to fears from the town of Red Cliff that Camp Hale would contaminate the Eagle River, the government helped develop a new source of fresh water for Red Cliff. The new source was Turkey Creek, located east of the town on the border with Camp Hale. The government gave Red Cliff water rights to Turkey Creek and reimbursed the town for expenses relating to piping, water storage facilities and water supply facilities from the new location.

219. Area Engineer, "Camp Hale Colorado," part 3, 1. The five deep wells went down as far as two hundred feet into the ground and were

drilled, cased, perforated and developed under contract by Roscoe Moss Company, well contractors from Los Angeles, California.

220. "Camp Hale Builders." One popular documented fishing destination for soldiers at Camp Hale was Twin Lakes, Colorado. The Twin Lakes are located south of Leadville and north of Granite along Colorado Highway 82, near the Southeast Ridge Trailhead for Mount Elbert. Both civilian workers and soldiers at Camp Hale took advantage of the many fishing opportunities in and around the cantonment.

221. Jay, "History of the Mountain Training Center," 41.

222. Ibid., 42. The change to enclosure one included lengthening the individual training program from thirteen to seventeen weeks in order to incorporate the extra ski training, mountain training and animal care.

223. Ibid., 46.

224. Ibid., 50.

225. "Camp Hale," *Pando Echo* 1, no. 9 (September 15, 1942).

226. Area Engineer, "Camp Hale Colorado," part 2, 6–9. Skis were issued to soldiers with a coat of paint on the bottom of them. Upon bringing them back to their barracks, many of the ski troopers stripped the paint off the bottom and applied ski wax to slicken them up using the appropriate type of ski wax. Three different types of wax were applied to skis based on snow conditions. Blue wax was used for dry snow. Red wax was for downhill speed, slalom or ski jumping. Orange wax was for climbing and wet and granular snow. For some at Camp Hale, the application of ski wax became an art form; soldiers spent a significant amount of time making sure they had just the right amount on their skis for the conditions.

227. Cassidy, *Off Limits*, 6.

228. Ibid., 9.

229. Lunday and Hampton, *Tramway Builders*, 10–11.

230. Richard (Dick) Over (85th, 86th and 110th Signal Company Veteran) in discussion with the author, July 2011.

231. Area Engineer, "Camp Hale Colorado," part 3, 50.

232. *Camp Hale Ski-Zette* 1, no. 49 (December 10, 1943). The kit also included a long pipe to vent the gasoline heater out the top.

233. Area Engineer, "Camp Hale Colorado," part 2, 14–18.

234. Ibid., part 6, p. 1.

235. Laundry service did not come to Camp Hale until January 1944 with the arrival of the 586th Quartermaster Laundry Company. The 586th occupied two warehouses in the Pando area and handled up to three thousand bundles of laundry per day. The 250-man company quickly

gained respect among the mountain troopers as an essential part of the mission of Camp Hale. Its members received the same basic training as any other soldier and continued to qualify with their M1 carbine rifles even while at Camp Hale.

236. *Camp Hale Ski-Zette* 2, no. 3 (January 21, 1943).

237. Ibid. 1, no. 31 (August 6, 1943).

238. Ibid. 2, no. 5 (February 11, 1943). Camp Hale bakers referred to their special concoction for making bread as a "formula" instead of a "recipe." Apparently, their formula turned out quite well, as they won second place in the 7th Service Command survey of all camp bakeries.

239. Fine and Remington, *Corps of Engineers Construction in the United States*, 342.

240. Ibid.

241. Sometime between April 18 and May 14, 1942, the army promoted Captain Ballard to major.

242. *Herald Democrat*, "Here's How."

243. Area Engineer, "Camp Hale Colorado," part 1b, 8.

244. Ibid., part 3, 58.

245. Smith, "Camp Hale, Colorado," 2.

246. Ibid.

247. *Herald Democrat*, "Postoffice [*sic*]."

248. Ibid., "Here's How."

249. Ibid., "Types of Workers."

250. According to the Camp Hale Completion Report (part 7, p. 8), Camp Hale experienced a higher labor turnover rate than most cantonments constructed during World War II given the altitude, the remoteness from activity, the great distances from home and family ties and the inconveniences of "roughing it" in a construction camp. Between the beginning and end of work at Camp Hale, about 40,000 individuals labored there, with a peak of 11,425 at one time.

251. Smith, "Camp Hale, Colorado," 2.

252. Thruelsen, "10th Caught It All."

CHAPTER 4

253. "Camp Hale Builders."

254. *Rocky Mountain News* "Army's Ski Camp."

255. *Herald Democrat*, "Handpicked Soldiers."

256. Ellis, "Mr. Irving Hale."

257. Ibid.

258. Taos, New Mexico, is located about seventy miles northeast of Santa Fe and fifty miles from the Colorado border. The arrival of Mexican Americans in Colorado for work at Pando was not the first time that Mexican Americans came to the state seeking employment. In an interview with Gustav Henry Meyer on December 27, 1944, by Erl H. Ellis at Eagle, Colorado, Meyer commented that Mexican Americans labored on the narrow-gauge railroad when it was constructed in the late nineteenth century.

259. *Pando Echo* 1, no. 8 (September 8, 1942).

260. Ibid.

261. Ibid.

262. *Herald Democrat*, "Dismissal of Men."

263. Ibid.

264. Ibid.

265. Ibid.

266. Ibid.

267. Ibid., "Discharged Camp Workers."

268. Ibid.

269. Ibid.

270. Ibid.

271. Ibid.

272. Ibid.

273. Ibid.

274. Ibid.

275. *Denver Post*, "Workers to Hold Jobs."

276. Ibid.

277. Ibid.

278. Ibid.

279. Ibid.

280. *Herald Democrat*, "Camp Hale, Construction Miracle."

281. Ibid.

282. Ibid., "Gym Will Be Used." Leadville High School, built in 1900 on 120 West Ninth Street, is now the Federally Chartered National Mining Hall of Fame and Museum.

283. Ibid.

284. *Pueblo Chieftain*, "CCC Camp Buildings." The Civilian Conservation Corps (CCC), established during the first one hundred days of President Franklin Delano Roosevelt's first term in office in 1933, provided jobs to

thousands of unemployed young men in the country. These men became part of a peacetime army that battled erosion and habitat destruction and planted billions of trees while building dams and other structures in state and national parks around the country. On June 30, 1942, Congress voted to cut funding for the CCC, effectively ending the organization. The CCC disbanded due to increased spending on the war, and therefore, the buildings sent to Camp Hale appropriately served the new wartime employees and eventually the soldiers in their training.

285. Ibid.
286. *Herald Democrat*, "Spanish-American, Negro Workers."
287. Ibid.
288. Ibid.
289. Ibid.
290. Ibid.
291. Ibid.
292. Ibid., "Workers at Pando."
293. Ibid.
294. Women also worked in many other jobs around Camp Hale during its construction. Some of these jobs included secretarial work, records management, cooking in the mess halls and typing. One soldier even recalled seeing some of these women greet him at the Pando, Denver & Rio Grande Western Railroad stop while passing through, as a gesture of support for the troops.
295. *Herald Democrat*, "Pando Bond Sales."
296. *Pando Echo* 1, no. 7 (September 1, 1942).
297. Ibid.
298. Ibid., no. 8 (September 8, 1942).
299. Ibid., no. 9 (September 15, 1942).
300. Carroll, "Feeding the Multitudes."
301. Smith, "Camp Hale, Colorado."
302. Ibid.
303. *Herald Democrat*, "Two Youths Jailed."
304. Ibid., "3,000 Workers."
305. Ibid., "Job of Constructing."
306. Ibid.
307. Ibid.
308. *Camp Hale Ski-Zette* 2, no. 3 (January 21, 1944).
309. *Herald Democrat*, "Army Opportunity."
310. Ibid.

311. *New York Times*, "Skiing Doctors Needed."
312. *Herald Democrat*, "Camp Hale Bulletin."
313. Ibid. The system of qualified enlistees training officers on the ski slopes created problems for Camp Hale officials, as some officers refused to listen to orders from lower-ranking soldiers.
314. Gilbert to Mr. and Mrs. Henry Gramlin, January 25, 1943.
315. *Camp Hale Ski-Zette* 1, no. 27 (July 9, 1943).
316. *Pando Echo* 1, no. 12 (November 4, 1942).
317. Smith, "Camp Hale, Colorado."
318. Ibid.
319. *Pando Echo* 1, no. 12 (November 4, 1942). The commissary section at the cantonment had to accommodate hundreds of new workers into barracks and feed them daily.
320. Smith, "Camp Hale, Colorado."
321. Area Engineer, "Camp Hale Colorado," part 1b, 1–2.
322. Ibid., 2.
323. Ibid., 3–5. The bakery had the potential to produce fifteen thousand loaves a day and four hundred at any one time. On average, the bakers turned out five thousand loaves a day.
324. One hospital recreation room was called the "Handcraft Shop," where patients could work with wood and tools in order to make artistic ashtrays, picture frames, figurines and paintings on tiles for the All-Camp Art Exhibit.
325. Area Engineer, "Camp Hale Colorado," part 1b, 6–7.
326. The army designated the four rope tows as A and B for the two on the slopes south of 21st Street in Camp Hale and 1 and 4 for the two located one mile northwest of the camp, near U.S. Highway 24. Tow A had a length of 590 feet between start and finish with a rise of 142 feet, Tow B was 730 feet in length with a rise of 177 feet, Tow 1 was 640 feet in length with a rise of 120 feet and Tow 4 was 572 feet in length with a rise of 111 feet. The ropes ran at a speed of about 900 feet per minute with a capacity of about nine hundred men per hour for each tow. The tows within the Pando Valley obtained the name the "Pando Ski Area." This area of training held one-third of the ski training classes while the others took place at Cooper Hill. One ski instructor recalled a competition between his group, called "Pando Schussing & Sliding Club," and the ski instructors of the 87th Infantry in which they competed down a three-quarters of a mile giant slalom slope above Pando nicknamed "Pandomonium." All ski slopes in and around Pando, along with Cooper Hill, were cut out by soldiers and engineers for Camp Hale's use.

327. Jay, "History of the Mountain Training Center," 35.
328. *Pando Echo* 1, no. 13 (November 18, 1942). Cooper Hill was located at the top of Tennessee Pass. Army officials chose the site first because of its location along the railroad, second because of its rugged mountainous terrain and third due to its 250-inch average annual snowfall. The 7,000-foot T-bar lift consisted of a lower terminal building (10,576-foot elevation), an upper terminal (11,698-foot elevation) and twenty-one intermediate towers. The lower terminal building housed a gasoline motor that provided eighty-five horsepower at an elevation of 11,000 feet. The upper terminal consisted of three bents built of round timbers that supported a 20,720-pound tension weight. The three-quarter-inch hauling cable had 130 towing bars and moved at a rate of 400 feet per minute while carrying two skiers on each bar for a total capacity of five hundred skiers per hour. Construction on the lift started on September 8, 1942, and was completed on December 3, 1942. Also, four 500-foot ski tows were constructed on the mountain. Of the ten ski runs, five were novice runs, four were intermediate runs and one was an expert run. Six of the runs returned to the lower terminal, while the other four ended up at a distance of up to one to two miles away. After the war, the hill was called "Ski Cooper," and it served the skiing needs of the local population. Today, it has grown into a modern, seven-day-a-week ski resort for skiers from around the world.
329. Gibson, "On Cooper Hill," 60. According to the Camp Hale Completion Report (part 3, p. 82), these twelve barracks and two mess halls were reconstructed from dismantled Civilian Conservation Corps buildings from Parkdale, Colorado. The winter camp at Tennessee Pass had a capacity of six hundred soldiers. The amount of land totaled 2,275 acres at Tennessee Pass reserved for the War Department's use for military training.
330. *Camp Hale Ski-Zette* 1, no. 34 (August 27, 1943). The PX offered this service for members of the 90th, 85th and 86th Regiments at either Cooper Hill or Gold Park while on bivouac. The truck and trailer left Camp Hale at around noon and did not return until around nine or ten o'clock at night.
331. Gibson, "On Cooper Hill," 61.
332. Jay, "History of the Mountain Training Center," 64.
333. Burton, *Ski Troops*, 126–27.
334. Ibid., 7–9.
335. Jay, "History of the Mountain Training Center," 41. Toward the end of February 1944, .22-caliber rifle competitions were being held between the different regiments in the training halls. The 10th Division Special Service planned and organized the events.

336. Ibid., 73. On October 27, 1942, the Army Ground Forces allotted an extra $15,000 to the newly formed Mountain Training Center as "Special Field Exercise Funds." One of the suggested uses for this money included the construction of mountain log shelters on the peaks of mountains to train ski patrols. Unfortunately, this never materialized but did become the basis and inspiration for the postwar development of the Tenth Mountain Division Hut Association, which now operates twenty-nine backcountry huts in Colorado connected by around 350 miles of trails. The association was formed in the early 1980s, with the first huts, McNamara and Margy's, being completed during the summer of 1982.

337. *Camp Hale Ski-Zette* 1, no. 21 (May 26, 1943). Since all of the Camp Hale Military Reservation fell under control of the army—and, more specifically, the post engineer—during Camp Hale's existence, a reservation forester was consulted for practices and methods relating to forest management, timber stand improvement, forest culture, forest fire control, soil and water conservation, wildlife conservation, the construction of access roads and trails and the preservation of the cantonment area.

338. *Herald Democrat*, "Camp Hale, Construction Miracle."

339. *Pando Echo* 1, no. 13 (November 18, 1942).

340. Ibid.

341. Ibid.

342. Ibid.

343. "Camp Hale Builders."

344. *Pando Echo* 1, no. 13 (November 18, 1942).

345. Area Engineer, "Camp Hale Colorado," part 8, form 39-A, 1.

346. *Camp Hale Ski-Zette* 1, no. 21 (May 26, 1943).

347. Ibid.

348. Robinson, "Building of Camp Hale."

CHAPTER 5

349. Reynolds, "Preventive Medicine."

350. McLane, "Of Mules and Skis," 33.

351. Jay, "History of the Mountain Training Center," 26. Captain Woodward taught ski troopers how to shoot at the ranges in Fort Lewis and also how to be ski instructors at Paradise Lodge. He pioneered ski instructing in the U.S. Army with the help of Sergeant Walter Prager and Corporal Hal Burton. Eventually, Captain Woodward worked his way up to be

Lieutenant Colonel Woodward, in command of the 1st Battalion, 87th Mountain Infantry Regiment.

352. Ibid., 79.

353. Ibid.

354. Ellis, newspaper clippings.

355. Imbrie and Imbrie, "Chronology of the 10th Mountain Division." The 87th Mountain Infantry Regiment activated its 1st Battalion on November 15, 1941; its 2nd Battalion on May 1, 1942; and its 3rd Battalion on June 1, 1942. The activation of the 87th at Fort Lewis marked the beginning of what eventually became the 10th Mountain Division. However, before it obtained the "mountain" designation, the 87th joined with the 85th and 86th Infantry Regiments to form the 10th Light Division (Alpine) on July 15, 1943, at Camp Hale, Colorado. On November 6, 1944, the army officially named it the 10th Mountain Division. Originally, the 10th Mountain Division patch consisted solely of the crossed swords in blue and white. The "mountain rocker" did not come until later. The *Blizzard Newspaper* made an announcement on December 9, 1944, with a headline reading, "The Tenth Gets Mountain Patch." However, the army did not issue the "mountain" patch until May 1945.

356. The army started activating the Mountain Training Center in late August 1942 from the command staff of the 87th Mountain Infantry Regiment. It officially organized on September 3, 1942, with Colonel Rolfe in command at Camp Carson, Colorado. The MTC served as the command staff for the newly forming mountain division from August 1942 until July 15, 1943, when Brigadier General Lloyd E. Jones took command of the newly established 10th Light Division (Alpine) at Camp Hale. The original purpose of the MTC was to organize the most highly skilled skiers and mountaineers in one location so that they could branch out to different training locations to train units in mountain warfare. Once Camp Hale was established, this became the one mountain training location for the entire army, and thus the MTC moved here on November 16, 1942. Colonel Rolfe gave up command of the 87th and took control of the MTC.

357. The MTC served as the provisional command of the newly formed mountain division, which initially only consisted of the 87th Infantry Regiment. By November 15, 1942, the original completion date for the cantonment, 1,071 troops occupied Camp Hale. One month later, on December 15, 5,866 troops lived in the camp.

358. Jay, "History of the Mountain Training Center," 37.

359. Ibid., 38.

360. *Denver Post*, "Ski Battalion."

361. Ibid.

362. Ibid., "Jeeps, Mules and Toboggans."

363. Ibid.

364. Mules were primarily used until the snow began to rise above their bellies. At that point, the mules became ineffective, and the soldiers had to take over in hauling the artillery pieces. After significant experimenting and new designs in the summer of 1942, the mountain troops eventually were able to put up to eight ammo chests, along with a mounted machine gun ready for action, on a single mule.

365. *Camp Hale Ski-Zette* 1, no. 21 (May 26, 1943).

366. *Rocky Mountain News*, "Camp Hale Troops."

367. *Army Hour*.

368. Almost directly across from the 10th Mountain Division memorial at the top of Tennessee Pass, bivouac campsites can still be found with various tin cans still lying around. The infantry soldiers of Camp Hale primarily used two bivouac sites: Cooper Hill/Tennessee Pass and Gold Park. The artillery bivouacked at Ptarmigan Hill and the engineers near Resolution Creek at McAllister Gulch. The artillery used Mitchell Creek as one of its primary heavy explosive areas for the 75mm rounds.

369. Ibid. Colonel Ruffner affectionately referred to all of his men as heroes, as they had to learn how to use newly issued snowshoes while pulling toboggans full of 75mm howitzer gun parts up and down steep slopes.

370. Jay, "History of the Mountain Training Center," 38.

371. Ibid., 38, 51. After an attempt to reorganize the 10th Cavalry Reconnaissance Troop in April 1943, General Rolfe eventually scrapped it from the 10th Light Division (Alpine) table of organization. The troops reformed on May 7, 1943, under the leadership of Captain John Woodward and then acquired experienced mountaineers, along with mechanized transportation in place of horses. During the summer of 1943, the unit taught rock climbing to elements of the 10th Light Division (Alpine). Since the unit basically consisted of all infantry soldiers highly skilled in mountaineering, attempts were made to change its name from the 10th Cavalry Reconnaissance Troop to the 10th Reconnaissance Company. However, this attempt failed, and the unit slowly faded away as soldiers were transferred to the Mountain Training Group and the 10th Light Division (Alpine).

372. *Camp Hale Ski-Zette* 1, no. 27 (July 9, 1943).

373. Ibid.

374. Imbrie and Imbrie, "Chronology of the 10th Mountain Division." The origins of the 99th Infantry Battalion date back to a May 9, 1942 letter from the War Department to the Army Ground Forces requesting the formation of a battalion of Norwegian nationals to serve as part of the U.S. Army. The unit formed up in the summer 1942 in Minnesota, which had a strong Norwegian heritage, and most soldiers completed basic training at Camp Ripley, Minnesota. The unit trained for just a couple months at Fort Snelling, Minnesota, from September to the middle of December 1942, when it moved to Camp Hale. The Norsemen of the 99th "Norwegian battalion" had only one requirement for membership: the ability to speak Norwegian. These first- and second-generation Norwegians formed a unique unit that kept its cultural heritage relevant and current through the publication of a newspaper called the *Viking* while training at Camp Hale and Camp Carson. The unit trained at Camp Hale for only a brief period of time as it left for Camp Shanks, New York, on August 27, 1943, in order to prepare for a landing on Omaha Beach on June 22, 1944, several weeks after D-day. The unit saw combat action throughout Europe until the end of the war in Europe in May 1945.

375. Nyquist, *99th Battalion*, 61.

376. The 126th Engineer Mountain Battalion emblem contained a beaver with Mount of the Holy Cross in the background. The Latin words *Aedificamus et destruimus* go across the emblem and mean "We build and we destroy."

377. Imbrie and Imbrie, "Chronology of the 10th Mountain Division." Also around this same time, members from the 110th Mountain Signal Company came from Camp Carson to Camp Hale. The signal company had an interesting existence from its start at Camp Hale. Eventually, over half of its members had to be transferred to a different unit and location because they could not handle the cold climate, high altitude and rugged mountain life.

378. *Camp Hale Ski-Zette* 1, no. 38 (September 24, 1943).

379. Camp Hale Public Relations Office, *Camp Hale Colorado*, 2.

380. *Camp Hale Ski-Zette* 1, no. 27 (July 9, 1943).

381. Jay, "History of the Mountain Training Center," 45–46.

382. Markwell, "War Stories."

383. *Camp Hale Ski-Zette* 1, no. 33 (August 20, 1943).

384. Ibid., no. 38 (September 24, 1943).

385. Markwell, "War Stories."

386. Govan, "Training for Mountain and Winter Warfare," 4.

387. Ibid. From August 2, 1943, to July 1, 1944, regimental combat teams from the 28th, 31st, 35th, 77th and 95th Infantry Divisions were given training in mountainous terrain.

388. Ibid.

389. Ibid.

390. Raffi Bedayn, quoted in Markwell, "War Stories." A plaque placed on a rock at Seneca Rocks, Monongahela National Forest, says, "In Honor of the 10th Mountain Division and the soldiers they trained here on Seneca Rocks. In 1943–44 these men climbed here to prepare themselves for the difficulties of mountain warfare before facing action during World War II."

391. Jay, "History of the Mountain Training Center," 53. The reason that a majority of the first mountain troops to make up the MTC came from the South was that at the time, the MTC needed cadre and these units were available to be pieced out for training purposes due to shortages of essential troops within their own ranks that prevented them from being used elsewhere. The MTC had to weed out soldiers who could not handle Camp Hale, which resulted in many lost training days.

392. Burton, *Ski Troops*, 124; *Camp Hale Ski-Zette* 1, no. 43 (October 29, 1943).

393. Gilbert to Mr. and Mrs. Henry Gramlin, January 25, 1943.

394. Sievers to Flora Sievers, August 11, 1943.

395. Burton, *Ski Troops*, 59.

396. *Camp Hale Ski-Zette* 2, no. 14 (April 14, 1944).

397. Ibid.

398. Gibson, "O.K., Fellows," 22.

399. Claus Høie, quoted in Nyquist, *99th Battalion*, 68.

400. A board of medical officers convened at Camp Hale on February 27, 1943, to discuss whether or not special physical standards should be set for soldiers entering the mountain troops. Ultimately, the medical officers concluded that the current standards were sufficient, and the surgeon general agreed. Thus, soldiers who could not mentally or physically handle the mountain training were reassigned only after this was proven while training at Camp Hale.

401. *Camp Hale Ski-Zette* 1, no. 42 (October 22, 1943).

402. *Herald Democrat*, "Camp Hale Chaplain."

403. Ibid., "Catholic Chaplains Now at Camp Hale."

404. The American Red Cross office at Camp Hale also contributed significantly to helping boost morale among the soldiers. According to Red Cross field director Howard E. Sherd in the January 1, 1943 issue of the *Ski-Zette*, the Red Cross had two primary duties: bolster morale by relieving anxiety

and worry of any member of the armed forces and collect confidential information about the home conditions of soldiers to warrant discharges and furloughs for the troops. Local Red Cross chapters in Colorado, such as those of Montrose, Delta and Hotchkiss, donated furniture and other goods, such as framed pictures, to the cantonment to help furnish the buildings and make the camp feel more comfortable during leisure time.

405. Smith, "Camp Hale, Colorado."

406. *Herald Democrat*, "Highway Is Open."

407. *Pando Echo* 1, no. 1 (December 18, 1942).

408. Corporal Ralph Pugh, member of the Headquarters Detachment DEML, contributed the winning name for the paper. Other top choices included the "Mountaineer," the "Mountain Echo," "Top of the World News," "Pandorama," "Snow Blizzard," "Mule Journal" and "Donkey Serenade." In the Christmas Day issue of the *Camp Hale Ski-Zette*, writers sought various correspondents from around the camp in order to make the newspaper a unique and diversified look at all aspects of Camp Hale life.

409. The army promoted Colonel Onslow S. Rolfe on December 11, 1942, to a brigadier general as the commander of Camp Hale. Prior to his position as camp commander, Rolfe served as a regular army cavalry officer who eventually received an assignment to the 87th Mountain Infantry Regiment. Apparently, the army found out he was born in New Hampshire and assumed he would be familiar with skiing. As it turned out, Rolfe knew little about skiing or the mountains but soon grew to appreciate their role in the war.

410. The Camp Hale Service Club was the only recreational facility in the camp reserved exclusively for enlisted men in December 1942. The club consisted of a lounge, a dance floor, a game room, a library with reading rooms and a phone room with ten phones for calling long distance.

411. Ibid.

412. *Camp Hale Ski-Zette* 1, no. 50 (December 17, 1943).

413. Ibid.

414. *Herald Democrat*, "Camp Hale Theater."

415. *Camp Hale Ski-Zette* 1, no. 2 (December 25, 1942). Gifts to the soldiers included books, comic magazines, games, puzzles and other small items.

416. Camp Hale even had guest quarters for enlisted men's families located at 11th and B Streets at a cost of seventy-five cents for a single room and one dollar for a double for a maximum of three nights.

417. *Camp Hale Ski-Zette* 2, no. 12 (March 31, 1944). In November 1942, members of the Mountain Training Center G-3 section began putting

together a manual that outlined the basics of what a ski trooper needed to know. However, the MTC never finished the manual and only completed three chapters: 4, Organizational Equipment; 10, Snow Avalanches; and 11, Military Skiing. The MTC labeled the document "Proposed Manual for Mountain Troops," and this is exactly the way it stayed since it never went into official publication. Chapter 4 (Organizational Equipment) details how mountain troopers were to attach the rifle to the rucksack and how it could be used in an emergency by quickly disengaging the sling strap from the ring. The manual says, "A quick downpull on the sling strap tab will disengage the ring from the left shoulder strap and free the muzzle of the rifle. Without disengaging the snap at the lower sling swivel, the rifle may be used from the hip in the assault position, or it may be unsnapped and freed completely." According to John Woodward, ski instructor at Paradise Lodge and Camp Hale, most instructors wrote their own manuals, and nothing was largely distributed to soldiers beyond those that were ski instructions. However, there is reason to believe that Frank Harper's book, *Military Ski Manual: A Handbook for Ski and Mountain Troops* (published in early 1943), may have been used by enlisted men at Camp Hale on a personal basis toward the end of 1943.

418. The trek uphill to Cooper Hill and on various other well-established paths around Camp Hale was difficult enough for most ski troopers. However, some received the order to blaze their own paths one hundred yards off to each side as "flank security." These soldiers not only had to blaze their own trail but also faced sinking into multiple feet of snow.

419. *Camp Hale Ski-Zette* 2, no. 12 (March 31, 1944). They constructed the snow huts out of hard blocks of snow and put pine boughs on the floors with their sleeping bags on top.

420. *What's My Name?* [*Camp Hale Ski-Zette*], December 18, 1942.

421. Jay, "History of the Mountain Training Center," 63. Camp Hale instructors taught all of the infantry regiments, the signal company and 10 percent of the other support units ski skills. Only the weapons platoons and the other 90 percent of support units received extensive training in snowshoeing.

422. Elkins, "GI Skiing," 50–51.

423. Ibid.

424. Ibid. Ski instructors taught the Arlberg System, the product of Austrian ski instructor Hannes Schneider. Schneider became a pinnacle instructor of skiing for the ski troopers after moving from Austria to Cranmore Mountain Ski Resort, North Conway, New Hampshire, in 1939. His son, Herbert, became a member of the Headquarters Company, 86th Mountain

Infantry Regiment. Instructors at Camp Hale manipulated his method to accommodate the heavy ninety-pound rucksacks the skiers carried.

425. Ibid.

426. Harper, *Skiing for the Millions*, 19.

427. *Denver Post*, "Camp Hale Dogs." Ski training ended during the summer of 1943 due to warmer weather melting all the mountain snow. However, training commenced once again beginning on November 15, 1943.

428. Sievers to Flora Sievers, April 11, 1943.

429. Ibid., March 23, 1943.

430. *Camp Hale Ski-Zette* 2, no. 4 (February 4, 1944).

431. Merrill J. Clark III, quoted in Jeffrey L. Meek, *They Answered the Call*, 97.

432. According to Hal Burton, the army knew little about ski training, mountain training and cold-weather survival. Thus, in early 1942, the army signed a written contract with the National Ski Association making the Ski Patrol an official recruiting agency for the strength and maintenance of the newly formed ski trooper units. The National Ski Patrol became the first and only civilian organization to recruit for the U.S. Army in the history of the country. Every prospective candidate for the ski troopers had to complete a questionnaire and submit three letters of recommendation, ensuring that they brought much-needed experience to the units. The National Ski Patrol also cooperated with the War Department to organize airplane crash rescue units for less densely populated areas in the United States.

433. The remnants of rock climbing at Camp Hale can still be seen today on the east side of the main length of the valley. Various rusted pitons remain in the rocks on the one-hundred-foot cliffs. There is a sign placed there on the side of the road, partially funded by a State Historic Fund grant awarded from the Colorado Historical Society. In August 1943, the rock-climbing school moved from Camp Hale three miles north to the cliffs along Homestake Creek. Training in rock climbing included techniques, route selection and navigation.

434. Jay, "History of the Mountain Training Center," 89; Dole, "President and Aide Go Travelling—II," 78. Later, a more advanced model of the Weasel came out under the nomenclature "M-29." Minnie Dole commented on the Weasel in the 1945 *Ski Annual*, saying, "I'm convinced it will do damn near anything." The Weasel series of snow vehicles were not the only ones tested. In March 1943, the Mountain and Winter Warfare Board assigned the 123rd Ordnance Company to test the newly developed T-28 Trailblazer snow vehicle. Tests were conducted around Tennessee

Pass with the help of soldiers who blazed snowshoe trails through the mountains while trimming brush so that the vehicle had a clear path to follow. This testing finally came to an end in May 1943 as the 123rd Ordnance "hillbillies" left the Tennessee Pass testing area and returned to Camp Hale proper.

435. Ibid. Camp Hale needed well-trained mountain firefighters given its remote location and the risk of setting forest fires due to the 75mm pack artillery shells exploding in the National Forest.

436. Earle, "History of the 87th."

437. "Skiing Heritage," *Journal of the International Skiing History Association*, 14.

CHAPTER 6

438. Jay, "History of the Mountain Training Center," 22.

439. *Camp Hale Ski-Zette* 1, no. 3 (January 1, 1943). What was truly unique about this school for cooks was that it trained students how to cook at high altitudes. Some soldiers joked about the difficulty of making an angel food cake rise in high altitude.

440. Ibid.

441. Jay, "History of the Mountain Training Center," 53–54.

442. Ibid., 54.

443. Ibid.

444. The 86th Mountain Infantry Regiment scored higher than any other unit at Camp Hale on just about every test, training exercise and evaluation given to it.

445. *Denver Post*, "Troops Training at Camp Hale."

446. Ibid.

447. Casewit, *Mountain Troopers!*, 21.

448. Dole, *One Soldier's Story*, 9.

449. *Camp Hale Ski-Zette* 1, no. 42 (October 22, 1943).

450. Ibid.

451. The MTC had no special physical requirements for mountain troops. Soldiers who passed the basic army entrance physical exam were eligible to enter the mountain troops. General Rolfe did not agree with this but was unable to change its reality.

452. Jay, "History of the Mountain Training Center," 58.

453. Ibid.

454. *Camp Hale Ski-Zette* 1, no. 16 (April 21, 1943).

455. Ibid., no. 24 (June 16, 1943).

456. Ibid., no. 25 (June 25, 1943).

457. Cossin, *I Soldiered*, 7.

458. *Camp Hale Ski-Zette* 1, no. 4, January 8, 1943. Almost a year later in February 1944, Camp Hale sent a fifty-man team to the Alta Snow Cup Races at Alta, Utah, to compete against civilian skiers. Corporal Freidl Pfieffer won the Giant Slalom, and MTG ski troopers took noteworthy places in many other races. Many of these same ski troopers competed in the Steamboat Springs, Colorado tournament on February 12–13, 1944, while a few members of the MTG, detached to the Mediterranean as ski instructors, also organized a downhill ski event competing against local European ski experts. The Steamboat Springs tournament had a ski jump competition that was easily won by world-famous ski jumper Sergeant Torger Tokle with a jump of 226 feet.

459. *Denver Post*, "Troops Training at Camp Hale."

460. Ibid., "Camp Hale Dogs."

461. Ibid.

462. Ibid. The army trained many different breeds of dogs for service. The *Ski-Zette* identified only four breeds—chows, whippets, spaniels and setters—that could not be trained as K-9 dogs. The army set stringent requirements for these dogs, including good overall physical condition, at least twenty inches at the shoulder height and fifty pounds in weight.

463. Ibid. However glorious General Rolfe made the dogs out to be, later camp officials found that many of the sentry dogs bit their masters repeatedly, required around fifty men for twenty dogs, were not available in sufficient numbers for a tactical division and became useless on anything but a packed trail. The entire dog initiative at Camp Hale was eventually discarded by the Army Ground Forces as wasteful and inefficient.

464. *Denver Post*, "Denver Club."

465. *Camp Hale Ski-Zette* 1, no. 5 (January 15, 1943).

466. *Denver Post*, "Troops Training at Camp Hale."

467. Camp Hale had its very own twice-a-month broadcast from the Service Club on Denver's 850 KOA.

468. *Denver Post*, "Troops Training at Camp Hale."

469. Lund, "Skiing Down Those Golden Years."

470. Ibid.

471. *Camp Hale Ski-Zette* 1, no. 6 (January 22, 1943). About seven months later, in the beginning of August, Warner Brothers released its film titled *The Mountain Fighters* in Denver at the Welton Theater located at 1530 Welton

Street. The company spent almost an entire month filming the movie at Camp Hale. It quickly became a hit with the mountain troops, who viewed it on the big screen in the Camp Hale theaters and in Leadville at the Liberty Bell Theater.

472. By the end of January 1943, all of the camp's theaters were in full operation. One of the army's largest field houses opened for soldiers to participate in many sports, including volleyball, basketball, wrestling, boxing, badminton and tennis. All of the service clubs, Red Cross buildings and post exchanges opened also. The post exchanges provided mountain troops with Camp Hale memorabilia to send home so friends and family could experience a little bit of the unique nature and notoriety of the camp.

473. Lund, "Skiing Down Those Golden Years."

474. Ibid.

475. Ibid.

476. *Camp Hale Ski-Zette* 1, no. 8 (February 15, 1943).

477. Ibid.

478. Ibid., 57.

479. *Rocky Mountain News*, "Ski Troops Relax Requirements."

480. The American Alpine Club, the National Forest Service, the National Geographic Society, the American Geographical Society and the National Park Service all helped the National Ski Patrol and the army with recruiting.

481. *Steamboat Pilot*, "Ski Patrol Handles Recruiting."

482. Dole, "National Ski Patrol System Carries On," 55.

483. Ibid.

484. Jay, "History of the Mountain Training Center," 55.

485. Ibid.

486. Harper, *Military Ski Manual*, 7.

487. Morten Tuftedal, quoted in Nyquist, *99th Battalion*, 72.

488. Jay, "History of the Mountain Training Center," 46.

489. Morgan, "Special Training," 81.

490. Ibid.

491. Shelton, *Climb to Conquer*, 59.

492. Ibid.

493. *Camp Hale Ski-Zette* 2, no. 2 (January 14, 1943). Major John Wood of the Mountain and Winter Warfare Board calculated that a typical mountain trooper load consisted of eighty-four pounds, four ounces. Mountain troopers loved to joke about how soldiers left Camp Hale

with a permanent curvature in their spine, which fit their rucksacks well but brought pain later on. One soldier joked that the command wanted them to have "two hooks attached to the top of the sack, each hook to accommodate a barracks bag—then over each shoulder we should have a leather strap with a hook at each end, each hook to be attached to a foot locker. On top of all this, just pitch in your bunk and you have the definition of a well-equipped ski trooper."

494. Jenkins, *Last Ridge*, 60.

495. Captain Jack Tappin, quoted in Jay, "History of the Mountain Training Center," 37.

496. Shelton, *Climb to Conquer*, 59.

497. Jay, "History of the Mountain Training Center," 47.

498. Ibid., 85. The third supply drop mission experimented with dropping mountain rations, five-gallon gasoline containers, field telephones, wire, rucksacks, snowshoes and skis without parachutes into five feet of snow at 110 miles per hour. Additional aerial training included the use of gliders to lay 2 miles of wire after being cut loose over Turquoise Lake. Glider pilots proved they could land on packed snow at a speed of 95 miles per hour.

499. Ibid., 83–84.

500. Harry Poschman, quoted in Shelton, *Climb to Conquer*, 63.

501. Parker, *What'd You Do in the War, Dad?*, 41.

502. Ibid., 42.

503. Burton, *Ski Troops*, 129.

504. Jenkins, *Last Ridge*, 61.

505. Charles Dole, quoted in Shelton, *Climb to Conquer*, 64.

506. Jay, "History of the Mountain Training Center," 48.

507. Jenkins, *Last Ridge*, 61.

508. Ibid., 60.

509. Jay, "History of the Mountain Training Center," 48. As a result of the command's recognition of shortcomings in training, it called in Canadian arctic explorer and Dartmouth College director of polar studies Dr. Vilhjalmur Stefansson. Dr. Stefansson taught lessons in snow craft and showed soldiers how to build igloos for survival in extreme winter conditions in September 1943.

510. Burton, *Ski Troops*, 129. The phrase referred to the multiple cases of withdrawal from Russia, including Napoleon's and Hitler's, due to the freezing temperatures and ill-prepared soldiers.

511. Jay, "History of the Mountain Training Center," 48.

512. Sievers to Flora Sievers, March 23, 1943.

513. Jay, "History of the Mountain Training Center," 38.

514. Ski instructors faced difficult roadblocks in obtaining promotions while their counterparts in less important jobs received them frequently. Some of these highly skilled instructors gave up their teaching positions in order to obtain a slot in a promotable specialty. However, most kept their instructing jobs and simply suffered for it due to issues in Washington with promotions within the MTC.

515. *Camp Hale Ski-Zette* 1, no. 9 (March 1, 1943).

516. *Denver Post*, "Serious Fire at Camp Hale."

517. *Camp Hale Ski-Zette* 1, no. 9 (March 1, 1943).

518. *Rocky Mountain News*, "$250,000 Fire at Camp Hale." Three months later, in May 1943, engineers finished constructing a new twenty-thousand-square-foot building that expanded the Ordnance Service Command Shop and included a supply room, a paint shop, a carpenter shop, a blacksmith shop, a heavy duty shop, a welding and brazing shop, a grease building, a tire shop, a parts room and an administration building.

519. *Camp Hale Ski-Zette* 1, no. 12 (March 23, 1943).

520. Ibid., no. 31 (August 6, 1943).

521. Ibid., no. 17 (April 28, 1943).

522. Ibid., no. 25 (June 25, 1943).

523. Ibid., no. 31 (August 6, 1943).

524. Ibid.

525. Ibid. The blacktopping of roads never became a reality at Camp Hale.

526. *Camp Hale Ski-Zette* 1, no. 16 (May 21, 1943).

527. *Rocky Mountain News*, "Camp Hale Artillery."

528. Ibid.

529. *Camp Hale Ski-Zette* 1, no. 21 (May 26, 1943).

530. Ibid.

531. Ibid.

532. By the end of the summer of 1943, the 10th Light Division consisted of the 85th Mountain Infantry, 86th Mountain Infantry, 87th Mountain Infantry (deployed to Kiska), the 90th Infantry, 604th Field Artillery, 605th Field Artillery, 616th Field Artillery, 110th Signal Company, 10th Medical Battalion, 10th Mountain Anti-Tank Battalion and the 126th Engineer Mountain Battalion. The new light infantry division was developed primarily because of jungle operations in the South Pacific that demanded a smaller, trimmer force with more individual firepower.

533. Imbrie and Imbrie, "Chronology of the 10th Mountain Division."

534. Ibid.

535. *Camp Hale Ski-Zette* 1, no. 39 (October 1, 1943); no. 42 (October 22, 1943). The 226th Motorized Engineer Company became the rival of the rest of the 126th Engineers because though all the men were engineers, they had different equipment and missions. The other company of the 126th had mules, and the 226th did not. The 126th were heavily involved in rock climbing while the 226th were more in tune with building aerial tramways. One soldier of the 226th commented derisively about the 126th, saying, "We went out in weather that was too tough for the rock climbers and put up a tramway so they could ride in style over the steeper slopes." The rivalry was real but all in good fun, as the two companies traversed the mountains together in support of the infantry.

536. *Camp Hale Ski-Zette* 1, no. 42 (October 22, 1943)

537. Ibid.

538. With the replacement of the Mountain Training Center by the 10th Light Division (Alpine), the army transferred the units of the MTC to the 10th Light Division. After July 15, 1943, only about one hundred officers and enlisted men remained in the Mountain Training Center, and all of them were unsuited for tactical combat due to either a lack of training or physical handicaps.

CHAPTER 7

539. *Camp Hale Ski-Zette* 1, no. 22 (June 2, 1943).

540. Ibid. Congress formed the Women's Auxiliary Army Corps (WAAC) through a congressional bill passed on March 15, 1942. Similarly, Congress introduced women into the ranks of the navy four months later, on July 30, 1942, by passing the Women's Naval Reserve Act. This act formed the WAVES (Women Accepted for Volunteer Emergency Service) and the Marine Corps Women's Reserve. The difference between women in the army and those in the navy was that the women in the navy were truly in the navy whereas women in the army were only part of an "auxiliary."

541. Ibid.

542. Ibid., no. 24 (June 16, 1943). Columbia Pictures Corporation produced a movie called *Lost Horizon* in 1937 that was directed by Frank Capra. In this movie, a British diplomat and his civilian staff crash-land their airplane in the valley of Shangri-la in the Himalayan Mountains. The local people of the valley, along with the mountains that surrounded the valley, protected them from the outside world, where the clouds of World War II were gathering.

Thus, a WAAC referral to this movie in describing Camp Hale makes sense, given the conditions and surrounding mountains.

543. Stone, "Food Was S.O.S."

544. The exclusion of the WAAC from the actual army did not change until July 3, 1943, when the WAAC became the Women's Army Corps by an act of Congress, giving women full military status. This meant that all the ranks of the WAAC switched over to the same rank system used by the soldiers of the army. Also, the WAC entitled all female personnel to government insurance (National Service Life Insurance), allotments and free mailing privileges.

545. The WAAC proved to be so successful that the army decided to more than double its numbers in 1943 from 60,000 to 150,000.

546. *Camp Hale Ski-Zette* 1, no. 22 (June 2, 1943).

547. Ibid., no. 26 (July 2, 1943).

548. Stone, "My Brother-in-Law."

549. Ibid., "We Knew We Had a Job to Do."

550. *Camp Hale Ski-Zette* 2, no. 24 (June 23, 1943).

551. Courting between soldiers and WAACs was not uncommon, but the army frowned upon it. Standard operating procedures developed around the country at air bases, posts and other military installations required soldiers to first have an invitation from a woman for him to pick her up and then he had to withstand inspection by the area guard. He then had to sign her out and, upon returning her to the post, sign her back in. The army had rules against fraternization and tried diligently to protect the WAACs.

552. *Camp Hale Ski-Zette* 1, no. 23 (June 9, 1943).

553. Ibid., no. 33 (August 20, 1943).

554. Ibid., no. 23 (June 9, 1943).

555. Ibid.

556. Ibid., no. 27 (July 9, 1943).

557. Ibid.

558. Camp Crowder was built in 1941 as a training site for the U.S. Army Signal Corps. The camp housed white and black soldiers, male and female, as well as German and Italian prisoners of war during its World War II years. The army deactivated the camp in 1958 and declared it surplus property in 1962. Crowder College now operates on the grounds and in the buildings once used by the army.

559. *Camp Hale Ski-Zette* 1, no. 24 (June 16, 1943).

560. Ibid., no. 25 (June 25, 1943). Most of the WAACs completed basic combat training at Fort Des Moines, Iowa, or Daytona Beach, Florida.

561. Ibid., no. 37 (September 17, 1943). The WAAC became the WAC, or Women's Army Corps, on September 1, 1943.

562. Ibid., no. 27 (July 9, 1943).

563. Ibid., no. 28 (July 16, 1943).

564. Ibid., no. 29 (July 23, 1943).

565. Ibid.

566. The WAAC Shack became the WAC Club in the beginning of December 1943.

567. *Camp Hale Ski-Zette* 1, no. 30 (July 30, 1943).

568. Corporal Ardes Porter came up with the idea of having indoor picnics. She obtained the nickname "the girl with the imagination plus." She left Camp Hale in September 1943 to attend the X-Ray Technicians Course at the Army and Navy Hospital in Hot Springs, Arkansas.

569. *Camp Hale Ski-Zette* 1, no. 33 (August 20, 1943).

570. Ibid., 1, no. 35 (September 3, 1943).

571. Hagen, "WACs of Camp Hale," 40.

572. *Camp Hale Ski-Zette* 1, no. 32 (August 13, 1943). The military's official designation of the WAC as being part of the U.S. Armed Forces did not actually occur until September 1, 1943. When the WAAC converted to the WAC, women were given the choice of enlisting in the army or to return to civilian life. Approximately 25 percent of women throughout the military returned to civilian life at this point. One WAC lieutenant by the name of Margaret E. Smith left the WAC detachment at Camp Hale due to physical reasons but returned shortly thereafter in a civilian capacity as director of the Service Club. She enjoyed Camp Hale so much that she desired to return after her discharge, and she accomplished this task. The *Ski-Zette* identifies that some women left the WAAC from Camp Hale and returned to civilian life, never to return.

573. Collinsworth, "Day We Took the Oath."

574. *Camp Hale Ski-Zette* 1, no. 33 (August 20, 1943).

575. Ibid., no. 40 (October 8, 1943). About 75 percent of the enlisted women reenlisted in the WAC during the transition.

576. Ibid., no. 44 (November 5, 1943).

577. Ibid.

578. Ibid., no. 47 (November 26, 1943). KP is a military acronym that stands for "Kitchen Patrol." Soldiers almost always enjoyed going to the field because there was no KP while on bivouac in the mountains. However, upon return, soldiers often times dreaded the duty, especially

over holidays. In addition to Thanksgiving, the WACs also volunteered for KP over Christmas.

579. Ibid., 2, no. 2 (January 14, 1943).

580. Ibid., no. 11 (March 24, 1944).

CHAPTER 8

581. *Herald Democrat*, "Leadville Is Whooping."

582. Ibid.

583. *Camp Hale Ski-Zette* 1, no. 36 (September 10, 1943).

584. Cassidy, *Off Limits*, 15.

585. *Camp Hale Ski-Zette* 1, no. 12 (March 23, 1943).

586. Ibid., no. 36 (September 10, 1943).

587. Ibid. 2, no. 4 (February 4, 1944).

588. Ibid. 1, no. 39 (October 1, 1943).

589. *Herald Democrat*, "Leadville Is Whooping."

590. Ibid. The Pioneer Club Bar originally opened on October 27, 1878, on Upper Chestnut Street and a year later moved to State Street, which is now West Second Street in Leadville. It served fine cigars, wines and liquors. The saloon also featured eight billiard tables, a bowling alley with two lanes and numerous gun fights during its heyday in the late nineteenth century. The establishment closed its doors in 1972 but then reopened in 1998 as the Pioneer Club Restaurant and Saloon, which still operates today in downtown Leadville, serving all-American food, including burgers, steaks and seafood. The saloon has been preserved to look today how it looked once it was rebuilt in 1881 after a fire burned it down.

591. Adolph Kuss, quoted in Lynda La Rocca, "Leadville's Last Whorehouse."

592. *Camp Hale Ski-Zette* 1, no. 35 (September 3, 1943).

593. *Herald Democrat*, "Leadville Is Whooping." The Leadville *Herald Democrat* reveals that, by this time, the official name had changed to West Second Street instead of State Street. However, many people still referred to it as "State Street."

594. Ibid. The individual who commented on the arrival of all of the workers was Garnett Murray. Murray played the piano in several Leadville spots for twenty-five years. The Pastime Bar, one of the locations at which Murray played, was founded in 1878. This bar claims to be the oldest original saloon on old State Street in Leadville while the Silver Dollar

Saloon claims to be the oldest bar. Both are still in operation today on West Second Street and Harrison Avenue, respectively.

595. *Camp Hale Ski-Zette* 1, no. 35 (September 3, 1943). Rumors of the streets being paved with gold were actually partially true. The slabs of concrete used to pave Harrison Avenue came out of the nearby mountains and contained gold deposits. In 1942, one thief made off with $500 worth of flagging.

596. Sievers to Flora Sievers, March 23, 1943.

597. *Camp Hale Ski-Zette*. 1, no. 9 (March 1, 1943).

598. Ibid., no. 10 (March 9, 1943).

599. Ibid. Taverns outside the city limits still remained out of bounds for soldiers.

600. *Denver Post*, "Leadville Welcomes."

601. *Camp Hale Ski-Zette* 1, no. 12 (March 23, 1943).

602. Ibid., no. 21 (May 26, 1943). By the end of December 1943, the *Camp Hale Variety Show at the Tabor Opera House* changed its name to *Halesapoppin*. The Tabor Opera House was built in 1879 by Horace Austin Warner Tabor. H.A.W. Tabor grew up in the Northeast working in stone quarries in Massachusetts and Maine. He married Augusta Pierce, his employer's daughter, in 1857. During the spring of 1859, the Tabors headed west through Denver to Leadville, fueled by rumors of gold. He struck it rich in various mining ventures in and around Leadville and quickly moved up in status as an influential individual in Colorado. He started in Leadville as a grocer and later became the town's first mayor and second postmaster. Along the way, he took up silver mining and eventually became a multimillionaire off the Matchless Mine and various other bonanzas. For the next twenty years, Tabor and his wife mined the surrounding land and became wealthy, eventually being worth about $10 million. In 1879, he built the Tabor Opera House as one of the most costly and solidly built structures in Colorado history. The materials for the three-story building were brought in by wagon and consisted of stone, brick, iron and Portland cement. The walls were sixteen inches thick, and surprisingly, the structure was completed in only one hundred days. During World War II, the Tabor Opera House was owned and operated by the Elks Lodge, which acquired it in 1901 and sold it in 1955. The Elks took great pride in bringing soldiers to the opera house and even held a large dance there for the soldiers on February 26, 1944, that featured a USO show and free refreshments upon the opening of their recreational center in the opera house. Today, the Tabor Opera House is undergoing restoration but continues to hold plays, concerts and operas.

603. Ibid.

604. Ibid., no. 25 (June 25, 1943). Camp Hale had a surprisingly large number of foreign soldiers who made their way into the U.S. Army. In the middle of June 1943, ninety-nine of them were given U.S. citizenship in proceedings in Leadville before Judge Luby.

605. Ibid., no. 30 (July 30, 1943).

606. The USO gave soldiers the opportunity to record their voice on a record and send it home to family or friends.

607. Brown, *Love Letter to Americans*, 230.

608. *Camp Hale Ski-Zette* 1, no. 24 (June 16, 1943). The Leadville Gulf Club was a nine-hole course located four miles west of Leadville. Soldiers were told to turn west from Harrison Avenue and Sixth Street by the Liberty Bell Theater. The road to the course left the Carleton Tunnel Road and turned left after a railroad track crossing and two bridges over the Arkansas River.

609. Ibid. 2, no. 3 (January 21, 1944).

610. Ibid.

611. In addition to providing many recreational opportunities, the surrounding communities also supported Camp Hale through the Camp Hale Camp and Hospital Council, which was composed of committees from fourteen different counties. By November 1943, the council had given Camp Hale 1,250 books, twenty-six radios, eighty-five card tables, fifteen rugs, seventy-one chairs, thirty-five lounge chairs, 114 lamps, 230 pairs of curtains, seven table tennis tables, thirty-two phonographs with records, tools, six desks, 150 ash stands, 101 pictures, nine pianos, nineteen davenports, two pool tables, games, puzzles and other items. Also, the Junior Red Cross, consisting of schoolchildren from around Colorado, helped make games, ping-pong tables, writing desks, tables, ash trays and various other items to furnish day rooms at Camp Hale.

612. *Grand Junction Daily Sentinel*, "Recreation Center Designated."

613. Ibid.

614. *Camp Hale Ski-Zette* 1, no. 17 (April 28, 1943).

615. Private Sievers was reassigned to the Headquarters Company 2nd Battalion, 86th Mountain Infantry Regiment, sometime between April 29, 1943, and May 14, 1943.

616. Sievers to Flora Sievers, April 6, 1943.

617. Ibid., April 19, 1943. Additionally, the rationing of meat and butter began on March 29, 1943, outside the army. This resulted in soldiers potentially facing the outside world without any ration books while on leave or even on weekend passes. As a result, the army sent out instructions

for soldiers to take their furlough papers to the local War Price and Rationing Board in whatever town they were visiting in order to obtain ration coupons. In order to combat meat shortage at Camp Hale, cooks began to serve venison that soldiers obtained during hunting season in and around Camp Hale. This provided them with a lean source of meat when rations were slim in the mess halls. Additionally, mess halls cooked up fish that were caught in the local streams, mainly from Homestake Creek and Lake Constantine.

618. Sievers to Flora Sievers, April 11, 1943.

619. Wallace Knutsen, quoted in Nyquist, *99th Battalion*, 63.

620. Gilbert to Mr. and Mrs. Henry Gramlin, January 25, 1943.

621. *Camp Hale Ski-Zette* 1, no. 17 (April 28, 1943).

622. Sievers to Flora Sievers, October 20, 1943. The War Production Board rationed ammunition for recreational use during World War II. Thankfully for the soldiers at Camp Hale, the board distributed enough ammunition to soldiers to make it through the fall hunting seasons. The army also authorized soldiers to bring their own guns and ammunition into Camp Hale for hunting purposes. All of it had to be registered with the post and stored by the quartermaster.

623. Hitchhiking in Colorado during World War II proved to be quite an easy task, according to several mountain veterans of Camp Hale. Soldiers commonly hopped rides with local residents, miners returning home from work and other GIs with vehicles.

624. Brown, *Love Letter to Americans*, 238.

625. Gale to Mrs. D.G. Gale, November 3, 1943.

626. Ibid., December 12, 1943.

627. Sievers to Flora Sievers, October 26, 1943. The high number of surprise visits from guests and family members of soldiers at Camp Hale resulted in the special services officer, Captain Ralph B. Major, to issue new regulations in the middle of March 1943 for visitors desiring to use the guesthouse. Rooms filled up quickly, especially on weekends. Guests were limited to a three-day stay at Camp Hale. Engineers constructed an enlisted men's guesthouse behind the Service Club and an officer's guesthouse south of the officer's club in between the 10th Division Headquarters and Highway 24. The American Red Cross recreation building at the station hospital at Camp Hale also hosted four rooms for visitors of patients.

628. Gale to Mrs. D.G. Gale, November 25, 1943.

629. *Denver Post*, "Denver Public Library." The Camp Hale library eventually had over two thousand books for circulation, national newspapers and

over seventy-five magazines on hand. Soldiers owed much of the success of the Camp Hale library to Miss Ann Leonard Samuels, who arrived on November 23, 1942, in order to establish a library. She later married Private Howard H. Dine of the 87th and helped establish the Camp Hale music room. She departed Camp Hale on December 23, 1943, in order to reside with her husband in Colorado Springs while he served at Camp Carson.

630. *Camp Hale Ski-Zette* 1, no. 16 (April 21, 1943). The music room in the Service Club was not the only place where ski troopers could hear some of the most popular tunes of the day. Camp Hale's loudspeaker system, which blasted retreat at the end of the day, also played some snappy tunes throughout the day and after retreat.

631. Camp Hale opened up a second Service Club in the middle of February 1944 in order to accommodate more recreational programs for the soldiers.

632. *Rocky Mountain News*, "Boxing Bouts Entertain Soldiers." Not only did Camp Hale soldiers box against one another, but big-name boxers, such as Sergeant Joe Louis and Corporal Ray "Sugar" Robinson, toured the country and performed exhibition fights for the soldiers as well. These two individuals visited Camp Hale in September 1943.

633. *Camp Hale Ski-Zette* 2, no. 19 (May 19, 1944).

634. Ibid., no. 21 (June 2, 1944).

635. Ibid. 1, no. 25 (June 25, 1943).

636. Ibid., no. 36 (September 10, 1943).

637. Ibid., no. 39 (October 1, 1943). The Climax Molybdenum Company is a subsidiary of Freeport-McMoRan Copper & Gold Inc. The company currently operates the largest molybdenum mine in the world, which is the Henderson Mine in Empire, Colorado. The Climax Mine originally opened in 1916 after a gray mineralized substance was found on the western slope of Bartlett Mountain in 1879. In 1895, Colorado School of Mines professor Rudolph George identified the substance as molybdenite. The mine soon went into full operation and provided metal for Allied armor plating and large gun barrels during World War I. During World War II, the company increased production of molybdenum, and in October 1942, Climax was awarded the army-navy "E" for an excellent record in contributing war materials for the war effort. It shut down most operations during the 1980s but regained prominence going into the twenty-first century as molybdenum prices rose to around $15 a pound. Freeport-McMoran has now spent around $700 million to revamp the mine into production, which began again in 2012.

638. Ibid., no. 8 (February 15, 1943).

639. Ibid.

640. Brown, *Love Letter to Americans*, 200.

641. The band moved from Camp Carson to Camp Hale under the name the 49th Engineers' Band.

642. *Camp Hale Ski-Zette* 1, no. 9 (March 1, 1943).

643. Ibid.

644. Ibid., no. 46 (November 19, 1943).

645. Ibid., no. 10 (March 9, 1943).

646. The Camp Hale Recreation Building was built using profits from the Camp Hale Theater, which showed movies to soldiers for a nominal fee. The total cost of the building was around $18,000.

647. *Camp Hale Ski-Zette* 1, no. 25 (March 25, 1943). The recreation building was open to enlisted men and women six days each week, with Wednesday evenings and Sunday nights being reserved for officers and civilian employees only.

648. Krear, *Journal of a U.S. Army Mountain Trooper*, 12.

649. Fay, *History of Skiing*, 60–68. Aspen became the premier skiing location for many soldiers who were serving at Camp Hale. Fay argues that the brief ban on soldiers mingling in Leadville might have cost the town a position that Aspen now holds. From the first arrival of soldiers at Camp Hale in October 1942 until February 1943, Leadville remained closed to soldiers. As a result, many of these soldiers took the train to the slopes of Aspen instead of those in and around the Leadville area. Fay additionally wrote that one such soldier who took advantage of Aspen was Friedl Pfeifer. In 1943, he met with the people of Aspen and expressed his interest to them in coming back after the war to build a ski area. While Pfeifer recovered from his combat injuries at a California hospital, Walter Paepcke contacted him and arranged for a meeting to discuss their mutual interest in Aspen.

650. *Denver Post*, "Tea Drinking 10th."

651. *Camp Hale Ski-Zette* 1, no. 18 (May 5, 1943). Miss Falkenburg starred in films such as *She Has What It Takes* and *Young and Beautiful* in 1943. She was born in South America but quickly became a magazine cover sensation in the United States during the war.

652. Ibid.

653. Ibid., no. 21 (May 26, 1943). During World War II, the technical name of this school was Eagle County High School. Locals oftentimes referred to it as Gypsum High School to distinguish it from other local high schools

with similar names. Today, the high school is called Eagle Valley High School, and it is still located in Gypsum, Colorado.

654. Ibid., no. 29 (July 23, 1943).

655. Ibid., no. 42 (October 22, 1943).

656. Ibid., no. 51 (December 24, 1943). By the end of December 1943, Camp Hale had its own skating rink located behind regimental headquarters of the 86th Mountain Infantry.

657. Ibid., no. 28 (July 16, 1943).

658. Ibid.

659. Ibid.

660. Some soldiers worked for free or for access to some type of recreation on the farm or ranch. Other soldiers worked through a program established by the U.S. Employment Agency that paid four dollars a day.

661. *Camp Hale Ski-Zette*, no. 28 (July 16, 1943).

662. Ibid., no. 34 (August 27, 1943).

663. Ibid.

664. Ibid., no. 33 (August 20, 1943).

665. Living off post proved to be a decent option for many because at the end of August 1943, the Office of Price Administration enacted federal rent regulations in the counties surrounding Camp Hale, including Chaffee, Lake, Eagle, Garland and Summit. This meant that renters could not charge more for houses, apartments, hotels, rooming houses, cottages, trailer camps and similar establishments than what they charged in March 1942 unless capital improvements had been made on the establishment.

666. Renovations included white asbestos siding, insulated walls and ceilings, modern plumbing, a shower in every apartment and hardwood floors.

667. The library obtained its first batch of eight cartons of books from the Denver Public Library in October 1943.

668. *Camp Hale Ski-Zette* 1, no. 40 (October 8, 1943). The Supply and Service Division's new commissary sales store opened at the end of November 1943 in the Pando area in order to benefit military personnel and their dependents. Groceries and other goods were sold at actual cost. However, the benefits of this store were not tailored to Camp Hale civilians.

669. Ibid., no. 42 (October 22, 1943). The Pando mess hall was constructed in order to handle 154 civilians at a time with a capacity of 1,000 per meal. Soldiers often envied the modern conveniences of this mess hall, as it had two electric ranges, an automatic dishwasher and a large walk-in refrigerator.

670. Ibid., no. 45 (November 12, 1943).

671. Ibid., no. 47 (November 26, 1943).

CHAPTER 9

672. Ibid., no. 44 (November 5, 1943).

673. Leland P. Bjerke, quoted in Nyquist, *99th Battalion*, 75.

674. Ragnar Abrahamsen, quoted in Nyquist, *99th Battalion*, 74.

675. Ibid., 75.

676. *Camp Hale Ski-Zette* 1, no. 45 (November 12, 1943).

677. Ibid., no. 45 (November 12, 1943).

678. Ibid.

679. Charles McLane, *Of Mules and Skis*, 21.

680. Jay, "History of the Mountain Training Center," 113.

681. Major John C. Jay in the *History of the Mountain Training Center* identified that "instruction teams" provided training three different times in the remaining few months of 1943. First, when the MTC transferred to the MTG, a team of twelve officers and twenty enlisted was already on the ground in Elkins, West Virginia, providing training in assault climbing for the 28th, 35th, 77th and 95th Divisions. Another group of thirty officers and one hundred enlisted men left in late October 1943 for Camp McCoy, Wisconsin, to provide training in cross-country skiing, snowshoeing and winter bivouacking for the 76th. Finally, a third group of officers and enlisted men traveled to Pine Camp, New York, to train soldiers of the 5th Armored Division.

682. Ibid. Nondivisional soldiers included anyone not assigned to the 10th Light Division. This included the Mountain Training Group; 10th Reconnaissance Troop; 10th Quartermaster Battalion; 7th, 37th and 38th Veterinary Companies; 126th and 226th Engineer Companies; and 252nd Quartermaster Laundry Company.

683. Ibid.

684. Ibid.

685. In September 1943, the 10th Reconnaissance sent a group of soldiers to Paradise Lodge at Mount Rainier in order to set up a school for ice and glacier work. The school had future plans to train units from other organizations that needed a background in movement on glaciers and in cold-weather survival. Some reference material still refers to the Mountain Training Group as the "Mountain Training Center" even after the army disbanded it. Captain Thomas P. Govan's "Training for Mountain and Winter Warfare Study No. 23" is one such document that makes references to the Mountain Training Center still supplying instructors to the West Virginia Maneuver Area up until March 15, 1944, when all instructors were transferred to the 8th Corps, which maintained the training in the

area. The West Virginia Training Area finally ceased operations on July 1, 1944, and the Mountain and Winter Warfare Board was disbanded. The interchangeable use of the two names is not a significant issue given that both essentially operated with the same mission of training soldiers for mountain and winter warfare whether they were at Camp Hale or somewhere else around the country.

686. Ibid.

687. Because the 10th Recon was never fully sourced for missions on a consistent basis, the men of the unit had the capability to go on long ski-mountaineering trips that lasted for three to five days. They also had the capability to scale Mount Massive (14,421) and Mount Elbert (14,433) on a consistent basis, especially during the winter months, when training for rock climbing slowed down.

688. *Camp Hale Ski-Zette* 1, no. 46 (November 12, 1943).

689. Ibid., no. 43 (October 29, 1943).

690. Ibid., no. 45 (November 12, 1943).

691. Ibid., no. 48 (December 3, 1943).

692. Cossin, *I Soldiered*, 6.

693. Gibson, "O.K., Fellows," 23.

694. *Denver Post*, "Many Refugees."

695. Ibid.

696. Camp Hale, "Prisoners of War," Metropolitan State University of Denver.

697. *Camp Hale Ski-Zette* 1, no. 49 (December 10, 1943).

698. Jenkins, *Last Ridge*, 111–12.

699. Ibid.

700. *Rocky Mountain News*, "Trespassing Led to Arrest."

701. Ibid., "Camp Hale Soldier." Maple and the two German prisoners of war entered Mexico near Ciudad Juárez but were stopped by an immigration official after trespassing on a private road near the town of Palomas, Chihauhua, three miles south of Juárez. The trio could not produce tourist cards and were therefore taken to Juárez in order to obtain them. Upon arriving at the station, a Mexican immigration official became suspicious of the two Germans, Earhard Schwichtenberg and Heinrich Kikilius, because they were both wearing blue denim shirts and of Maple because he was wearing his U.S. Army uniform. After running a check with U.S. data supplied to the immigration officials, they quickly realized that the trio was wanted in the United States, and they eventually revealed their identity without resisting arrest. U.S. officials moved the

two German prisoners of war to Camp Phillips, Kansas, while they took Maple to Fort Leavenworth, Kansas. The court-martial sentenced Maple to death by hanging, but President Roosevelt commuted Maple's sentence to life imprisonment and hard labor at Fort Leavenworth. The army further commuted his sentence to ten years in prison, and he was released in February 1951. Maple was a stellar student at Harvard University, but as the FBI had picked up on, he had pro-Nazi tendencies, which resulted in him getting kicked out of the ROTC program. He joined the army in February 1942 after graduating from Harvard and completed basic training at Fort Bragg. The army then sent him to Camp Hale with the 620th Engineer General Service Company in order to guard prisoners of war. Given that the FBI and the army both had files of suspicion on Maple, they assigned him to one of the only units unable to bear arms.

702. Ibid.

703. *Rocky Mountain News*, "Camp Hale Becomes POW Camp."

704. *Denver Post*, "German POWs Build Still."

705. Ibid.

706. *Rocky Mountain News*, "Camp Hale Becomes POW Camp."

707. Ibid.

708. *Camp Hale Ski-Zette* 1, no. 52 (December 31, 1943).

709. Ibid. 2, no. 3 (January 21, 1944).

710. *Denver Post*, "They Climbed."

711. Ibid.

712. At the summit, the soldiers all signed the summit registry, which was placed there by the Colorado Mountain Club in an iron container among the rock cairn. Even today, the Colorado Mountain Club continues to place summit registries on the top of Colorado's fourteeners. When the registries are full, they are removed and placed in the club's archives. Currently, some old and deteriorating registries are being restored by the American Alpine Club so that future generations can view the summit comments made by climbers and soldiers of the 10th Infantry.

713. *Camp Hale Ski-Zette* 2, no. 1 (January 7, 1943).

714. Ibid., no. 2 (January 14, 1943).

715. The engineers constructed a road going north out of Camp Hale following McAllister Gulch. The road today on maps is Road 708, which branches off northwest from Resolution Creek Road, just outside Camp Hale proper.

716. *Camp Hale Ski-Zette* 2, no. 23 (June 16, 1943). Meager also encouraged the soldiers to limit their use of branches off Engelmann Spruce trees,

which made tender, soft beds for soldiers in the field. He understood the sacrifices that soldiers had to make in the field on bivouac, but he also resented wanton destruction of the forest and its wildlife. On one occasion, he found a dying beaver left with a weak and irregular heartbeat after a bivouac in the area, which caused quite a stir in Camp Hale given that the female beaver was a protected species and this one was found with her head battered and teeth knocked out. Soldiers had killed her for the fun of it, according to witnesses, and little did they realize that she was also carrying five beaver pups inside of her.

717. Ibid.

718. Ibid., no. 4 (February 4, 1944).

719. Ibid., no. 6 (February 18, 1944).

720. Ibid.

721. Some soldiers used snowshoes instead of skis. The cross-country ski trails atop Tennessee Pass can still be seen and used in the winter months extending out west from Cooper Hill across Highway 24.

722. *Camp Hale Ski-Zette* 2, no. 7 (February 25, 1944).

723. Dole, "The President and Aide Go Travelling—II," 77.

724. Ibid.

725. Ibid.

726. *Camp Hale Ski-Zette* 2, no. 8 (March 3, 1944).

727. Ibid. Nothing but the Malta schoolhouse and its outhouse remain as remnants of the 1875 smelter town, located just outside the city limits of Leadville at the mouth of California Gulch, where Highway 24 turns south. From this staging area, the soldiers followed Half Moon Creek trail in between Mount Massive and Mount Elbert as they made their way up and over Champion–Deer Mountain Pass to the north fork of Lake Creek. On the third day, they crossed the Continental Divide around thirteen thousand feet in the Sawatch Range and then progressed through the Williams Range to the north fork of Hunter Creek. On the fourth day, they traveled down Hunter Creek and across Thimble Rock Ridge in order to gain an old pack road for the last eleven miles into Aspen.

728. Ibid., no. 16 (April 28, 1944).

729. Ibid.

730. Ibid., no. 17 (May 5, 1944).

731. Ibid.

732. Ibid., no. 18 (May 12, 1944). Also, the name, rank and organization of the winner were added each year to the trophy. Master Sergeant Clarence Campbell of the MTG took first place, Private First Class Robert D.

Wright of the 86th took second and Private First Class Armas S. Takola of the 86th took third. Thor Groswold of Denver also won a contract to make skis for the ski troopers at Camp Hale.

733. Ibid. The 87th Mountain Infantry Regiment returned from Kiska to Camp Hale on February 23, 1944, and joined the rest of the 10th Light Infantry Division.

734. Ibid., no. 10 (March 17, 1944).

735. Ibid.

736. Krear, *Journal of a U.S. Army Mountain Trooper*, 19.

737. Ibid., 20.

738. Ibid.

739. Ibid.

740. *Camp Hale Ski-Zette* 2, No. 9 (March 10, 1944).

741. Ibid., no. 11 (March 24, 1944).

742. Ibid.

743. Ibid.

744. Ibid., no. 12 (March 31, 1944).

745. Ibid.

746. Ibid. The original proposal according to the *Ski-Zette* included five weeks of training in the D-Series Maneuvers, but only three were used in reality. The harsh blizzard conditions led the command to shorten the training to just three weeks. Little did Colonel Strong realize that the weather was about to take a turn for the worse and the injuries were going to mount up significantly.

747. Casewit, *Mountain Troopers!*, 26.

748. Ibid.

749. *Camp Hale Ski-Zette* 2, no. 13 (April 7, 1944). Exceptionally deep snow in 1944 caused the mules of the 10th problems in transporting supplies up the mountains.

750. Casewit, *Mountain Troopers!*, 27.

751. Ibid.

752. Frank Harper, *Night Climb*, 160.

753. Krear, *Journal of a U.S. Army Mountain Trooper*, 22.

754. Johnson, *Soldiers of the Mountain*, 55.

755. *Camp Hale Ski-Zette* 2, no. 11 (March 24, 1944). The enemy force consisted of Colonel Paul G. Goode's 87th Infantry Regiment and its supporting artillery, the 616th Field Artillery, under the command of Lieutenant Colonel Philip C. Wehle. Colonel Goode proved his expert leadership capabilities during the D-Series Maneuvers. However, the

army transferred him to the European theater, where the Germans eventually captured him in combat. At the end of the war, he survived life in a Polish prisoner of war camp and gained the respect of those who survived with him.

756. *Rocky Mountain News*, "Battle Tactics."

757. Ibid.

758. Ibid.

759. Ibid. The enemy forces did not literally destroy most of what the umpires deemed as "destroyed." However, for the sake of the three-dimensional war games, they were quite effective. They did literally cut communication lines, which made the games even more real.

760. Umpires, who drove around in Weasels, often lost track of units and got lost in the blizzards. Some veterans of the D-Series Maneuvers recounted how all the umpires really did was complain about the cold, which led them to make bad judgments in officiating the war games.

761. Ibid.

762. Jenkins, *Last Ridge*, 119.

763. *Camp Hale Ski-Zette* 2, no. 19 (May 19, 1944).

764. Jenkins, *Last Ridge*, 119.

765. *Camp Hale Ski-Zette* 2, no. 19 (May 19, 1944).

766. Dusenbery, *Ski the High Trail*, 145.

767. Ralph Lafferty, quoted in Moran, "Camp Hale."

768. *Camp Hale Ski-Zette* 2, no. 19 (May 19, 1944).

769. Ludwig Foeger, quoted in Burton, *Ski Troops*, 138.

770. Burton, *Ski Troops*, 138.

771. Paul Goode, quoted in Burton, *Ski Troops*, 138.

772. Dusenbery, *Ski the High Trail*, 145.

773. *Camp Hale Ski-Zette* 2, no. 17 (May 5, 1944).

774. Ibid., no. 20 (May 26, 1944).

775. Ibid.

776. Ibid., no. 21 (June 2, 1944). Mountain warfare added an extra level of complexity for the artillery due to the changing elevations between mountain peaks, valleys and hills. Artillery observers could see only so much in the field, and so the school planned to train ten officers from each infantry regiment to assist when needed in directing fire through difficult terrain. These lieutenants went through a one-week course that taught them a scaled-down code of calling in their observations to the batteries for fire missions.

777. Minot Dole, quoted in Burton, *Ski Troops*, 139.

778. *Rocky Mountain News*, "March in the Infantry?" Infantry Day was a celebration of the infantry and, specifically, of the unique nature of the 10th Infantry Division. Soldiers scaled cliffs and repelled down in front of reporters and cameras, demonstrating the expertise and discipline of the mountain troops.

779. Sievers to Flora Sievers, September 16, 1943.

780. McLane, "Of Mules and Skis," 34.

EPILOGUE

781. *Denver Post*, "Plan to Junk Camp Hale."

782. Imbrie and Imbrie, "Chronology of the 10th Mountain Division."

783. Wilson, *U.S. Skiing*.

784. Ibid.

785. In 1992, Camp Hale was placed on the National Register of Historic Places.

BIBLIOGRAPHY

PRIMARY SOURCES

Adjutant General's Office, Record of Communication Received. "Report of Investigation by Board of Officers, Eighth Corps Area, of Proposed Camp Site in Pando, Colorado, Area." June 23, 1941. Metropolitan State University of Denver, Government Records and Documents. https://www.msudenver.edu/media/content/camphale/chh_003_Report_of_Investigation.pdf.

Area Engineer, Pando Constructors Engineering Section. "Camp Hale Colorado: 1942 Completion Report, Job Number Pando T1." Lake County Public Library, Colorado Mountain History Collection, Leadville Room, March 15, 1943.

The Army Hour. Camp Hale, Colorado Portion. January 17, 1943. Camp Hale History. Metropolitan State University of Denver. https://www.msudenver.edu/media/content/camphale/chh_003_The_Army_Hour.pdf.

Bradley, Charles C. "A Mountain Soldier Sings." In *American Ski Annual 1945*. Edited by Roger Langley. N.p.: Your Sport, Inc., 1944.

"Camp Hale Builders Win Race Against Time: The Job Is Done." Memoir, Tenth Mountain Division TMD1, Box 2, Range 18B, Section 1, Shelf 2, FF 28. Denver Public Library, Western History and Genealogy, circa 1942.

Camp Hale Public Relations Office, ed. *Camp Hale Colorado*. N.p.: Parade Publications, Inc., 1943.

Camp Hale Ski-Zette 1, nos. 1–6, 8–10, 12, 16–18, 21–40, 42–52. Lake County Public Library, Leadville, Colorado, Colorado Mountain History Collection.

————. Vol. 2, nos. 1–14, 16–24. Lake County Public Library, Leadville, Colorado, Colorado Mountain History Collection.

Carroll, J. Hunter. "Dismantling and Salvage: Camp Hale, Pando, Colo." Memoir, M1966 Carroll, J. Hunter Papers (TMD Related) STX V; RG 4; Section 3; SF 5; Box 33. Denver Public Library, Western History and Genealogy.

————. "Feeding the Multitudes in the Mountains." Memoir, M1966 Carroll, J. Hunter Papers (TMD Related) STX V, RG 4, Section 3, SF 5, Box 33. Denver Public Library, Western History and Genealogy.

Collinsworth, Emily. "The Day We Took the Oath of Regular Army." Video interviews. Women in the Military. Metropolitan State University of Denver. https://www.msudenver.edu/camphale/resources/interviews/emilycollinsworth/.

Dole, Charles Minot. "The National Ski Patrol System Carries On." In *American Ski Annual 1944*. Edited by Roger Langley. N.p.: Your Sport, Inc., 1944.

————. "The President and Aide Go Travelling—II." In *American Ski Annual 1945*. Edited by Roger Langley. N.p.: Your Sport, Inc., 1944.

Elkins, Frank. "GI Skiing." In *American Ski Annual 1945*. Edited by Roger Langley. N.p.: Your Sport, Inc., 1944.

Ellis, Erl H. "Camp Hale Construction." Notes (typed). Colorado History Project–Camp Hale. Erl H. Ellis Collection, WH1737 Box 1, Range 9A, Section 12, Shelf 3, FF 20. Denver Public Library, Western History and Genealogy, 1945.

————. Correspondence Received, Sent (typed) August 1942. Colorado History Project–Camp Hale. Erl H. Ellis Collection, WH1737 Box 1, Range 9A, Section 12, Shelf 3, FF 5. Denver Public Library, Western History and Genealogy.

————. Correspondence Received, Sent (typed). Colorado History Project–Camp Hale. Erl. H. Ellis Collection, WH1737 Box 1, Range 9A, Section 12, Shelf 3, FF 18. Denver Public Library, Western History and Genealogy, 1945.

————. Correspondence Received, Sent (typed) February 7, 1945. Colorado History Project–Camp Hale. Erl H. Ellis Collection, WH1737 Box 1, Range 9A, Section 12, Shelf 3, FF 8. Denver Public Library, Western History and Genealogy.

————. Correspondence Received, Sent (typed) October–December 1944. Colorado History Project–Camp Hale. Erl H. Ellis Collection, WH1737 Box 1, Range 9A, Section 12, Shelf 3, FF 6. Denver Public Library, Western History and Genealogy.

———. "Mr. Irving Hale, Attorney at Law, First National Bank Bldg, Denver, Colorado." Hale, General Irving: Correspondence Regarding, Biographical Sketch. Erl H. Ellis Collection, WH1737 Box 1, Range 9A, Section 12, Shelf 3, FF 16. Denver Public Library, Western History and Genealogy.

———. Newspaper clippings (typed). Colorado History Project–Camp Hale. Erl H. Ellis Collection, WH1737 Box 1, Range 9A, Section 12, Shelf 3, FF 14. Denver Public Library, Western History and Genealogy.

Gale, Donnell G. Letters, November 1, 1943; November 3, 1943; November 25, 1943; December 12, 1943. In author's personal collection.

Gibson, Edwin. "O.K., Fellows." In *American Ski Annual 1944*. Edited by Roger Langley. N.p.: Your Sport, Inc., 1944.

———. "On Cooper Hill." In *American Ski Annual 1945*. Edited by Roger Langley. N.p.: Your Sport, Inc., 1944.

Gilbert, Clarence E. Letter, January 25, 1943. In author's personal collection.

Govan, Thomas P. "History of the 10th Light Division (Alpine)." Study No. 28, 1946. DTIC Online, Information for the Defense Community. Historical Section Army Ground Forces. http://www.dtic.mil/dtic/tr/fulltext/u2/a954912.pdf.

———. "Training for Mountain and Winter Warfare." Study No. 23, 1946. DTIC Online, Information for the Defense Community. Historical Section Army Ground Forces. http://www.dtic.mil/dtic/tr/fulltext/u2/a323076.pdf.

Hale, Irving. "Biographic Sketch of Brigadier General Irving Hale." Hale, General Irving: Correspondence Regarding, Biographical Sketch, Erl H. Ellis Collection, WH1737 Box 1, Range 9A, Section 12, Shelf 3, FF 16. Denver Public Library, Western History and Genealogy, 1944.

Harper, Frank. *Military Ski Manual: A Handbook for Ski and Mountain Troops*. Harrisburg, PA: Military Service Publishing Company, 1943.

Jay, Major John C. "History of the Mountain Training Center." June 30, 1948. Revised by Dr. Sina K. Spiker. DTIC Online, Information for the Defense Community. "Historical Section Army Ground Forces." http://www.dtic.mil/dtic/tr/fulltext/u2/a955065.pdf (accessed July 29, 2011).

Laughlin, James, IV. "Ski Parachute Troops." In *American Ski Annual 1943*. Edited by Roger Langley. Your Sport, Inc., 1943.

McLane, Charles. "Of Mules and Skis." In *American Ski Annual 1943*. Edited by Roger Langley. N.p.: Your Sport, Inc., 1943.

McNeil, Fred H. "Skiing and National Defense." In *American Ski Annual 1942*. Edited by Roger Langley. N.p.: Stephen Daye Press, 1941.

Morgan, John E.P. "Special Training." In *American Ski Annual 1944*. Edited by Roger Langley. N.p.: Your Sport, Inc., 1944.

Pando Echo: Published on the Summit of the Nation 1, nos. 5, 7–9, 12–13 (August 25, 1942; September 1, 1942; September 8, 1942; September 15, 1942; November 4, 1942; November 18, 1942). Denver Public Library, Western History and Genealogy.

Reynolds, Whitman M. "Preventive Medicine in Winter and Mountain Warfare." Tenth Mountain Division Camp Hale–MTC Reports TMD1, Box 3, Range 18B, Section 1, Shelf 2, FF 29. Denver Public Library, Western History and Genealogy, circa 1942.

Ricker, R. Brooke. "The Invasion of Kiska." In *American Ski Annual 1945*. Edited by Roger Langley. N.p.: Your Sport, Inc., 1944.

Robinson, Erma Paul. "Camp Hale by Erma Paul Robinson Casper, Wyoming." Online Memoir. *Camp Hale WAC Detachment Segments*. Metropolitan State University of Denver. https://www.msudenver.edu/camphale/thewomensarmycorps/camphalewacdetachment/segments.

Robinson, H.R. "The Building of Camp Hale." Poem copy. Erl H. Ellis Collection WH1737 Box 1, Range 9A, Section 12, Shelf 3, FF 16. Denver Public Library, Western History and Genealogy, December 22, 1942.

Sievers, Victor J. Letters, March 23, 1943; April 6, 1943; April 11, 1943; April 19, 1943; September 16, 1943; October 20, 1943; and October 26, 1943. In author's personal collection.

Smith, J.R. "Camp Hale, Colorado." Memoir, Tenth Mountain Division TMD1, Box 2, Range 18B, Section 1, Shelf 2, FF 28. Denver Public Library, Western History and Genealogy, circa 1942.

Sorensen, Harald. "Ski Patrol U.S. Army." In *American Ski Annual 1942*. Edited by Roger Langley. N.p.: Stephen Daye Press, 1941.

Stone, Mary. "Camp Crowder Compared to Camp Hale." Video interviews. Women in the Military. Metropolitan State University of Denver. https://www.msudenver.edu/camphale/resources/interviews/marystone.

———. "The Food Was S.O.S." Video interviews. Women in the Military. Metropolitan State University of Denver. https://www.msudenver.edu/camphale/resources/interviews/marystone.

———. "My Brother-in-Law Did Not Respect the WACs." Video interviews. Women in the Military. Metropolitan State University of Denver. https://www.msudenver.edu/camphale/resources/interviews/marystone.

———. "We Knew We Had a Job to Do." Video interviews. Women in the Military. Metropolitan State University of Denver. https://www.msudenver.edu/camphale/resources/interviews/marystone.

Thruelsen, Richard. "The 10th Caught It All at Once." *Saturday Evening Post*, December 8, 1945.

"Treaty with the Utah, Tabeguache Band." University of Tulsa: Index of Treaties Entered into by the Various North American Indian Tribes, Bands, and Nations. Accessed online. URL no longer valid.

NEWSPAPERS

Denver Post. "Army Reveals Camp Hale Job." October 28, 1964.

———. "Camp Hale: Army Testing Arctic Arsenal." January 30, 1963.

———. "Camp Hale Dogs Being Trained to 'Fight' Anywhere in World." January 17, 1943.

———. "Camp Hale Sports Project Probable." May 15, 1945.

———. "Denver Club Gives Forty Pigeons to Camp Hale Group." May 31, 1943.

———. "Denver Public Library Furnishes Camp Hale Books." January 24, 1943.

———. "German POWs Build Still." March 7, 1944.

———. "Jeeps, Mules and Toboggans 'Tote' Camp Hale Guns in Snow." December 29, 1942.

———. "Leadville Welcomes Camp Hale Troops as Army Eases Its Ban." February 24, 1943.

———. "Many Refugees from Fascism at Camp Hale." January 2, 1944.

———. "Pando Health Record Is Boost for Colorado." February 4, 1943.

———. "Plan to Junk Camp Hale Is Being Held Up." September 21, 1944.

———. "Serious Fire at Camp Hale." February 21, 1943.

———. "Ski Battalion of All Nations Typical of Camp's Quality." April 6, 1943.

———. "Ski Troops to Train in Leadville Area." March 29, 1942.

———. "Soldiers' Winter Carnival: 511th Cadre Holds Snow Contests." January 24, 1954.

———. "The Tea Drinking 10th." January 10, 1943.

———. "They Climbed Colorado's Mt. Elbert and Mt. Massive in Mid-Winter." January 16, 1944.

———. "Troops Training at Camp Hale Are Tough Triple-Threat Men." January 13, 1943.

———. "Workers to Hold Jobs Regardless of Color, Creed." June 28, 1942.

Grand Junction Daily Sentinel. "Recreation Center Designated." January 7, 1943.

Herald Democrat. "Army Opportunity for Local Boys." October 29, 1942.
———. "Camp at Pando will Put Leadville in Spotlight." April 2, 1942.
———. "Camp Hale Builders Win Race Against Time—The Job Is Done." December 9, 1942.
———. "Camp Hale Bulletin: Headquarters Office of Public Relations Camp Hale, Colorado." October 30, 1942.
———. "Camp Hale Chaplain Is a 'Ski Pilot.'" November 18, 1942.
———. "Camp Hale, Construction Miracle, Fast Nearing Completion at Pando." November 21, 1942.
———. "Camp Hale Theater Open for Soldiers." November 27, 1942.
———. "Catholic Chaplains Now at Camp Hale.'" November 23, 1942.
———. "Discharged Camp Workers Petition for Jobs at Pando." June 25, 1942.
———. "Dismissal of Men at Pando Protested." June 23, 1942.
———. "Gym Will be Used to House Workers." July 23, 1942.
———. "Handpicked Soldiers Will Be Trained at Camp Hale, Named for State Hero." June 26, 1942.
———. "Here's How Leadville Can Help U.S. Army with Big Cantonment Built at Pando." May 14, 1942.
———. "Highway at Pando to Be Relocated." April 22, 1942.
———. "Highway Is Open Thru Pando Again." December 2, 1942.
———. "Job of Constructing Camp Hale Is Rushed." October 6, 1942.
———. "Leadville Is Whooping It Up in Wartime." August 31, 1942.
———. "Pando Bond Sales: $680 in Two Hours." September 3, 1942.
———. "Pando Construction Gets Weather Break." May 11, 1942.
———. "Postoffice [*sic*] Planning Service for Pando." May 26, 1942.
———. "Spanish-American, Negro Workers Accepted at Pando." September 23, 1942.
———. "3,000 Workers Needed at Pando." October 5, 1942.
———. "Two Youths Jailed for Pando Thefts." September 30, 1942.
———. "Types of Workers Needed at Pando." June 9, 1942.
———. "A U.S. Army Winter Training Camp at Pando." February 27, 1942.
———. "What Pando Construction Will Mean to This Area." April 18, 1942.
———. "Workers at Pando Buy Lots of Bonds." October 5, 1942.
———. "Work Starts on Army Camp at Pando." April 10, 1942.
Lewiston Evening Journal. "28th Infantry Ends Ski-Fighting Games." February 27, 1940.
New York Times. "Skiing Doctors Needed." October 19, 1942.
Pueblo Chieftain. "CCC Camp Buildings Moved to Camp Hale." September 5, 1942.

Rocky Mountain News. "Army's Ski Camp at Pando Named for General Hale." June 24, 1942.

———. "Army to Start Ski Camp Construction at Pando at Once." April 14, 1942.

———. "Battle Tactics, Art of Supply Superb in Hale War Games." April 17, 1944.

———. "Boxing Bouts Entertain Soldiers." February 28, 1943.

———. "Camp Hale Artillery Makes 170-Mile Hike." May 15, 1943.

———. "Camp Hale Becomes POW Camp and Sensational Story of Treasons Unfolds." March 10, 1944.

———. "Camp Hale Site of Top Secret Test Program." January 17, 1959.

———. "Camp Hale Soldier Is Caught in Mexico with 2 Escaped Nazis." February 20, 1944.

———. "Camp Hale Troops Deadly in Rockies—Or in the Alps." April 5, 1943.

———. "Gung Ho, With the Ski Troops." February 2, 1947.

———. "March in the Infantry? Yes, and Climb, Too—Straight Up." June 16, 1944.

———. "Ski Troops Relax Requirements," January 11, 1943.

———. "Trespassing Led to Arrest of Maple, Two Germans." February 24, 1944.

———. "$250,000 Fire at Camp Hale." February 21, 1943.

Steamboat Pilot. "Ski Patrol Handles Recruiting." January 14, 1943.

Secondary Sources

Baker, John Harvard. *Camp Adair: The Story of a World War II Cantonment, Today: Oregon's Largest Ghost Town.* N.p.: John H. Baker, 2005.

Baumgardner, Randy W. *10th Mountain Division.* New York: Turning Publishing Company, 1998.

Benson, Jack A. "Skiing at Camp Hale: Mountain Troops During World War II." *Western Historical Quarterly* 15, no. 2 (April 1984): 163–74. http://0-web.ebscohost.com.iii-server.ualr.edu.

Blair, Edward. *Leadville: Colorado's Magic City.* Boulder, CO: Fred Pruett Books, 1995.

Bolton, S. Charles. "Turning Point: World War II and the Economic Development of Arkansas." *Arkansas Historical Quarterly* 61, no. 2 (June 2002): 123–51. http://0-web.ebscohost.com.iii-server.ualr.edu.

Brown, Donald G. *Love Letter to Americans: Observations of a Ski Trooper and Journalist*. Victoria, CAN: Trafford Publishing, 2003.

Burton, Hal. *The Ski Troops: A History of the 10th Mountain Division, Its Battle Record in World War II and the Influence It Has Had on the Development of Skiing in the U.S.* New York: Simon and Schuster, 1971.

Buys, Christian J. *A Quick History of Leadville*. Lake City, CO: Western Reflections Publishing Company, 2004.

Camp Hale: Military Munitions Project. "Munitions Response Activities." http://www.camphale.org/Cleanup/Cleanup.htm.

———. "Project Information." http://www.camphale.org/ProjectInfo/ProjectInfo.htm.

Camp Hale. "Prisoners of War." Metropolitan State University of Denver. https://www.msudenver.edu/camphale/camphalehistory/prisonersofwar.

Casewit, Curtis W. *Mountain Troopers!: The Story of the Tenth Mountain Division*. New York: Thomas Y. Crowell Company, 1972.

Cassidy, Maribee. *Off Limits: Leadville in the Early 1940's*. Leadville: Herald Democrat, 1983.

Colorado State Archives: Civilian Conservation Corps Collection. "The Civilian Conservation Corps in Colorado." http://www.colorado.gov/dpa/doit/archives/ccc/cccscope.html#history.

Coquoz, Rene L. *The Invisible Men on Skis: The Story of the Construction of Camp Hale and the Occupation by the 10th Mountain Division, 1942–1945*. 3rd ed. Chicago: Johnson Publishing Company, 1986.

———. *The Leadville Story: Brief Story 1860–1960*. Boulder, CO: Johnson Publishing Company, 1971.

Cossin, Carl V. *I Soldiered with America's Elite 10th Mountain Division of W.W. II*. N.p.: Authorhouse, 2001.

Dawson, Louis W., II. *Colorado 10th Mountain Huts & Trails*. 3rd ed. Basalt, CO: WHO Press, 2003.

Dole, Charles Minot. *Adventures in Skiing*. New York: F. Watts, 1965.

Dole, Robert J. *One Soldier's Story: A Memoir*. New York: HarperCollins Publishers, 2005.

Dusenbery, Harris. *Ski the High Trail: World War II Ski Troopers in the High Colorado Rockies*. Portland, OR: Binford & Mort Publishing, 1991.

Earle, George F. "History of the 87th Mountain Infantry in Italy." 1945. National Association of the 10th Mountain Division. www.10thmtndivassoc.org/87thhistory.pdf.

Ellis, Robert B. *See Naples and Die: A Ski Trooper's World War II Memoir*. Jefferson, NC: McFarland & Company, Inc., 1996.

Fay, Abbott. *A History of Skiing in Colorado*. Ouray, CO: Western Reflections Inc., 2000.

Fetcher, Bill. "Camp Hale: B-Slope." Colorado Ski History. http://www.coloradoskihistory.com/lost/camphale_bslope.html.

Fine, Lenore, and Jesse A. Remington. *World War II: The Corps of Engineers; Construction in the United States*. Vol. 6, pt. 6, vol. 3 of *U.S. Army in World War II: The Technical Services*. Washington D.C.: U.S. Government Printing Office, 1972.

Fire on the Mountain. DVD. Directed by Beth Gage and George Gage. New York: First Run Features, 2003.

Hagen, Monys A. "The WACs of Camp Hale." *Skiing Heritage: Journal of the International Skiing History Association* 17, no. 3 (September 2005). http://books.google.com/books?id=clgEAAAAMBAJ&pg=PA41&dq=Monys+Hagen+Skiing+Heritage&hl=en&sa=X&ei=tvl0VK_GGKbfsAT69IGIAQ&ved=0CC0Q6AEwAA#v=onepage&q=Monys%20Hagen%20Skiing%20Heritage&f=false.

Harper, Frank. *Night Climb*. New York: Longmans, Green & Co., Inc., 1946.
———. *Skiing for the Millions*. New York: Longmans, Green & Co., Inc., 1945.

Imbrie, John, and Barbara Imbrie. "Chronology of the 10th Mountain Division in World War II: 6 January 1940–30 November 1945." June 2004. National Association of the 10th Mountain Division, Inc. http://www.10thmtndivassoc.org/chronology.pdf.

Jenkins, Mckay. *The Last Ridge: The Epic Story of America's First Mountain Soldiers and the Assult on Hitler's Europe*. New York: Random House, 2004.

Johnson, Norma Tadlock. *Soldiers of the Mountain: The Story of the 10th Mountain Division of World War II*. Frederick, MD: PublishAmerica, 2005.

Krear, H. Robert. *The Journal of a U.S. Army Mountain Trooper in World War II*. Estes Park, CO: desktop publishing by Jan Bishop, 1993.

La Rocca, Lynda. "Leadville's Last Whorehouse Will Re-open as a Restaurant." *Colorado Central Magazine*, November 1998. http://cozine.com/1998-november/leadvilles-last-whorehouse-will-re-open-as-a-restaurant.

The Last Ridge. DVD. Directed by Abbie Kealy. Harrington Park, NJ: Janson Media, 2007.

Lunday, Philip A., and Charles M. Hampton. *The Tramway Builders: A Brief History of Company D, 126th Engineer Mountain Battalion, United States Tenth Mountain Division*. Santa Fe, NM: privately printed, 1994.

Lund, Morten. "Skiing Down Those Golden Years with John Jay: The First Man to Show His Ski Lecture Films, Coast to Coast, Year After Year."

Skiing Heritage: A Ski History Quarterly 8, no. 2 (Spring/Summer 1996). http://www.skiinghistory.org/john%20jay.html.

Markwell, John. "War Stories." Training at Seneca Rocks West Virginia. http://homepage.mac.com/galaher/10thMountain/seneca.html.

Meek, Jeffrey L. *They Answered the Call: World War II Veterans Share Their Stories.* Bloomington, IN: AuthorHouse Self Publishing, 2011.

Moran, Lauren. "Camp Hale: Military Maneuvers in Extreme Weather." SummitDaily.com, January 14, 2011. http://www.summitdaily.com/article/20110114/NEWS/110119902.

Nyquist, Gerd. *The 99th Battalion.* Reading, PA: Aperture Press LLC, 2014.

Over, Richard (Dick). Interviewed by David R. Witte, July 24, 2011, transcript.

Parker, Robert W. *What'd You Do in the War, Dad?* Santa Fe, NM: Rio Grande Publishing, 2005.

Pote, Winston. *Mountain Troops: Camp Hale—Colorado.* Camden, ME: Down East Books, 1982.

Putnam, William Lowell. *Green Cognac: The Education of a Mountain Fighter.* New York: AAC Press, 1991.

Sanders, Charles J. *The Boys of Winter: Life and Death in the U.S. Ski Troops During the Second World War.* Boulder: University Press of Colorado, 2005.

Shelton, Peter. *Climb to Conquer: The Untold Story of WWII's 10th Mountain Division Ski Troops.* New York: Scribner, 2003.

"Skiing Heritage." *Journal of the International Skiing History Association* 7, no. 2 (Fall 1995).

Varney, Philip, and John Drew. *Ghost Towns of Colorado: Your Guide to Colorado's Historic Mining Camps and Ghost Towns.* Stillwater, MN: Voyageur Press, Inc., 1999.

Westerlund, John S. *Arizona's War Town: Flagstaff, Navajo Ordnance Depot, and World War II.* Tucson: University of Arizona Press, 2003.

Whitlock, Flint, and Bob Bishop. *Soldiers on Skis: A Pictorial Memoir of the 10th Mountain Division.* Boulder, CO: Paladin Press, 1992.

Wilson, Richard M. *U.S. Skiing—and Men of the 10th Mountain Division: They Made It Happen!* N.p.: self-published, November 1992, revised July 1995.

Wolf, Tom. *Ice Crusaders: A Memoir of Cold War and Cold Sport.* Boulder, CO: Roberts Rinehart Publishers, 1999.

INDEX

Index

Index

INDEX

About the Author

Chaplain (CPT) David R. Witte currently serves as the battalion chaplain for the 777th Aviation Support Battalion, Arkansas Army National Guard. On the civilian side, he is the military and veterans' affairs representative for Congressman Bruce Westerman. During his leisure time, he is an avid outdoorsman and frequent climber of Colorado's fourteeners. Over the past twenty-four years, he has climbed all fifty-four of Colorado's fourteen-thousand-foot mountains and plans to continue mountaineering into the future.

He holds a master of arts degree in public history from the University of Arkansas at Little Rock and is an army chaplain endorsed by the Lutheran Church–Missouri Synod. David; his wife, Megan; and their three children reside in Little Rock, Arkansas.